MW01259206

FRANÇOIS Coty

This logo designed by René Lalique and François Coty shows the founding year of the company (1905), Coty locations across the globe, the Spoturno family crest, and the official crest of Corsica. (Elizabeth Z. Coty Collection)

FRANÇOIS Coty

FRAGRANCE, POWER, MONEY

Roulhac B. Toledano
and Elizabeth Z. Coty

PELICAN PUBLISHING COMPANY
GRETNA 2009

Library of Congress Cataloging-in-Publication Data

Toledano, Roulhac.
  François Coty : fragrance, power, money / by Roulhac B. Toledano and Elizabeth Z. Coty.
    p. cm.
  Includes bibliographical references and index.
    ISBN 978-1-58980-639-9 (hardcover : alk. paper) 1. Coty, François, 1874-1934. 2. Businesspeople—France—Biography. 3. Industrialists—France—Biography. 4. Politicians—France—Biography. I. Coty, Elizabeth Z. II. Title.
  HC272.5T65 2009
  338.7'66854092—dc22
  [B]
                                    2008043835

Page 1 illustration: René Lalique designed this logo for François Coty, who used it on stationery, advertisements, and building facades worldwide. (Elizabeth Z. Coty Collection)

Printed in the United States of America
Published by Pelican Publishing Company, Inc.
1000 Burmaster Street, Gretna, Louisiana 70053

In remembrance of

Yves Michel Coty (1931-74)

Maud Monnier Gewin, Demopolis, Alabama

Lutie Allen Bunkley, Honey Grove, Texas

Hilda Weil Casanas, Clinton, Louisiana

who fancied Coty Fragrances

François Coty. (Elizabeth Z. Coty Collection)

Contents

PREFACE

Perfume and Prejudice

[François Coty] has passion, animation, eloquence, a remarkable
memory and a prodigious faculty of assimilation.

Arthur Train Jr., 1932

Known by the First World War as the Emperor of Perfume, and
soon thereafter as France's first billionaire, François Coty (1874-
1934) revealed himself to be more than the words beside the name
on his calling card: Industrialist, Artist, Technician, Economist,
Financier, Social Scientist. Add architect, news magnate, politician,
philanthropist, and lover, and note that he omitted the basis for his
unequalled fortune—*parfumeur.* Based in Paris, this Corsican, this
lover *extraordinaire,* a man who appreciated women, forged an
international career that exalted women. Between 1920 and 1960,
"Coty," his cosmetic label, was probably the best-known French
name on five continents, including Asia, South America, and North
America. The United States was the major source of his millions of
dollars and billions of francs.

The perfume magnate's monthly spending exceeded 3 million
francs by 1926, and his perfume empire reached its apex in 1929,
thanks to American sales.[1] Coty Inc. in the United States sold 500
million francs worth of cosmetic or perfume products in 1929. Coty
SA in France had 9,000 workers and garnered 300 million francs
a year.[2] In 1929, Coty SA sold 17 percent of the perfume in Paris,
while Guerlain and Lanvin earned 16 percent and Chanel claimed
7 percent of the market share. According to his attorney, Justinius,
Coty spent about 7 million francs per month by 1929 and 1930 on
himself, his friends, his philanthropies, and his various journalistic
and political projects.[3]

François Coty embraced life passionately, with a number of interests
worldwide. He wove into his life the glamor, art, and culture of turn-
of-the-century Paris and, later, the tensions and resentments of post-
World War I Europe. After rebuilding fourteen French architectural
landmarks and châteaux, he became advisor to two French presidents

and an emissary representing French business and political affairs in England and Italy, where he owned vast factories and retail shops. Coty also owned or controlled about forty French newspapers, and he owned and wrote in *Le Figaro,* Paris's preeminent newspaper from 1922 until 1929. For him, his most important journalistic achievement was the 1928 founding of the influential conservative daily, *L'Ami du Peuple.* Perfume as well as prejudice and excitement permeated François Coty's life. A man with billions, strong opinions, and a corporatist agenda, Coty proved to be a figure of consequence in France between the two world wars.

His life provides a window into Europe at that time. His political agenda reveals how a fortune made by a genius was misspent by that same man in his sincere belief that he was saving his country. What he actually funded within France was an anti-Semitic movement and anti-freemasonry attitudes while financing Mussolini's march on Rome in 1921. He contributed to the demise of the Third Republic of France, the same government that had provided the atmosphere and opportunity for him to acquire his fortune in the first place. The imbroglio that Coty created in his personal life parallels the cauldron of France's experiment with democracy during the Third Republic.

Corsican and French sources, Coty family documents and memories, as well as contemporary European and New York newspapers inspired this narrative that delineates the meteoric rise to fortune and influence of Corsican-born Joseph Marie François Spoturno, called Coty, relative of Napoleon, his idol and his paradigm. The text follows Coty's much publicized extramarital love life and its consequences: five illegitimate children. Coty's story does not end with his untimely death before World War II. His legacy was France's largest business, a cosmetic multinational that had spread to eighty countries before 1934. This empire, based in Suresnes, near Paris, and in New York City, was left in the hands of Yvonne Le Baron Coty, his first wife, mother of his two legitimate children, Roland and Christiane.

Having divorced Coty in 1929 to marry Moldavian Léon Cotnareanu, Yvonne, against the advice of her bankers and her two children, allowed her new husband to seize management of the multinational company. By World War II, the company, operating as Coty Inc., was based primarily in New York City, since the United States had become the source of most of its profits. Ironically, under Cotnareanu's leadership, the firm embarked on a worldwide mass-marketing strategy that by 1963 brought Coty products back to drugstores around the world, the places from which Coty had wrested them in 1904, elevating his scents and cosmetic products to luxury status.

Because Yvonne Coty relinquished all involvement in the Coty empire, Léon Cotnareanu controlled the destiny of the Coty descendants and their fortune for thirty years until Yvonne's lonely death at eighty-three in Paris in 1965. Cotnareanu's sale of Coty Inc. to Pfizer Pharmaceuticals, a Canadian-based company, for $30 million two years before her death had been a bitter blow to Yvonne and Coty's grandsons and their children. The 1992 sale of Coty by Pfizer to Benckiser, a German pharmaceutical company, further incensed the powerless heirs of François Coty, both in France and in the United States. The Coty company became a far cry from the Coty that had reigned in Paris's Place Vendôme from 1907 until World War II, and in every prestigious department store in thirty countries from 1913 on.

After 1960, prestige and high-end marketing no longer ruled: profits did. In 1986, under Pfizer, net sales for women's fragrances alone in Coty U.S.A. were $51.9 million, and net sales for all products exceeded $142 million. That year, the four most popular original Coty scents in America, out of ten still available, were *Muguet, L'Aimant, L'Origan,* and *Emeraude,* which brought in net sales of $19.5 million. The fragrance *Paris* topped sales for Coty in Great Britain. These scents, which still sell today under the name Coty, represent the low end of fragrance in the United States, retailing between $12 and $20, but sales across the globe are huge.

In 2004, 100 years after François Coty started his perfume enterprise, Benckiser's Coty Inc. reaped sales of over $1.6 billion. Since then, Coty has surged ahead and is the licensee for over thirty-five brands. Besides Calgon, Vanilla Fields, Jovan, Stetson, Adidas, Yue-Sai, Rimmel, and Margaret Astor in mass distribution, the company controls Davidoff, Joop!, Jil Sander, Chopard, and Lancaster in selective distribution. Coty distributes major brands in the United States that are owned by its competitor, Puig of Spain. These include Nina Ricci, Carolina Herrera, Prada, Paco Rabanne, and Comme des Garçons.

The purchase of Unilever's fragrance division added to the Coty company's roster the licenses of Calvin Klein, Marc Jacobs, Vera Wang, Kenneth Cole, Vivienne Westwood, Cerruti, and Chloé. Coty is currently a leader in men's fragrances, cosmetics, and skin-treatment products in the mass market. Such an eventuality would have been unimaginable to the woman-loving François Coty. Coty Inc., an independent division of Benckiser, continues to add names to its roster.

Headquartered in the United States and operating on a global basis, Coty has facilities in more than thirty countries and sales in over eighty countries. A recently acquired manufacturing and distribution center in China is committed to the vast Asian market. Ironically, Coty manufactures products for France in Sanford, North Carolina, on a 258-acre site the company purchased in 1971, a reversal from

François Coty's day when great vats of formula were shipped from Suresnes to New York to be assembled and boxed.

Even though Coty claims the number-one slot in worldwide perfumery, the name Coty is seldom in evidence. Instead, Coty has initiated the biggest innovation in fragrance—celebrity perfumes— since Paul Poiret brought perfume into the fashion houses in 1904. Celebrity perfumes began to go over the top when Coty came out with Jennifer Lopez's *Glow* in 2002. Eight million bottles were sold before 2005.

François Coty's determination to make the name Coty shine worldwide in perfume, and to be remembered for helping to preserve France's cultural heritage through architecture, philanthropy, and journalism, has resulted in something quite different in the twenty-first century. In his day, François Coty was the "nose" who created the scents, developed them, bought the supplies from Ferminch in Switzerland, and produced the perfumes. He directed and created bottles and packages, advertisements, and even displays, inventing the vertical-organization method to run his business and all its allied industries. He did it all!

The letters of Coty's name, stretched into a sensuous logo on all his products and in Coty advertisements, symbolized beauty, romance, and fragrance to women the world over. In Europe, François Coty reigned as the Emperor of Perfume, the Napoleon of the Press, and France's first billionaire. An ego and a flamboyance such as his would never have allowed the diminution of his name and logo, much less its disappearance from bottles, packaging, advertisements, or retail shops, for any amount of money. Today, in a global perfume market worth over $30 billion, a celebrity's name on a fragrance is worth the removal of the name Coty. A best-selling *luxe* perfume with a celebrity name might net $20 million or more in profits in just one year.[4] François Coty's name is no longer his legacy. His achievement is the international business he established before his 1934 death. His perfume and the industry it launched comprise a notable legacy. After 100-plus years, it is his accomplishments that are presented and elucidated in the following pages. His personal saga and his interests drove one of the most remarkable lives among the rich and famous in the first third of the twentieth century.

An Eight-Year-Old's Love,
by Elizabeth Coty

Some scents can permeate all substances
Even glass seems porous to their power.
Charles Baudelaire, "The Flask"

My fascination with François Coty began in 1934 far from France, in the Blue Ridge Mountains of Virginia. Grandmother Mims introduced me, as a child of eight, to her collection of Coty perfumes in lovely Baccarat and Lalique flasks. They stood regally on her dressing table in the suite of her Mimslyn Hotel in Luray, Virginia. I gingerly touched the satin-tufted powder boxes, trimmed in silk and lace, thrilling to the glamorous containers adorned with golden puffs that I rubbed against my face. I was mesmerized by the etched stoppers of the delicate flasks, which depicted ethereal ladies' faces with flowing hair that seemed to float in the heady fragrances. That day I learned an enchanting story from Gram when I asked about this sparkling collection.

She told me that a Frenchman named François Coty had created these treasures. "He lives in exotic 'Paree,'" she said. A hinged metal case with an empty perfume flask caught my eye, and Gram smiled as she presented it to me. We put tiny jet beads inside to make my own special *Perfume Noir.* "The designs of these perfume flasks and their beautiful stoppers were inspired by ancient images—figures of ladies from the imperial courts of Rome, China, and Egypt," Gram told me. My idea of Monsieur Coty was so romantic that, without ever seeing his black-brown eyes, wavy chestnut hair, or creamy skin, I fell in love with him, as only a child can.

Twenty-five years later in New York City, I became the first woman product manager at Coty Inc. On the second day of work, while being shown my new office, I saw François's image standing before me like a mirage. This reincarnation was his grandson, Yves Michel Coty, who resembled my own imaginary François. Both of us recognized the significance of that moment, and our instant attraction culminated in our secret marriage within three months, in 1960.

François Coty would have been eighty-six years old had he lived to attend our wedding, which we were able to keep secret for three months. He would have reveled in its gleeful chaos as we ducked away from the stern eyes of Léon Cotnareanu, chairman of the board of Coty Inc. and Coty SA, the man who had hired me. He was also Michel's step-grandfather, married to Michel's grandmother, Yvonne Le Baron Coty.

François had lived his own romantic intrigues to the hilt; now his grandson and I continued this tradition in operatic fashion. Our stories kept colliding with those of François and Yvonne, his talented wife, just as theirs had melded with the myths and lives of Napoleon and Josephine. My knowledge and love of Michel brought the awareness that François Coty and Napoleon might have shared many similarities in their own powerful and compelling life stories. Certainly François thought so, as he often invoked his relative's name.

As Michel Coty's wife, I came to know and admire Michel's French grandmother, Yvonne Le Baron Coty Cotnareanu, heiress to François Coty's empire. As François's beautiful and intelligent wife, she had decorated and created packaging for her husband's first perfumes. A sophisticated woman, she made up her own mind and with her own family, the Dubois and Le Baron lineages, had helped put the Coty perfume business on its feet. When I knew her in the 1960s, she was a grande dame with homes in New York, New York; Madison, Connecticut; Warrenton, Virginia; and Geneva, Switzerland and on the Rond-Point des Champs-Elysées in Paris, in addition to being entitled to use châteaux that François had owned across France.

Michel and I would enjoy our brief stays in the châteaux and *hôtels particuliers* that François had built or restored with great care and passion—in Touraine, Normandy, the Dordogne, Louveciennes, the Bois de Boulogne, the Riviera, and Corsica. We would wander awestruck through La Cité des Parfums in Suresnes, where François, the Emperor of Perfume and the world's foremost "nose," had developed a gigantic complex to research, process, manufacture, package, market, and ship perfume as well as the related cosmetic products that he conceived. His vertical process, whereby he owned and managed every aspect of his business from the flowers in the fields to delivery trucks, fascinated me.

The life of France's first billionaire, one of the most influential men in Europe in his day, with a financial empire that crossed the world, captivated me. I envisioned François when Michel and I visited the various Coty plants, headquarters, and shops in Canada, France, England, Australia, Japan, Egypt, and Argentina. We imagined how he had set up his shops in Moscow, Johannesburg, even Peking and Rio. Here were the footprints of the man who had created the artifacts that beguiled me as a child. Now I was more impressed to learn that he had lent millions to the France he loved and had provided pensions and trusts to so many old friends while leaving fortunes to the cities that he remembered with affection. He even devised and financed projects to save Corsica, his homeland, from collapse due to rampant emigration.

As a couple, Michel and I grew agreeably close to François's family: Yvonne Coty—we never said Cotnareanu—his grandmother, who raised him, and especially Michel's father, Roland, and his only aunt, Christiane. We listened to their reminiscences and observed the effects of wealth and passion on the children, grandchildren, and great-grandchildren of this legacy. When I learned that my French father-in-law called himself Roland Spoturno dit Coti, I began to understand the Italian and Corsican origin of François Coty. Just as he transformed everything he touched—whether château, scent, flask, or female—to suit his own tastes, desires, and needs, François had changed his mother's name, the Corsican "Coti," to the French "Coty." François's family name on his father's side was Spoturno. I had not just married a Coty but a Spoturno dit Coti.

In 1963, I drove to Spotorno, Italy, after reading that the medieval town on the Ligurian Sea between Monaco and Genoa was the Spoturno family seat before they settled in Ajaccio, Corsica by the early 1500s. Finding the place, I climbed a hill, trekking through wiry grass to see the abandoned fortress at Spotorno. I imagined the ancestors of Michel and François as they were in the Middle Ages when the castle bustled with citizens and soldiers ready to defend the village from neighboring Noli. The migration 500 years ago from Spotorno to Ajaccio presented itself to me in a mirage as I looked far down at the thundering sea from the windswept fortress.

Later that same year, Michel and I flew to Corsica, where his aunt Christiane provided us with a driver to visit the five-story Spoturno house adjacent to Napoleon's family home in Ajaccio. Christiane had instructed a guard to remain beside us at all times; we understood that, as Cotys in Corsica, we had to be protected. Walking through the church in Ajaccio where François, in 1874, was baptized like Napoleon Bonaparte more than a century before him, I reflected on how the Corsican Catholic Church had taught and raised François.

Joseph Marie François Spoturno, a member of the Ajaccian gentry in provincial Corsica, had become the unimaginably rich Parisian François Coty with a beautiful and talented wife, Yvonne Le Baron. I thought of them as emperor and empress. But what about their descendants, like the grandson I had married in New York? Through the years of our marriage, Michel's eldest brother, Henri, a resistance fighter and a prisoner of the Germans in World War II, resented my very American attitudes and background. Christiane, François's only daughter, and her only daughter, Rolande Dubonnet, have led tumultuous and sometimes tragic lives, always in conflict with one another. Bitterness toward François filled them, while at the same time they secretly adored him. How had François's five children by his mistress, Henriette Dieudé, fared?

I saw my in-laws try unsuccessfully to convince themselves that there was nothing difficult in being descended from a genius of such fame and controversy. While they were impressed with their ancestor, recognized as the world's most innovative and successful *parfumeur* and businessman of his time, his very public excesses, passions, politics, and opinions embarrassed them.

François Coty became to me a very real person whose life had penetrated mine, though I had never known him, since he died in 1934, when I was eight years old. My vision of François is as the world-renowned creator of beauty, a man with unparalleled wealth whose benefactions fill pages and would empty banks today. Others know the François whose patriotism and lust for influence engendered controversy during his lifetime. His contemporaries never looked at him as a Frenchman set firmly within France's eventful Third Republic. Perhaps they were right, because his intuitions were those of a Corsican. Much as he was a nationalist and loved France, his persona was that of an islander.

The Coty name and history were imprinted on me. Am I the only person on the planet who knows and loves this man today, when just 100 years ago he was among the most admired and adored men in the world?

From the moment I walked into the Coty offices in New York in 1960 as a new product manager, I have been determined to restore the image that was both Coty Inc. in New York and Coty SA in France between the two world wars and even afterward. I realized immediately that, once the company got into volume and mass marketing and distribution, it would lose identity and prestige. François Coty himself, while creating and selling the most expensive perfumes in the world in his day, had also managed to offer to women of all economic levels the allure of appropriate cosmetics and toiletries without losing the Coty image.

My husband, Michel, François Coty's grandson, had worked at Coty Inc. since he was a student at Yale, living with his grandmother Yvonne in Madison, Connecticut, and expecting to take over the reins of Coty from his step-grandfather, Léon Cotnareanu. His first position after our marriage was president of Coty, Canada. We worked tirelessly together to reaffirm Coty's international prestige from Montreal. The sale of the company by Léon Cotnareanu, then chairman of the board, to Pfizer while we lived in Canada nearly destroyed Michel, but it made me determined to get the company back for the family. After all, I was pregnant with our baby girl.

Michel died suddenly at forty-two in Charlottesville, Virginia in 1974—like his grandfather, because of an aneurysm. Our daughter, Patrice, was in school in Switzerland and I was living in Marbella, Spain after a painful divorce from Michel. I was determined to reacquire Coty on behalf of Patrice, Michel's daughter Yvonne by his first marriage, Michel's half-brother, Yvon, and his nephew, Stephane. He had remarried after our divorce, but I proceeded ahead undeterred. I engineered an attempted buyout from Pfizer in 1987. When that attempt failed, and Benckiser bought Coty in 1992, I approached Benckiser to turn their new Coty division over to the Coty family for marketing and sales. Reuniting this great family business with its founding heritage continues to excite me. It all came to nothing, though. Restoring the image of François Coty is my goal in telling his life story.

I had to wait over forty years before writing about François and those eclectic people, the Spoturno-Coti family. My primary interest was always François's life story. From my first visit to Paris in late 1960 to meet Yvonne Coty and the family, I enjoyed the world, the drama, and the fortune that François had left. On that first visit, I also began thinking about the incidents and stories that had never been recorded. I began to collect Coty memorabilia and I devoured everything I heard or saw about my new family and its business, because I had been a businesswoman since my late teens.

Soon it became clear to me that François's story could teach everyone about the problems that wealth brings. The universal motifs underlying his life and the lives of his descendants motivated me to contribute my personal experiences and memories to this history of François and the rise of Coty SA and Coty Inc. Interwoven throughout this biography is a second track, in italics, that intimates the joys and the sorrows of great wealth.

FRANÇOIS Coty

PART I

Emperor of Perfume

CHAPTER 1

France's First Billionaire

Coty has rattled the bogy of communism enough to give colic to the bourgeoisie.

Arthur Train Jr.

Not one man in France would have predicted that the country's first billionaire would be a Corsican who launched a cosmetics and perfume business in 1904 that would become a worldwide enterprise before his death in 1934. François Spoturno, called Coty, had astounded the business world in 1906 by becoming a multimillionaire within two years of creating his first perfume, *La Rose Jacqueminot*. Soon after the end of World War I, he was a billionaire *parfumeur* and industrialist in the manufacture of cosmetics and their distribution worldwide.

François Coty's wealth surpassed that of the industrial magnates operating in the conventional pillars of the French economy, such as the Merciers, electricity producers who had brought this form of energy to Paris; automobile pioneers Louis Renault and André Citroen; and André Michelin, whose tires rolled the world over at the same time that Coty was selling powder puffs on five continents. The Coty firm's small consumer items—cologne, powder, soap, lipstick—outsold capital goods and big-ticket items. A Frenchman acquired unimaginable wealth during the most devastating war in the history of Europe, fought on French soil. It seemed impossible, yet it happened.

By 1917, the war against Germany had become a disaster for France. Serious mutinies had broken out among the starving and distressed soldiers in sixteen French army corps. At the last moment, the United States entered the war in France, moving swiftly to save the country. By March of 1918, Gen. Douglas MacArthur, chief of staff of the Forty-second Rainbow Division, had landed soldiers from twenty-six states. On June 2, 1918, at the Supreme War Council in Versailles, Gen. John J. Pershing, commander of the American Expeditionary Forces, promised to supply 250,000 American soldiers a month to bolster the Western Front. His First Army grew so large that he divided it into two armies—216,000 to attack the Meuse River area for the Saint-Mihiel offensive and 300,000 for an attack centering on the Argonne forest in September of 1918.

The American presence in Paris and its environs consisted of civilians as well as the military. America shored up the French economy for four years during and after the war while the allies debated the Treaty of Versailles. The American Red Cross, with administrative offices for the European theater filling the Hôtel Crillon, ran the American Hospital at l'Avenue du Bois de Boulogne, as well as an installation at Saint-Pierre-des-Corps, where Coty financed transporting the wounded to his own château-turned-hospital. Much of the staff that ran these operations consisted of wealthy American men and women. Well-to-do Americans also attended an officers' school at Tours or the French Artillery School at Fontainebleau, and filled managerial posts in the Post Dispatch Service and the State Department. These moneyed Americans not only filled the hotels and restaurants, the theaters and the Opera House, they also proved to be big shoppers for clothes, perfume, and jewelry. The French *luxe* trade could not be put down by a devastating world war.

Once World War I ended in November of 1918, the American Service of Supply had to plan and organize the return to the United States of 2 million Americans, a project not completed until August of 1919. In the interim, American soldiers and civilians, glad not to be among the 116,000 dead Americans or the hundreds of thousands of badly wounded, swarmed about Paris and ports such as Nice and Bordeaux, where François Coty had shops, and they bought perfume and cosmetics. Coty perfume and powder caught the eyes of these legions of American doughboys, as well as other allied soldiers and service personnel, anxious to buy something to take home to their loved ones.

Precisely because of these American civilians and soldiers in war-torn France, François Coty became France's first billionaire, by 1919. The idea of including fragrance in sets of cosmetics, scented identically and packaged together, had come to François and Yvonne Coty when they marketed their products in the twentieth century's first decade. The concept of cosmetic gift boxes, containing cologne, powder, soap, and crèmes all scented to match the purchaser's preferred perfume, was a first for the cosmetics industry and wildly successful.

Since 1904, François Coty had been creating fragrances, scented powders, soaps, face creams, lipsticks, and other cosmetics at the château he renovated, Longchamp, and, from 1909, at his growing industrial complex in Suresnes, across the Seine River. Throughout the war, the Coty employees worked feverishly to manufacture and package all the products for which they could acquire the basic ingredients.

Sales spiked for Coty's luxury items by the time the armistice was signed, as the craze for Coty products continued. Pres. Woodrow Wilson landed with his vast entourage at Brest on December 13, 1918, in time for Christmas in Paris. Kings, presidents, heads of states, and thousands of staff members from the countries of both victors and vanquished crowded the hotels of Paris, refurbished to accommodate this huge boon to Paris's desperate economy. President and Mrs. Wilson, whom the French insisted on calling Madame Galt, since she was the widower's second and recent wife, stayed at Hôtel Le Murat with their entourage.

Coty's signature retail sales shop on rue de Faubourg Saint Honoré at Place Vendôme, as well as his display windows in the major hotels, featured *Chypre, Emeraude, Paris, l'Origan, l'Aimant,* and other expensive perfumes in their exquisite Baccarat and Lalique flasks. Coty's sophisticated and beautiful window displays attracted men and women from the Old World and the new. The diplomats and officers with their retinues remained for months, sightseeing and buying, while Paris became the center, once more, of the European universe. By day and by night, President Wilson's Fourteen Points were debated, along with the futures of Germany and Eastern Europe, and the allies parceled out colonies to the various victors of World War I, but time was found for the purchase of lovely mementos of Paris, most obviously, Coty perfumes and powders.

By war's end, Coty, besides being France's and the world's premier *parfumeur,* was France's greatest captain of industry, measured on a global scale. At his Cité des Parfums in Suresnes, ateliers continued to churn out Coty products for the European market and raw materials to ship in vast quantities for assembly in the United States. Factories throughout Europe, even in Germany, were back into production within the year, and fields for François Coty's flowers, dormant during the war, were plowed and sown throughout Europe and the French colonies.

No matter how hard the times, how little food, electricity, and currency were available, women could scratch together enough money to buy fragrance and powder from Coty. His product delivery system never failed because he had developed "Le Système Coty," a vertical system wherein he owned and ran every aspect of his perfume businesses worldwide—not just wholesale factories and retail stores. Glassblowing, labeling, and packaging ateliers as well as shipping-box factories along the Seine near Suresnes employed over four thousand workers, the stacks exuding smoke throughout the suburbs. Coty owned fleets of delivery trucks and vast research and marketing divisions.

Coty had joined the Nineteenth Infantry Regiment of Ajaccio in response to the French war decree of August 1, 1914. He was released in December of the same year in Paris because of an astigmatism in his left eye. He lost all sight in the eye in 1920, reportedly due to a thrombosis of a central vein of the retina.

He spent the war years in Paris overseeing the operation of his growing enterprise. World War I did not prevent Coty's production, distribution, or sales of his merchandise, at least in France and Italy. During the war, a 1917 Maison Coty catalogue of about twenty-eight pages, produced in French and Italian by Coty's printer, Georges Draeger, featured twenty-one scents, along with *eau de toilette* (infamously mistranslated as "toilet water" in English), cologne, toothpaste, soaps, sachets, powders, brilliantines in crystals or liquid, and a plethora of other products for women. Lotions and powder, scented to match the perfume or cologne of choice, rested in beautiful boxes of Moroccan work.

François created and produced one of his most important perfumes during the war. *Chypre* came out in 1917. He called it "a perfume of amber froth emanating at certain hours from the woods and the forests," having in mind the odors and the forests of his Corsican childhood. While his *Chypre* collected a huge following and instigated the creation of other important scents because of its success, oils and resins from the chypre shrub had been used previously by competitors: Guerlain's Eau de Chypre was offered in 1850, their Cyprisine in 1894, and Chypre de Paris in 1909. Before the turn of the twentieth century, at least Roger et Gallet and Lubin produced scents based on chypre. *Coty's work as a parfumeur with chypre, blending naturals with chemicals, paved the way for the use of chypre in some of the most important perfumes of the world.*

Coty did not limit himself to focusing on business throughout World War I. He worked toward some kind of relief for the most severely wounded or mutilated French soldiers. Along with his good friend and mentor, François Carnot, brother of a former president of the Third Republic, Sadi Carnot, Coty developed *Le Jouet de France* in January of 1917, a society to hire the war wounded. Other sponsors included Georges Chiris, Count Hubert de Ganay, and the sculptor Gaston Etienne le Bourgeois. They put up an atelier in L'île de Puteaux, among Coty's factories, to employ the wounded. Coty went further, installing a military hospital at his Château d'Artigny. His mother-in-law, Virginie Dubois Le Baron, unable during the war to cross the Atlantic to the United States, where she had been developing an American clientele for Coty, put herself in charge of this undertaking.

Coty vans transferred the wounded from the train at Saint-Pierre-des-Corps to the château.

A brilliant and passionate man, Coty needed little rest and acted on his own whims, whether to fund a hospital or a great philanthropy, or to acquire a new mistress, or to create a new scent based on an aroma or a visual or even literary inspiration. Coty described himself as "a laborious artisan, perfected in ten different trades to assure the success of one." He observed, "Perfume is a luxury and can be sold at a high price. If it is to be sold at a high price, it must be the best that can be made. Finally, a beautiful setting must emphasize the perfume's luxuriousness."[1]

In droves, between 1917 and 1920, soldiers bought Coty's decorative gift sets while still in France. As mothers, wives, sisters, and sweethearts of soldiers received Coty's beautifully packaged products, his firm received free advertising throughout the allied countries. Back in New York, Benjamin Levy, Coty's sole agent in the United States since 1910, had been frantically working throughout the war to expand Coty's sales of perfumes, colognes, powder, soap, lipstick, and gift sets. Coty Inc., with a shop at 714 Fifth Avenue decorated by René Lalique, profited tremendously from the homecoming flood of soldiers. Only François Coty could find a way to use a war to open new avenues for a worldwide perfume business and bring fragrances to women of widely diverse backgrounds.

Recipients of these gifts in the United States and Canada rushed out to buy more Coty products from stores that had remained open throughout the war. After World War I, the largest part of François Coty's immense fortune emanated from the United States.

By 1925, François Coty's role in the renaissance of perfume in France and his success in marketing French perfume all over the world were such that France dubbed him the Emperor of Perfume. He oversaw the installation of a spectacular exhibition space at the 1925 International Exposition of Decorative Arts in Paris. A book called *La Parfumerie Française et l'Art dans la Présentation* featured Coty, recognizing his role in the complete revolution that had taken place in the perfume industry:

> Frankly speaking, this revolution has a promoter and a dictator whose name is Coty. Before his arrival, the French perfume industry was already known for its incontestable superiority; but we have to attribute to Monsieur Coty the renovation of *parfumerie*. This irresistible growth in the trend of the art of presentation is not a small trifle. Not only the commerce of *parfumerie* in France has been transformed and increased for the past ten years, but also the exportation has grown in the same

proportions. This prodigious success does not cease. The result is that today the perfume industry is one of the most important branches of French industry. It is our most exported industry.

After World War I, because of François Coty's vision, perfume was no longer a mere accessory for seduction, a means to enhance the beauty and aroma of royals, or a way to disguise odors. It had become a vital aspect of social rituals across the spectrum of society. He managed to keep the *luxe* trade while at the same time making products available to a large population of women. François Coty perceived that his personal legacy to women everywhere was empowerment: when they applied cosmetics and scent, women felt good about themselves. His goal was to enhance women's outer beauty and self-awareness. He felt that, through his beauty products, he prepared women to succeed in life. Perfume became just one part of the set of scented beauty products perceived as desirable, if not essential, to all women for everyday use.

François Coty was at his professional apogee, the most talented *parfumeur* in the world and a mighty industrialist. His wealth was built on profits from perfumes and consolidated by markups on powders and cosmetics, as well as all the industries associated with their development, marketing, and distribution. He flourished during and at the end of a war that ruined so many of the great fortunes of Europe. His metal compacts and perfume bottles became the symbol of his conquest of the United States market. In 1914, Coty Inc. sold 30,000 compacts a day in the United States alone. After World War I, the number tripled. The world was his.

François Coty: His Persona

At war's end, in November of 1918, François Coty was forty-four years old, a handsome, small man with a beautiful and increasingly sophisticated wife and a teenage son, Roland, and daughter, Christiane. The family lived at any one of the various residences that Coty enjoyed restoring, either at Longchamp, at Suresnes, or on the grounds of the historic d'Artigny property that he bought near Tours in 1912. Before and after World War I, Coty indulged his passion for architecture by designing and building France's last great château on this property.

His reputation as a womanizer followed him everywhere; women recognized him on the streets of Paris and ran to touch him or bring their cologne-laden bodies in front of him to show that they used his scents. Before long, he had seven bodyguards and multiple drivers. A chauffeur drove his recognizable custom-designed Hispano-Suiza automobile, but François was not in it; the perfumer followed in a taxi to avoid the crowds of women admirers. Special suites occupying an entire floor at the Hotel Astoria housed his mistresses. He acquired a tailor, seamstress, dressers, and manicurist, among other staffers, to attend to his daily personal needs. An increasing need for privacy followed his ballooning fame and his always-blossoming love life. This last he pursued with vigor in spite of a continuing admiration and love for his wife, Yvonne.

François Coty's stationery, as early as 1910, foretold his immense ambition and ego. He included the coat of arms of his ancient Ligurian family, the Spoturnos, who had settled in Corsica as leaders in Ajaccio soon after its redevelopment by the Bank of Genoa in 1492. Napoleon had presented the *titre d'Empire* to Lt. François-Joseph Spoturno, a second cousin to Joseph Bonaparte, Napoleon's father. Napoleon made this relative of François's a baron for saving his life at Vilnius. The young man died (1788-1812) during the retreat from Russia. François Coty considered the coat of arms his own. Under a crown, within an oval appeared an eagle surrounded by three stars and holding three balls in its talons. All this hinted of François Spoturno dit Coti's ambitions to be worthy of Napoleon. His stationery also bore a beautifully designed inscription: "Coty, founder of Perfume City at Suresnes near Paris, France. Research and development at his private residence at the Château de Longchamp; original designs exhibited at 23, Place Vendôme, Paris; 714 Fifth Avenue, New York; 20, Cheapside, London; 33 Djamagoroff Passage, Moscow." Brevity was not François's style.

Having built his fortune with comparative ease and a felicitous combination of talent and energy in the shortest time of any early twentieth-century magnate, Coty then pursued his quest for fame and public appreciation. One means by which he captured the attention of the press and the social world was through philanthropic projects throughout France. Since there was little that did not spark his interest, he also spread

François Coty used the Spoturno coat of arms on many of his perfume labels. (Elizabeth Z. Coty Collection)

his wealth by buying or building *châteaux* and *hôtels particuliers* throughout the country. He became Europe's most avid collector of various possessions—mistresses, automobiles, art, architecture, racehorses.

By 1911, he had begun sailing regularly to the United States and on trips throughout the world. Curtailed by the war, his voyages resumed in 1922. He brought Yvonne, Roland, Christiane, and his grandmother Anna Maria Belone Spoturno on various trips. Virginie Dubois Le Baron, his mother-in-law and an official employee of Coty Inc., was one of François's favorite companions. After the war, combining business with pleasure, he treated all his relatives and business connections to trips from France to New York, where he continued to enjoy spending his money lavishly. Christiane Coty met the young man whom she later married, Paul Dubonnet, on one of these ocean voyages; the Dubonnet family, wealthy from their vineyards, sailed on the same ship.

Even when most of his fortune emanated from Coty Inc., François Coty continued his love affair with France, just as he continued to create fragrances at his properties, all furnished with white-tiled laboratories for his convenience. Jean Despres, executive vice president of Coty Inc. after World War I, wrote that he and his associates "would take the Pan American clipper to England, and sleep overnight in real beds on this huge plane." He continued, "Then we'd fly to Paris to visit with François Coty. . . . We would drive out to his Château d'Artigny in the Loire Valley. There were flowers everywhere—*muguets,* lilies of the valley, of course."[2]

As the richest man in France by 1926, and one of the five richest in the world by 1928, François was attracted to famous, important, or wealthy people, whom he sought out wherever and whomever they were: artists, musicians, dancers, opera stars, and impresarios in the visual and performing arts. He acted as patron to Russian ballet and stage refugees whom he had met in Saint Petersburg and Moscow when he bought perfume factories and set up retail shops there. Few French politicians and journalists of his day, whatever their persuasion, did not eat at his table. He sailed with kings, shahs, sheiks, and czars. Royals from many nations were his guests. He became an intimate and a financial supporter of Italy's Benito Mussolini, and he dined in London with Sir Austen Chamberlain, British foreign secretary from 1924 to 1929 and older brother to the future prime minister. Always supportive of the Holy See, where he was granted audiences with Pope Pius XI, he donated millions for the Church's fight against communism.

In 1923, Coty was elected senator from Corsica to the Palais du Luxembourg in Paris, but the Senate later refused to seat him, claiming that votes had been bought. His appearance before the body that day in 1924 was, perhaps, Coty's most humiliating moment. It galled and saddened him for the rest of his life. He continued, though, his nationalistic activities to an unusual extent, developing a sinking fund project of 1926, worked out with Prime Minister Raymond Poincaré, to prevent the collapse of France's national currency. Its conception and deployment were informed by all that François had learned while developing his global cosmetics industry. Like so much that Coty did, it was not appreciated. He never collected on the 3 percent bonds; the 100 million francs he "lent" the government became a gift to his nation. The sinking fund and the airplanes he provided the nation for flights around the globe were probably Coty's outstanding philanthropy for France, but the way the government and the people of France ignored his largesse became one of his greatest disappointments. So often, his name was eliminated from the membership lists of the committees and boards that he had founded and financed.

His personality was enigmatic. One contemporary wrote, "No respecter of persons, he is always ready for a good scrap, but he does not look the part. He is small, well-kept, with a clean-shaven, rather expressionless face and intelligent eyes. A French writer has made the cruel observation that one is tempted to mistake him for his own valet."[3]

Appreciated or not, in Corsican fashion Coty bounded ahead, taking financial leadership in projects that ensured glory for France or boosted its image in the international community. From the moment his name appeared on the masthead as owner and director of *Le Figaro* newspaper in 1925, until his removal from the board and the disappearance of his name from the masthead in 1928, Coty never stopped writing or having his comments published by his staff or ghostwriters. Throughout this time, his interests in his other projects never diminished. He developed fragrances, built and renovated châteaux, traveled around the world, and ran for office in Corsica all at the same time.

The years between the two world wars were tumultuous ones for France. Events between 1922, when Coty acquired *Le Figaro,* and 1934, when he died, set the stage for World War II. François had become so important internationally that the *New York Times* often picked up his comments in *Le Figaro*. By July of 1926, Coty had become vociferously upset about the payments that France had to make to the United States to settle war debts. The *New York Times* on July 1 wrote about "the steadily growing suspicions of American

This caricature by André Sikorska of Maurice Hanot d'Hartoy, a friend of Coty, was published in *Le Figaro* in 1928. (Library of Congress)

motives in the debt settlements . . . thus, in the *Figaro* today, François Coty, who at least knows America, can write, 'America wishes to profit from her position as the creditor of Europe to place a mortgage on her [France] and prevent her economic organization by her [own] efforts and means.'"[4] His voice, between the two world wars, reflected the feelings of many of France's great industrialists and of the conservative nobility or Bonapartists.

François Coty's life is, in many ways, a metaphor for France between the wars. In the wake of the Bolshevik revolution, the French communist party took root in France, officially at Tours in 1922. François had long abhorred the communists for confiscating his eight factories in Russia. He was infuriated by the loss of all his investment in Russia—his stores, his stocks, and his deposits at the Crédit Lyonnais of Moscow—over 4 million francs.[5]

His fondest aim, which he called the "crusade of nations" against the Reds, took more and more of his time. He felt it was a fine thing to champion law, order, and discipline in France, a nation where individualism prevailed and so many people represented extremes of political thought. To combat communism, some French industrialists, royalists, and conservatives, inspired by Mussolini's development of fascism in Italy, wanted to replace the Third Republic that had disillusioned so many. Coty leaned more and more in that direction. The *parfumeur,* like other French industrialists of the period, tried his hardest to influence French thinking by taking a leading position in the economic and political life of France. In an effort to bring down the Third Republic, he used his millions and his ownership of newspapers throughout the country to develop a Cotyiste party. Fortunately for his family and for France, as well as his worldwide perfume and cosmetics interests, his frantic efforts to replace the Third Republic began to fail just before his death in 1934.

François Coty was known as the heir of a great old Corsican family—not well off, but with talent and ability. However, he did not think that a mere businessman could aspire to fame. In his mind, his talent as a parfumeur *and an artist should trump his success in business. He lusted for recognition in those fields, but fame, as he understood it, eluded him. His destiny was to be among the first French industrialists in the luxury business to attain global renown after World War I. This was of little consequence to him. It was not real fame—not like the fame Napoleon had achieved. When I try to understand how all this happened, I always think of Corsica, where François was born and bred.*

CHAPTER 2

Corsica: 1874-98

You want romance, read history.

François Guizot

Neither the thick walls of the ancient Spoturno townhouse nor the waves crashing against the boulders protecting the nearby citadel could cover such a wail! The tiny baby cried with all his might, as if to announce that his was not an ordinary birth. The midwife, familiar with such times in the houses of the old Ajaccian families, hoped that this boy-child, of the hundreds of babies she had pulled from the womb, could be somebody. There had been bad blood among the men in the Spoturno family for a long time. Perhaps this baby will bring the father and grandfather together again. Why did the ancient families of Ajaccio from Liguria, like the Spoturnos, hold themselves so high?

On May 3, 1874, at eight in the evening, Joseph Marie François Spoturno dit Coti, later called Coty, was born in Ajaccio. He was at least the tenth generation of Spoturnos to be born in that city since the early 1500s. The birth is said to have taken place three blocks from the sea in the five-story masonry Spoturno house, located on Ajaccio's historic main street, *Carrughju drittu,* now known as rue Bonaparte, at the corner of rue Saint-Charles. The house had belonged to the Spoturno family since 1720. In the neighboring house on rue Saint-Charles that came into the Bonaparte family in 1743, Napoleon had been born.

The priest from the oratorio was delighted when the midwife paused in her rush homeward to tell him about the new Spoturno baby. He strolled up the block to welcome this newborn son of an ancient family. He was glad to hear about the birth of a boy, because it just might clear up the bad feelings that for twenty-five years now had dogged the Spoturno family—especially this newborn's father, Jean-Baptiste, and his father, Domenico. The troubles dated back to old mayor Jean-Baptiste Spoturno, who was a stickler for tradition and proper marriages.

The priest's robe billowed around his legs as he walked the short

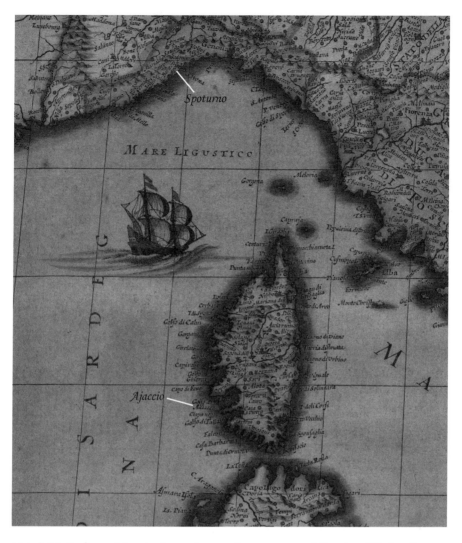

Coty's birthplace, Ajaccio, is on the southwest coast of Corsica. His family was from Spotorno on the mainland, southeast of Genoa on the Ligurian coast.

distance to the Spoturno home, pausing, surely, to enjoy the aroma of blossoms in the newly established plaza across the street. The small park memorialized the 1769 birthplace of Napoleon I. Napoleon III, latter-day emperor of France, had paid for the flower-laden park just across the narrow street from the Bonaparte house. As the priest ascended the stone stairs of the Spoturno house on the corner, he knew that this new Spoturno was born in a room sharing a wall with the birth room of Nabuléone Buonaparte, as the emperor was called in the old Corsican language. That the child's mother was

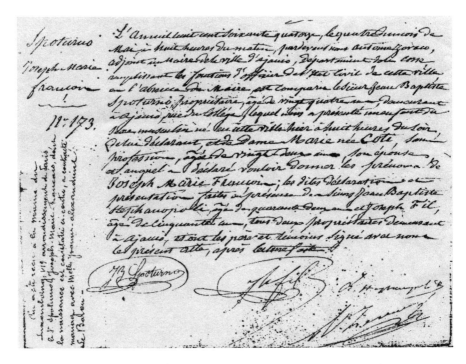

According to this birth certificate, Joseph Marie François Spoturno, later François Coty, was born May 3, 1874, in Ajaccio, Corsica. (Elizabeth Z. Coty Collection)

brought to bed at the longtime Spoturno residence, where ordinarily she was not welcome, was a good sign.

The baby's mother, Marie-Adolphine-Françoise Coti (1852-77), had been just seventeen in August of 1869 when her natural child, who had died, was legitimized by her marriage to Jean-Baptiste (Balta) Spoturno. The Spoturno family did not care for the alliance. The young woman had been born in Paris to one Marie-Adolphine Ledoux, a couturière who was not married to the child's father, François-Marie Coti. The father, Coti, had recognized the little girl and brought her to Ajaccio, where he worked. There he arranged a dowry of 5,000 francs when she married Spoturno.

In fact, the Spoturno family had spurned Jean-Baptiste's father, Joseph-Marie Domenico Spoturno, from the day in 1849 that he fell in love with Anna Maria Belone, from a family considered of an inferior rank in almost tribal-oriented Corsica. Domenico's father, also named Jean-Baptiste Spoturno (1776-1869), administrator of the Civil Hospital and mayor of Ajaccio from 1822 to 1826, had garnered the Legion of Honor in 1824. Such honors were expected of the Spoturnos, as were appropriate marriages. The mayor had followed the tradition, marrying a suitable bride, Lucie Colonna Leca, also of Ligurian extraction. The couple had three sons and a daughter, but trouble developed between the firstborn, Joseph-Marie Domenico (born 1820), and his father, who disinherited him because of his dalliance with a daughter of the Belones. Domenico moved in with the Belone family on rue Notre Dame, unmarried, and his son Jean-Baptiste, also called Balta, was born to Anna Maria Belone in 1850. The parents lived together on rue Notre Dame until Domenico's father, the old mayor, died in 1869. Five days afterward, on August 5, 1869, Anna Maria Belone and Domenico Spoturno were married at last; their son Jean-Baptiste was nineteen years old.

In 1875, Domenico appeared in court in an effort to recover his share of the well-known Spoturno family property, Barbicaja, located on the route des Sanguinaires between Ajaccio and the sea. The effort failed. His brother Philippe-Gabriel inherited the family property. Domenico's son Jean-Baptiste knew about the property and later lamented its loss to his own son François.

The new father, Jean-Baptiste, met the priest at the door and led the way to the bedroom. The two approached the ancient bed where Marie lay. The mother was bursting with pride since the baby was a male and patently healthy. I can just imagine that the priest greeted her warmly and laid an aromatic rose beside her shoulder, the baby's introduction to fragrance.

The boy looked much as his father Jean-Baptiste had looked before him—indeed, not much different from any number of the children born to the old Ligurian nobility of Ajaccio. The child showed the strong inherited trait of the Spoturnos: a broad forehead below tawny hair, already forming a widow's peak. The morning after the birth, the mayor, Monsieur Michel Zebaco, arrived to congratulate the couple, and he notarized the birth at the nearby city hall. The mayor was a writer and a politician, who, like many Corsicans of the period, leaned toward anarchism. Nobody would have guessed that the same mayor would be imprisoned at Saint-Pélagie for his anarchistic writings in 1892, a preview of the new Spoturno's own politics forty years later.

Family Tree

One legend has it that François's paternal progenitor from Italy was a bishop of Savona, who fathered a son by a woman of Spotorno, Italy. Another story goes that this son was recognized by the bishop and given the generic name of a person from his mother's village. This son, it is whispered, came to Ajaccio, where he started a dynasty of Ajaccian leaders from the early 1500s.

Ajaccio, now Corsica's capital, was reestablished in 1492 by colonists from Italy's Ligurian coast who were sent by the rich Bank of Saint-Georges in Genoa. The settlement was planned as an extension of the sixth-century Roman settlement, Adjaccium. The bank in Genoa, the only bank in Europe that sponsored entire colonies and owned cities, was planning Ajaccio when Christopher Columbus, a citizen of greater Genoa but claimed as a native of Calvi by most Corsicans, requested funds for a sailing voyage to discover a new route to the Far East and India. Ironically, the bank refused his petition in favor of the project on the island of Corsica.

Records indicate that by 1325, a Spoturno was a director of the Republic of Genoa. Another sailed as a settler to Ajaccio by the early 1500s, with 100 other families originating from the Riviera di Aponente. In this way, the Spoturnos became a founding family of Ajaccio, one of fourteen leading families always permitted to live within the walls of the old city.

Corsica became French in 1769, after about four centuries as part of the Republic of Genoa. In 1811, Napoleon made Ajaccio the capital of French Corsica—or Corse, as the French called the island. In the 1860s, Napoleon III purchased and refurbished Napoleon's birthplace on rue Saint-Charles, adjacent to the Spoturno house. During François Spoturno's childhood, Ajaccio received money and organization from France's Third Republic, resulting in new roads, ferries, and schools. The funding was given in honor of Napoleon Bonaparte, who had brought international recognition to his birthplace.

François's genealogy shows eleven unions between Bonapartes and Spoturnos through the centuries. Stefano Spoturno, son of Giuilio Spoturno, of a Genoese family from the Savona area, was living in Ajaccio in 1605 when he married Gieronima Buonaparte. Two centuries later in 1803, Giovanni Battista Ornano, whose mother was Isabella Buonaparte, married Maria Gieronima Spoturno. By 1890, some Ornano descendants lived in Paris and the Tours area, and in the early twentieth century, François Coty solicited their friendship. Later, he placed members of the Ornano family in administrative positions of Coty SA; these Ornano connections founded Lancôme.

While the maternal side is seldom mentioned in the Spoturno family's oral history, it is François's mother's name, Coti, altered to the French Coty that the young man adopted after he arrived in Paris. The Cotis, also of Ligurian-Genoese extraction, had come to Corsica centuries before the Spoturnos, and a village, Coti-Chiavari, sixteen kilometers south of Ajaccio, carries their name.[1]

Other members of the family of Marie Coti's father were government pensioners for their service to France. Jean-Baptiste Coti of Ajaccio received the Legion of Honor in 1833. Jean Coti was nominated in 1851 and Jacques-Dominique Coti in 1880. The Cotis from the Ajaccio area married into the Leca, Canavaggio, and Prunetti families, all Genoese-Corsicans. The reinforcement of the old Genoese strain continued until well after World War II, and many persons named Coti remain in the vicinity today.

Young François Spoturno grew up in Napoleon's own neighborhood at a time when the emperor's memory was undergoing an apotheosis under the aegis of his nephews, cousins, and Napoleon III. The imposing bronze statue by Viollet-Leduc, *Napoleon et Ses Frères*, one of many gifts of Napoleon III to Ajaccio, was erected in 1855 at la Place du Diamant. This immersion in things Napoleonic made a lasting impression on young François.[2]

The Death of François's Parents

Tragedy struck the Spoturno family in 1877 when Marie Coti Spoturno died at twenty-five. Her death occurred less than a year after another son, François-Henri, was stillborn on August 27, 1876. Little François was just three years old. From 1870 until the time of his wife's death, Jean-Baptiste (Balta) Spoturno had made his living as a soldier, often stationed abroad. Now, he came home to Ajaccio to take care of his young son, but when François was just seven years old, his father disappeared. Some say Jean-Baptiste sailed to Livorno, Italy in search of work, where he may have died. The reason for the father's disappearance remains a mystery.

Since his parents were dead or gone, seven-year-old François had no choice but to listen, learn, and obey his great-grandmother Marie-Josephe Spoturno. His father's mother, Anna Maria Belone Spoturno, who lived in Marseille, spent months in Ajaccio to help. Despite the bad feelings between the Spoturno and Belone families, François was raised by the two women and the Jesuit priests of his school.

Without a father figure and little male guidance, François looked to the father figure of Ajaccio itself: Napoleon. He fashioned himself after this great Corsican, and François's loyalty to his idol never wavered, carrying him through difficult times in his life. François's boyhood was not much different from that of the young Napoleon a century earlier, except that François had an idol to dream about, which the boy Napoleon did not. François played on the same streets where Napoleon had played and attended school at l'Ecole Saint-Paul, once the home of Elisa Bonaparte.[3] The Hôtel de Ville was fitted out with a *Salon Napoléon,* which François knew well.[4] The rue du Cardinal-Fesch carried the name of an uncle of Napoleon who built a palace there by 1837. In François's day, the complex served as the Musée Fesch and a library; all the young boys of the neighborhood passed these landmarks daily and played in their courtyards.

On colorful fall days, the auburn-headed boy could be seen walking hand in hand with one of the priests, who puffed on his curved burl pipe as they followed the narrow pathways through the maquis to the old Greek cemetery overlooking the Bay des Sanguinaires. The aroma of marjoram, chypre, and oregano from those walks stayed with François throughout his life.

Occasionally, during his late childhood, several boys of the Coti family rowed into the port from the coast to take him fishing. He never forgot one outing with these same cousins from their village of Coti-Chiavari to the great round Genoese tower high on the promontory jutting into the gulf, the Tour de la Castagna. They hiked from the Plage de Verghia into the Forêt de Chiavari, where dense masses of scrub-oak trees, gnarled eucalyptus, squat cork trees, and tangled rosemary shrubs shrouded the slopes above the shore. The aromas stayed with him always, along with that of the maquis that covered the sandy rock-strewn fields.

Marie-Josephe—"Mamie"—and François passed the years together. One cold morning, François awakened alone. His Mamie had not come to his room to get him. Frightened, François worked up his nerve to enter her bedroom. Mosquito netting hung around a bed as big as his whole bedroom. There his Mamie lay, oblivious to her great-grandchild's attempts to rouse her. François realized that his efforts were futile. He turned and ran to the oratorio to find her priest.

The women of the community as well as family friends gathered to comfort young François, who stood by the head of the casket. The boy was just thirteen when his great-grandmother died in 1887, and he moved to the mainland to live with his grandmother Anna Maria Belone Spoturno in Marseille.

When he left Ajaccio, he was small, but not much smaller than his friends on the rue Bonaparte and rue Notre Dame. Everyone knew that the boys of the old families of Corsica were shorter than the French boys on the island. His reddish hair shone in the evening sun as two priests from the oratorio walked him to the harbor, just five minutes from his Mamie's house. The steamship rocked in the harbor of Ajaccio, its sails in a tight roll. As the trio marched along, François tried to remember what he could about the life he was leaving.

The family priest had told François that Papa was gone now six years, but his father's image still lingered in his memory as handsome and strong. They had walked together in the orange groves at Barbicaja, and his papa had carried him when he was tired. His father had been so proud of the family property that had won the prize at the Exposition générale de Corse, four hectares planted with grapes, olives, citrus, pomegranates, apricots, and figs. The young François remembered every minute of those days and decided right then to buy the property and build a villa on the hillside.

Each of the Jesuits held one of François's hands, and they pulled up just as the lugger's horn moaned, signaling that it was time to weigh anchor for Calvi on the way across the Mediterranean to Marseille. "You are a good boy, François, from a fine old family of Corsica." The young priest tousled the boy's hair and pointed up, facing the western sun. "Your people have been here as long as la cittadella, and they have served Corsica well." He spoke in the old Corsican language that the child understood better than French, the official language of his country. The island was known officially as Corse, but forever as Corsica to him and his neighbors, and the old Lombard-Genoese-based language they spoke was redolent of Italy.

The older priest spoke, inspired by the striking sunset beyond the harbor of Ajaccio. "Now it's your time, François. You will be to all France what your ancestors have been to Ajaccio. We have taught you from your infancy. I christened you myself. It is your work and the work of God that you must prevail in when you reach the greater world you are about to enter."

One of the sailors stumbled down from the ship's deck, gathered the boy's hand in his own, and turned to lead him aboard. François, standing on the rolling deck with his hair blowing in the breeze, waved toward the Jesuits on the dock until the sun disappeared. Silently he said goodbye to the red-tiled roofs of his home city. He watched the men unrolling and setting the sail, but he could not make out the song they sang. He heard only the wind and the lapping of the clear aqua sea against the side of the boat.

Searching out an empty corner of the gently rolling deck, François kneeled to take out the strong, aged ham and sour cheese that the fathers had provided for the trip. Later, one of the sailors brought him a hammock, and he dreamed of the future as he sailed toward Marseille. The young boy did not know it, but his departure marked the end of nearly four centuries of Spoturno family predominance in Ajaccio. The mark of Corsica and Ajaccio were on him, though. His ambition and character were as Ajaccian as his genes, his size, and his complexion.

Marseille: 1887-93

Dawn with its riot of color was eclipsed by François's first glimpse of Marseille's skyline. He recalled what the priests of Ajaccio had told him—that the city of Marseille was even older than Christianity and that he would have to guard himself against the sins he would find along the harbor. He pulled out the paper with directions to Grandmère's house. He knew that she lived not far from the harbor, high on the hill in the Vieux Port. If he just knew the look of the building, he might see it from the dock. Then, one of the sailors from Ajaccio hoisted François's small sack of belongings on his shoulder and led the boy by the hand to his new life on the French mainland.

Grandmère Anna Maria came to the door dressed for the day, with her thick brown hair twisted into a high bun on the top of her head. François had to avoid her needle-like hairpins when she embraced him. Her starched white batiste blouse fairly crackled when they hugged. They turned arm in arm into her parlor to begin their new life together. Grandmère had not changed a bit since François had last seen her in Ajaccio.

In a short time, François found that Marseille's urban district near the wharves was far more exciting than Ajaccio. Anna Maria lived in the Vieux Port in the flat she bought after her husband died. From there, François had a view of the ancient, bustling harbor of Marseille.[5] In the distant future, François's daughter, Christiane, would live in the same flat.

Full of acumen and energy, Anna Maria was a businesswoman, unusual for her time and background. She became François's best friend and benefactor. The boy was grateful for her beneficent nature, while she appreciated her grandson's brilliance. The two visited Ajaccio from time to time, as Anna Maria had a brother who still lived there.[6] On one trip back to Corsica when he was sixteen, François was caught in some high jinks, reportedly having stolen a parrot from an old lady. He was sentenced on December 5, 1890, and went to jail in Ajaccio for eight days. The Ajaccians expected something of their first families, and the judge, who had known the boy's grandfather, may have decided to teach this Spoturno a lesson.

François needed pocket money, and he loved the hustle and bustle of Marseille's seaport. Realizing that sailors from all over the world docked there, he collected trinkets and mementos typical of France and sold them to sailors and foreigners on the waterfront. He knew instinctively what they wanted. Later, it was reported that he moved about Marseille as a young haberdasher and a dealer in small wares and notions, even lace. Learning how to project himself, he used his energy and personality to sell.

Young François also learned something about the newspaper business. Working for one of the local papers, he created his own stories about the neighborhood and harbor. These became the "run-over dog stories" to which Coty often referred later in life. This early introduction to journalism initiated a lifelong interest in the field.

Marseille taught François something about wealth as well. François-Charles Roux, a Marseille shipbuilder who had made a great fortune, served as an idol for many young boys in those days. His successes were visible throughout Marseille and in the roadstead of the harbor. This glimpse of what money could do motivated François to become successful, and Roux served as one of a number of role models for François.

François could have attended the Ecole Normale or the Polytechnique in Marseille; Anna Maria had saved some money. However, she did not consider education for the youth as important as business experience. In her day, the streets of Marseille seemed sufficient for François to learn all that was necessary, and the boy took to them with his own energy and acumen. Young and restless, he was full of wanderlust, which was no surprise to Anna Maria. She realized that her grandson was as strong-willed as he was intelligent. She perceived his passion for life and his determination to make something of himself. Despite François's lack of formal schooling, he was constantly striving, working, and thinking. Years later, he explained his education: "At the beginning I succeeded brilliantly in school. But after a few years of success, I had to stop school because my kind grandmother, who was paying for my education, was no longer willing to make the same sacrifices as the families of my schoolmates."[7]

In 1893, nineteen-year-old François registered for his military service, in the reserves of the French army at Ajaccio. The municipal archives in Ajaccio describe him as "blond, with green eyes, medium face, big mouth, round chin, one meter 65 centimeters tall" and as of September 12, 1897, list him as a corporal of the Fifty-fifth Regiment of Infantry.[8] A "Certificate of Good Conduct" followed in 1898 when he was released in good standing in September, although as late as 1905, he was listed in the reserves. The records preserved in Ajaccio indicate that he was to appear for duty in 1906 in Paris, which did not occur. Records there state that "his right eye had no mobility." Photographs of François throughout his life indicate that his right eye was stationary, but he always arranged his pose carefully so that the eyes tracked together.

CHAPTER 3

Paris, 1899-1902: La Belle Epoque

Day dreamers are dangerous men, for they can play out their dream
with their eyes open and make it possible.

T. E. Lawrence

As soon as he was released from the army, young François called
on his family connections in Ajaccio. Seeing his potential, an old
friend of the Spoturno family gave him the opportunity of a lifetime.
Jeanne Forcioli, mother of the future Corsican senator Emmanuel
Arène, was a native of Ajaccio whose ancestors shared the Spoturno's
history on the island, where family connections always count and
where loyalty to family is paramount. Madame Arène arranged for
François to meet with her son Emmanuel. Arène, whose paternal

Emmanuel Arène, senator from
Corsica, was Coty's mentor and
first employer. (Elizabeth Z.
Coty Collection)

family had come from Provence to
Corsica three generations prior to his
birth, had become France's youngest
deputy in the Palais Bourbon in Paris
in 1881 when elected to represent
Corte, Corsica. He became deputy
for Ajaccio in 1897. An ally of Léon
Gambetta, Arène had also become
secretary to the minister of the
interior and of culture, propounding
Gambetta's republican sentiments
in Corsica in an effort to overcome
the prevalent Bonapartism. In 1904,
Arène would be elected senator from
Corsica. Over time, he became known
as the viceroy of Corsica because of
his passionate and informed work to
address the economic problems that
plagued the island.

Recognizing the charm of the
Spoturnos in this orphaned son of the

family, Arène said to François, "If you decide to come to Paris, be sure to come to see me. I think you will work handsomely in a government office." The discharged soldier agreed wholeheartedly. He returned to the mainland to tell Grandmère Anna Maria of this opportunity, and she was as excited as he was. He boarded the train in Marseille for the most important journey of his life. At dawn, he arrived at Paris's Gare du Nord for the first time, in the early spring of 1899. Delighted with Paris, he set off to find Arène's office, arriving there far in advance of the deputy himself.

François was seeking fame and fortune, but first he had to find a career. His work for Arène introduced him to Parisian political and social life. The newspaper *Le Crapouillot* reported Arène as saying to him, "You will not be paid, but when I take my meals at home your place will be set. I will even give you a little money when I earn some. In short, you will have a title, parliamentary attaché. Put it on your calling cards and manage for yourself." François Spoturno followed this advice, using the calling card to great effect. He took advantage of all that life had to offer in the Paris of *La Belle Epoque,* becoming, in the process, a sophisticated Parisian. The career could wait until he found it.

Through Arène, François met senators, ministers, and bureaucrats in the French government. Rubbing shoulders with the French leadership became an everyday affair. He also learned about what had occurred in French government since his hero Napoleon's exile in 1816. He learned to consider the reign of Napoleon III a disaster because of the loss of Alsace and Lorraine to the Germans in 1870. François took a lifelong dislike to the people across the Rhine because they threatened France, a country he had come to love. He learned that Léon Gambetta, Arène's own mentor as well as hero of the Commune and the first Radical-Socialist party leader, had made possible the transition from the Second Empire to the Third Republic. There was much for François to observe, absorb, and question, and he spent many days and nights in the library of Arène's residence at 86, rue d'Amsterdam in Paris.

Arène circulated among the broadest social circles in Paris, and François went everywhere in his company. A day with Arène at the Longchamp races was not just a social occasion but a ritual and a gourmet's delight. There was the grand Sunday buffet at the Jockey Club and an afternoon at the adjoining raceway. Among the spectators, François met Gabrielle (Coco) Chanel with her English escort. Theirs became a friendship that lasted through the decades. The races themselves provided never-forgotten moments with the best horses in France; François declared to himself that one day he would enter his own thoroughbreds in these races.

On several occasions, the Arène group attended duels. An insult to a gentleman's honor or contested claims to the heart of a woman were matters regulated through dueling. What many considered an amusing pastime became a frightening experience for François when his own Arène became involved. Arène was infuriated at the young American-born journalist Arthur Meyer, who had insulted him in *La Lanterne* by calling the deputies from Corsica bandits. Arène's honor and the honor of Corsica were impugned. So the deputy challenged the journalist to a duel.

Family lore has it that François spent the night before the duel in the deputy's apartment so that he could help him prepare. This glorified valet position both attracted and frightened him. Arène remained closeted all night with his friends in the salon. François finally fell into a troubled sleep on the lit de repos *at the foot of the deputy's bed. Before dawn, after an elaborate toilette, the deputy set off in a coach-and-four to the appointed site in the Bois de Boulogne, with François teetering upon the driver's bench. François's real fear for the deputy turned to comic relief when he saw two almost simultaneous shots puff into the air, missing both men. Meyer would later become the editor of* Le Gaulois *and one of François's many enemies in the newspaper business.*

François soon realized that more than boulevardiers and artists characterized *La Belle Epoque.* On January 13, 1898, author Emile Zola released *J'Accuse,* in defense of Capt. Alfred Dreyfus. In it, Zola criticized the anti-Semitism of the army's general staff. Sen. Georges Clemençeau's newspaper, *L'Aurore,* published 300,000 copies of *J'accuse.* Clemençeau, leader of the radical-Socialist party, was Arène's colleague, so François and his employer read everything they could about the issue and observed the furor Zola's piece caused in France. Zola's work articulated the battle between justice and the ancient concept of military honor, but Zola met a violent death for making a stand in favor of Dreyfus. François thereby became aware of the problem of anti-Semitism that pervaded France.

The global business of elegant *couture* was centered in Paris at the House of Worth and of Poiret, but women such as Gabrielle Chanel and Jeanne Lanvin had come from the provinces and, despite their undistinguished backgrounds, they had begun to broaden the scope of chic French fashion. François observed these talented women and realized that they were breaking ironbound French traditions with success.

In 1894, the grand department store, Galeries Lafayette, had opened, and that same year, René Lalique received the Legion of

Honor for his jewelry at the Brussels Exposition. These events proved important for François's future. The advent of multilevel department stores offered marketing opportunities for the perfumes and cosmetics he would soon develop.

At this time, visual artists in Montparnasse were rebelling against *l'Académie.* François took notice of the new symbolist and abstract styles. He lingered in the cafes and bistros in Montparnasse to meet these artists who, he was surprised to find, lived unkempt in their dirty studios. Already a dandy, he was offended, but it did not matter, because during his first spring in Paris, François fell in love with the city: the cuisine, the women, the customs, the buildings, the shops and their display windows. He watched the *boulevardiers* and listened to them talk in the sidewalk cafes and bistros; among them were journalists and intellectuals who wrote for *Le Figaro,* Paris's literary newspaper.

As drama critic for *Le Figaro* and a regular contributor to *Le Matin,* Arène introduced François to editor Louis Latzarus and journalist Alfred Capus at *Le Figaro.* François realized that Arène was also a performed playwright and a published author of *romans.* Arène's novel *Le Dernier Bandit* (1887) recalled life in Corsica. His debut with author Alfred Capus in the newspaper *L'Adversaire* launched Arène into the world of well-known authors. Arène wrote *Le Roi* with Robert de Flers and Arman de Caillavet, two respected intellectuals and journalists for *Le Figaro,* the newspaper that François would eventually buy. François, in the company of the renowned deputy, his apprentices, and mentors, witnessed the literary revolution of *fin de siècle* France. The time had come for new genres and writers, including Marcel Proust, Charles Maurras, and André Maurois. No one would have dreamed that most of these same luminaries, authors, and artists would become François's own employees within a decade. Already, he developed a close relationship with Robert de Flers.

François benefited from the four-year education he received as Arène's aide, but his work was hardly demanding. "Actually the job as secretary of Emmanuel Arène consisted of throwing letters from the voters into an old suitcase," François said many times much later. No wonder he developed a lifelong distaste for the ineptitude of the parliamentary system and the Third Republic itself. Yet under the aegis of Arène, he met some of the most cultured, powerful, and influential men of France.

Arène was one of the last representatives of the *boulevardiers.* His protégé adopted the style as his own. As a mentor, Arène was influential in François's later careers as a *parfumeur,* newspaper magnate, and politician. A man of indefatigable curiosity, Arène had branched out from the political arena to that of journalism and literature, balancing it all with aplomb, and he probably served François as the father he barely remembered. Certainly, Arène was a worthy role model. Later, François took advantage of Arène's social, political, and literary experience, not just by writing for *Le Figaro* but by purchasing France's oldest premier newspaper. He even tried to become a senator from Corsica, like Arène.

When Arène died on August 14, 1908, at Saint-Gervais-les-Bains, his body was returned to his native land, where a street was named for him in Ajaccio. A monument in his honor was erected in 1929; the ornate base, adorned with a bronze medallion by sculptor Louis Patriarchs from Bastia, Corsica, was paid for by *Le Figaro* upon instructions by François Coty, who owned the newspaper at that time.

Raymond Goëry, Who Transformed François's Life

Nineteen hundred, the turn of the century, might be considered the most important year in François Coty's life. He met and married Yvonne Dubois Le Baron. At age twenty-six, he met Raymond Goëry, who introduced him to the world of perfume, and he discovered the 1900 Universal Exposition in Paris, with all its opportunities.

Meeting Goëry inaugurated a sea change in François's life and unexpectedly launched the career he had been seeking. Arène had asked François to select some pomade at the pharmacy of Raymond Goëry on the Avenue de la Motte-Piquet. On that first visit, François looked around the shop, taking his time with his errand. He saw and sniffed a few heavy fragrances packaged in pharmaceutical bottles and became interested in the chemicals and scents in the pharmacy. François asked to see the work in the laboratory behind the pharmacy, and Goëry led him to the back room, filled with chemicals. To the chemist's amused surprise, François asked intelligent questions about the pharmaceutical business. When François demonstrated that he could identify by smell most of the ingredients blended to create Goëry's fragrances, the two men realized in amazement that the Corsican had "a nose." A "nose" is the perfume industry's term for a person with no chemical training, like François, whose nose is so sensitive that he or she is able to identify the ingredients and composition of a fragrance. Then and now, the world has known few natural parfumeurs *or "noses," able to differentiate from among as many as two hundred different "potions" or natural ingredients.*

These include the basic essences of spice, oil, bone, leaf, citrus, wood, leather, amber, and the most popular, flower. Jokingly, the pharmacist attributed François's talent to his Corsican background. "You must have been raised near the maquis. I've heard it told that when the wind is right on the island, the whole place has the aroma of a fine perfume." François remarked that he had been able to distinguish from among the herbs and bushes for as long as he could remember.

François noticed that Goëry's fragrances were strong and heavy and that they were presented in bottles styled for medicinal use. That the same kind of bottles that held perfume and cologne also dispensed medicine baffled François. "Isn't fragrance made especially for women?" he asked himself. François did not suppose that the ladies of Paris would enjoy these thick bottles, nor the commonplace labels identifying their scent.

The young pharmacist, Raymond Goëry, and François immediately liked one another, and a friendship developed. Over time, François persuaded Raymond to let him try his hand at making cologne. He mixed some basic ingredients, aiming for a light, misty, citrus cologne. A mature fragrance had a more complex formula, and François had no training for such a project. Working in the pharmacy in the evenings, François created his first fragrance and called it Cologne Coti, *after his mother. He bought some of the less offensive-looking bottles, hoping the product would appeal to women. Raymond assured him that his cologne was enticing. "It isn't bad and it is light and fresh. There is an accord."*

Cologne interested François more than politics did. He was not ready for the fast pace of Parisian politics, an alternative idea for his future. Besides, François knew that without an education at l'Ecole Polytechnique, the leg up for a Third Republic politician, his way would be difficult. An unknown person needed money and a strong base of support before challenging experienced politicians face to face in an election. While he enjoyed the cat-and-mouse games the politicians played, François knew he needed to have his own philosophy. What were his beliefs? When he was growing up, he had taken no notice of how a city or province was run or who was in power. He had not considered these complex subjects. His political positions would coalesce later. Right now he had made cologne, and he wanted to promote it.

Back at the Chamber of Deputies, François discussed this development with Arène. The two Corsicans, mentor and protégé, decided that François should try to market his product in the provinces. Why not?

The young man was single and needed a little money. The venture would decide if he was a businessman or a politician. Arène provided one further piece of advice. "Use your mother's name. You may say Coti, but I would write Coty with a 'y.' I know what it is like to be a provincial and a Corsican on top of that. What I've had to overcome is not worth talking about. You will do better to abandon Spoturno in Paris and in the world of business. The name Coty will suit you better." Despite the fact that Napoleon himself was a Ligurian Corsican, the French denigrated Corsicans. François recalled the duel: Arène had been forced to risk his life for the honor of the islanders. François determined to rename himself Coty.

Adventure in the Provinces

The renamed François Coty set off for the provinces as a salesman and marketer of his new product, now called *Cologne Coty.* He knew that the deluxe perfume market was lucrative, but for the elite few. The inexpensive perfumes were heavy, old-fashioned, and unexciting, but they sold well since there was nothing else. François dreamed of a feminine world not yet in existence where women appreciated themselves as much as they loved their loved ones, where all women pampered themselves with scent and powder. Optimistic by nature, François did not hesitate to borrow money from his grandmother in Marseille, who had money when he needed it. The energetic, hardworking, charming young man, using the salesmanship he had learned in Marseille, placed the cologne in shops everywhere. He made a sizable amount off his first cologne, and his grandmother paid for the bottles and the labels on which the words *Cologne Coty* were printed, using the new name for the first time.

Marketing his product was a dream about to be tested. He had to get women's attention, but he had no money to advertize. François hired a pony cart, loaded it with cologne, and made his way throughout the southern provinces. Selling in small towns and villages, François created an original marketing concept. He bought ripe and inexpensive country sausages and, before entering a village, he tied them to the back of his wagon, dragging them toward the town's center. He knew that stray dogs, a country institution, were always hungry and would create a ruckus, thereby getting the attention of the townspeople.

Barking, growling dogs ran after François's wagon, fighting over the meat. Men and women emerged from their houses and shops, and crowds collected around the water fountains, wondering about the commotion. When women approached the cart, François sprayed them with his cologne, after which they clamored for more. Women, young and old, bought the cologne. Before his trip was over, he had sold everything. Farmers bought bottles for their wives, knowing it was unwise to return home surrounded by a cloud of cologne unless they brought it as a gift. The selling experiment worked, and young François could smell success. His good looks and manners appealed to the provincials.

During the long nights, François would lie beside a stream under the stars and analyze his experience. He recalled what the buyers had said to him about the cologne and realized that he would become a parfumeur and a marketer of fragrance. He knew that all women loved fragrance, regardless of age or wealth. Women would buy perfume if they possibly could. It made them feel good about themselves; it made them feel attractive. He observed that the men loved the fragrances, too, and they did not hesitate to spend hard-earned francs on his bottles of cologne.

François later recalled, "I had been told that I had a real talent for creating scents. The nose was there. Now I learned the reason for making perfume and for whom I was going to make it. Parfumerie was a career made for me." In a period of months, fragrance became François's lifelong passion and the road to his riches. Years later, he told his close friend Gérard d'Houville that, despite his financial success, he was never entirely happy "because I never mastered honeysuckle!"

François Meets Yvonne

The second life-altering event of 1900, after François's return to Paris from his sales trip, was his meeting Yvonne Alexandrine Le Baron. She worked as a milliner with her widowed mother at the department store Les Grands Magasins du Louvre. One story goes that they met at the pharmacy of Raymond Goëry, meaning that Coty had Goëry to thank for his career in perfume as well as for his wife. No wonder Goëry was their first child's godfather.

Born in Paris on November 14, 1882, Yvonne was living in Passy near Clamart with her mother and brothers the year she met François. Her deceased father, Charles Aimé Le Baron, had worked at the Monnaie de Paris along the Seine in Saint-Germain-des-Pres, where he was recognized as a talented designer and engraver of French coins and medals.[1] Her mother, Virginie Dubois, had married Le Baron in 1879 when she was sixteen years old. Widowed early with three young sons and a daughter, she went to work as a hat designer.

Yvonne's elegance was startling, her olive eyes set above high cheekbones. She had an abundance of golden-red hair, styled to frame her face. Even in Paris, where beautiful women abounded, Yvonne Alexandrine Le Baron stood out. Her personality was sure and steady, and she possessed a distinctive sense of humor. Having selected the love of his life and a career at the same time, François asked the young woman to marry him, and they married before he left for Grasse to acquire the necessary training for the perfume business. Perceiving in the dashing young Corsican the talent and brilliance that lay dormant within his small body, she suspected that, after instruction and experience, he would become a great man.

Yvonne Le Baron and François Spoturno were married on June 12, 1900, at the town hall of Luxembourg, in the sixth arrondissement of Paris. Virginie Dubois Le Baron and her clan were supportive of the alliance. In fact, Virginie would become one of François's closest friends and business associates over the years. Her extraordinary creative talent, like that of her daughter, helped François in his career as a *parfumeur*.

Madame Le Baron's father, Alphée Dubois (1831-1905), also a celebrated medalist and coin designer, had been inducted into the Legion of Honor on December 30, 1882, after winning the Grand Prix de Rome for engraving medals in fine stones. The design and engraving of medals was a Dubois family tradition, and Alphée Dubois's father, Joseph Eugène Dubois (1795-1863), won awards for French coin designs. Yvonne's father and brothers continued the tradition.

The Universal Exposition of 1900

The Universal Exposition in Paris heralded the arrival of the twentieth century. While Paris had held annual international expositions since 1855, this turn-of-the-century event was particularly grand. The 350-acre site of the main fairgrounds bordered the Champs-Elysées, the Hôtel des Invalides, the Champs de Mars, and the Trocadero. Napoleon's old military school ran beside the fairgrounds, and Raymond Goëry lived down the street. François had found a tiny flat at 46, avenue Bosquet, near the Ecole Militaire and in the midst of the fairgrounds area.

The Universal Exposition was seminal to the development of François's career, providing a frame of reference that would both inspire creative ideas and business plans and give context for them. He and Yvonne practically lived at the fair, which attracted 45 million visitors. François met other *parfumeurs;* saw the work of modern artists such as Picasso,[2] soon to be his neighbor; and admired the architectural wonder of the new Grand Palais. Within little more than two decades, he would have an office and elegant apartments nearby on the Rond-Point des Champs-Elysées. Then he would look out of his windows at the Grand Palais and reminisce about these early years when he was beginning to make his mark.

François Carnot, president of the *Union Centrale des Arts Décoratifs,* was in charge of the exposition's perfume section. François Coty had met Carnot at one of the fashionable literary and art salons that he attended with Arène. Carnot, only two years older, became François's mentor and teacher during the period of the fair, and their friendship continued throughout François's lifetime. Carnot served, in fact, as a paradigm for François Coty, beginning with the year of the fair. He was a man of wealth and impeccable lineage as well as a man of letters, a great-art collector, and an activist in the cultural life of France. By 1901 he was elected chevalier of the Legion of Honor and became a *commandeur,* something that always impressed François because his great-grandfather in Corsica had been a chevalier. In 1902, Carnot, following in his family's footsteps, was elected deputy from the Côte d'Or. To Coty, Carnot represented the best of France.

Their friendship helped to further François's education and provided future inspiration for his perfume industry. The decorative arts had become François Carnot's passion, especially the incipient art nouveau and fauvist styles. He bridged the gap between art and science when he became an active proponent of using art to promote or improve industry. He became a key member of the Chamber of Deputies' Beaux Arts Commission. Carnot lived on the avenue Montespan, and François not only spent many evenings there with him but also accompanied Carnot to the fashionable literary salons.

During the run of the 1900 exposition, Carnot introduced Coty to René Lalique, who was exhibiting his prizewinning jewelry. Four years later, François would seek out Lalique's collaboration in product design for his perfume presentation and advertising. Among the *parfumeurs* displaying at the fair were Houbigant, Guerlain, L. T. Piver, Rigaud, and Lubin. By 1900, the perfume business employed 20,000 men and women, with 300 factories and 2,000 retail outlets in France. Exports accounted for one-third of the French business. Within five years, François would have a retail boutique on the Place Vendôme across the street from Lalique and near L. T. Piver at La Madeleine.

The star attraction of the exposition, however, was electricity. Paul Morand, a writer at *Le Figaro,* marveled at the aesthetic miracle wrought by electricity: "At night searchlights sweep the Champs de Mars and the water tower cascades with vivid colors—a symphony of liquid fire, an orgy of electricity." Fifteen years later, Coty would bring electric streetlights to Ajaccio, one of his many gifts to the town from which he hailed. The Mercier family, industrialists who brought electricity to Paris, would later work with Coty in the political sphere. Ernest Mercier would found Redressement Français in the 1920s, an economic and political movement, though by that time François Coty had surpassed him in fortune and influence.

François noted the coverage of the fair by James Gordon Bennett, Jr., the American-born publisher of the *Paris Herald*. This four-page French version of the *New York Herald*, founded by Bennett's father in 1835, had been in circulation since 1897.[3] François was impressed enough to emulate Bennett in later years by going into the newspaper business. François would buy Bennett's residence, La Namouna, at Beaulieu-sur-mer even before Bennett's 1918 death.

The Paris Metro, with art nouveau entrances by Hector Guimard, also opened in July of 1900, in time for the fair. The metro's success would transform Paris's way of functioning, as the architect and designer, Guimard, would transform Paris's streets and neighborhoods, especially the ones where Raymond Goëry and François Coty lived. The metro would soon make possible François's employment of 4,000 men and women at his factories in La Cité des Parfums industrial park in Suresnes. The metro also made Longchamp, the Bois de Boulogne, and Passy accessible to François Coty, who, seeing opportunity, snapped up real estate everywhere.

The Birth of François's and Yvonne's Children

Just after the fair closed, François and Yvonne's first child was born at 204, boulevard Raspail in 1901. They named him Roland Alphée after Yvonne's grandfather; Raymond Goëry was chosen as his godfather. By the time of Roland's birth, a home had been established apart from their laboratory on the rue de La Boetie. Two years later, in 1903, their daughter, Christiane, was born. She and Roland were to be Yvonne's only children, though this would not be the case for François. In those days, Yvonne and François worked together frantically to expand their business through the production, packaging, and sale of *Cologne Coty*. They were also raising money for the production and distribution of François's new scent, *La Rose Jacqueminot*.

CHAPTER 4

The Nose and Grasse

A woman who doesn't wear perfume has no future.

Paul Valéry

Once François discovered his "nose," he knew that a career in the field of *parfumerie* awaited him. What he did not yet know was that his energy and intellectual curiosity would serve him as well as his nose would. Yvonne Le Baron sensed this before he did, and she was prepared to work with him so that he might achieve his goal. François did realize, however, that he was interested in women: the way they looked, the way they dressed, and the way they comported themselves. Most women attracted him in some way. He could not have guessed in 1900 that within fifteen years he would transform the habits of women the world over and make billions of francs in the process.

Arène had arranged two benefits for François that altered his future: an introduction to Sen. Antoine-Léon Chiris in Paris and an internship for François in Grasse, where the Chiris family ran the world's largest perfume production business. Coty's good friend François Carnot, married to one of the Chiris daughters and a director of the Rallet fragrance factories in Russia, owned by the Chiris family since 1898, was involved in this important decision to study perfume making in the world capital of perfumery. François had seen Grasse, east of Nice in Provence, briefly on his travels with the pony cart. Now he was determined to master the details of the perfume industry.

The Chiris family had long been award-winning perfume fabricators and wholesale distributors of perfume raw materials throughout Europe. They owned flower fields in Europe, Africa, and Asia. Antoine-Léon Chiris was Arène's close friend and political ally. He was born to Antoine-Anselme-Léopold Chiris and Marie-Claire-Paul Isnard in Grasse on December 13, 1839. He had continued his father's perfume work, winning the Gold Medal at the Paris exposition of 1867. Then, in 1874, the year François was born, Antoine-Léon was elected to the Chamber of Deputies, representing the center-left. In 1882, he became a senator as a conservative republican who supported maintaining Nice's union with France.

Chiris and his family emerged third on the list of mentors to François and became his friends for life as well as business associates. Here was an early example to François of a creative *parfumeur* who became a successful politician. This was a sign of things to come for François's own career. Another fortuitous connection for François was that his good friend François Carnot was married to Valentine Chiris. In 1902, while François was in Grasse, Antoine-Léon's son Georges married the granddaughter of French president Sadi Carnot. To cement the connection further, in the French manner, Ernest Carnot was married to Marguerite Chiris. The upshot was that François was received well in Grasse because of the Arène-Carnot-Chiris connection.

At the Chiris factory, François was greeted by Antoine-Léon sons, Georges and André, both active in the operational and industrial aspect of the business. François soon learned that the Chiris family ran the largest perfume enterprise in the world. Their cargo boats shipped everywhere from Cannes to Russia to New York. He felt fortunate to have obtained a position in their training program for young hopefuls, recognizing once more the importance of the Spoturno family's longtime friendship with Madame Arène. The opportunity to study with Chiris emanated from that connection, although the Chiris family immediately recognized his talent as a "nose." The lesson in power impressed him as much as the aroma of flowers destined for use in perfume. Arène had opened many doors for him in Paris and had encouraged him in his field of choice. His nose would do the rest. Trusting in his ability, talent, and friendships, François felt that his future was secure.

Parfumerie in Grasse

Spending long days at the laboratory, François soaked in, along with the allure of natural fragrance, detailed lessons of chemistry. He became close to Georges Chiris, who came to appreciate François's nose as well as his energy, hard work, and business acumen. Within a short time, Georges decided to sponsor the young Corsican.

François passed long evenings in the library of Georges Chiris, hard at work with scientific research. He also acquired information about Grasse and the perfume industry's development. At one time, Grasse's largest industry had been the tanning of hides for glove makers. Gloves had become popular in France during the sixteenth century. Throughout the seventeenth century, the demand for gloves—whether for ladies promenading along the boulevards and

private pleasure gardens or for gentlemen driving their phaetons or
fighting duels—created a demand for Grasse's herbs, which acted
as tanning agents, rendering the leathers fragrant and supple. The
resulting financial boom ended with the demise of traditional glove
making during the Industrial Revolution. The small town was hard
hit.

Yet, this was not the end for Grasse, because the ancient town
possessed all the elements necessary for its future prosperity. The
families that had formerly engaged in tanning had begun to specialize
in the production of raw materials for fragrances. Prior to the
establishment of the Chiris manufacturing facilities, parfumerie had
been a minor aspect of the tanning business. After Chiris's factories
were developed, other perfumers collected around them, settling
into the city's convents that had been abandoned since the French
Revolution. Working together, these manufacturers conquered world
markets and made Grasse the global capital of perfume. Many exotic
ingredients arrived in ships from all over the world. These included
vetiver, incense, vanilla, and nutmeg. Men had toiled for centuries
to perfect the extraction techniques. François mastered the Chiris
family's collective knowledge of fragrant-oil extraction.

The perfume industries traded in both French and international
markets. Fortunately for Grasse, the climate, soil, and availability of
experienced agricultural labor made the area ideal for the cultivation
of roses, jasmine, tuberoses, and other flowers. However, flowers
were not the complete roster of perfume ingredients. Certain animal
products were also essential to the fragrance business. Civets,
belonging to the Viverridae family, were imported from southwestern
Ethiopia. They were desired for their crescent-shaped pouches close
to the genitals that secrete viverreum. The pouches were surgically
removed so that the viverreum could be extracted. It was then
blended with other ingredients, imparting a long-lasting sensuality
to a perfume.[1] Another animal product essential to the perfume
business was ambergris, a concretion formed in the intestines of
sperm whales, which served as a fixative for volatile fragrances. The
Chiris laboratory received it in kidney-shaped blocks, weighing from
a few ounces to over six hundred pounds. After drying for several
months and cold maceration in pure alcohol, ambergris became a
fixative for the highest-quality perfumes.[2]

The list of fragrant "notes" associated with jasmine was endless
to François. In Grasse, where all flowers were called by their proper
names, jasmine was known simply as "the flower." The Chiris family
harvested these blossoms from their own fields in Italy, Egypt,
Tunisia, Morocco, Madagascar, and the former French colony around

Pondichéry, India, because over four thousand flowers were required to make a single pound of jasmine essence, sometimes referred to as "absolute." It is difficult to imagine the vast number of workers and fields involved in bringing about just one pound of this product.

The fragrance industry had changed dramatically after 1850 due to the introduction of extraction techniques using volatile solvents. Chiris had obtained the patent on these techniques and created the first factory to employ chemicals. When François arrived, about the turn of the century, Louis Chiris had set up his first workshop based on solvent extraction. Fragrant components could be extracted when flowers, mosses, resins, or leaves were dissolved in a volatile liquid and then evaporated.

Houbigant had already used synthetic molecules in their fragrance *Fougère Royale,* the formula with cumarin that recalls the scent of sweet grass. In 1872, Roger and Gallet had used ionone as a substitute for the scent of violets, producing *Vera Violetta,* a popular scent during the Second Empire. Guerlain had used the chemical substitute vanillin in *Jicky.* Through Chiris's work, these chemical advances in the creation and manufacture of perfume became available to a larger number of manufacturers. Perfume became more profitable for producers and more affordable for consumers.

François saw to it that he was well trained in all these processes. He realized that by combining natural essences with synthetic ones, he could preserve quality and tradition while reducing cost. These thoughts germinated as he sat at the "fragrance keyboard," a table that had about as many bottles of scent as an organ keyboard has keys; they were arranged in descending rows, recalling a church organ. By selecting from the bottles arranged before him, he learned how to combine the various scents to create a fragrance.

With the experience and knowledge he acquired in Grasse, François worked out a combination of natural floral essences, animal extracts, and synthetics to use for his own fragrances. But if this were all, the mixture would evaporate. To stabilize the fragrance and ensure that the perfume would last, he balanced it with balsams, gums, or oleoresins, which retarded evaporation. With his natural talent— some called it genius—he perfected this combining process.

The world of perfume enveloped François. Through conversation and reading, he discovered that Catherine de Medici's arrival in France in 1533 had contributed to making the country the capital of perfumery. After her marriage to Henri II, she brought with her from Italy a private *parfumeur* named René, and she sponsored the cultivation of flowers for perfume manufacture and development.

Surprised that the concept of cologne was anything but French, he also learned that an Italian, Paul Fenimo, working in Cologne, Germany, developed a perfume product in the early eighteenth century. The word "cologne" came to mean fragrance. Fenimo's innovation was to make an aroma that was not a single note but rather a composite of several essences of separate flowers, herbs, and extracts. The resulting multiscent had a unified and unique bouquet.

François perceived that the history of fragrance paralleled the history of cultural aesthetics and the story of man's efforts to express emotion through the olfactory system. If the sense of smell is psychologically connected to color, taste, and memory, wouldn't fragrances be more appealing to the buyer if allied with the other senses? Voilà! He conceptualized the entire presentation of a scent, from aroma to bottling, labeling, packaging, and displaying, as an aesthetic experience designed to attract women, just as perfume and other cosmetics made the women themselves more attractive to men.

François, as a man of the world, realized that fragrance and cosmetics had long been known to empower women in their interaction with not only men but society in general. If more women had access to cosmetics, he thought, these women might influence society in a new way. Beginning to understand the core social function of perfume, he determined to design more popular and profitable perfume, and the information he acquired in the process would inform his displays and advertising. He discovered the role of scent in religious and social rituals. Fragrance and its secrets passed to the Romans from the Greeks, Carthaginians, and Egyptians. Weren't two of the first three gifts to the baby Jesus scents—frankincense and myrrh—according to published tradition?

François not only learned this history, but his mind teemed with ideas of how this tradition of scent might become available to all women instead of the few in the elite classes around the world. His attention turned from chemistry and the uses of his now educated "nose" to the business that could develop through expansion of the availability of perfume. First, though, he had to use his new knowledge to create another scent.

La Rose Jacqueminot

The result of François's studies, training, and process development was *La Rose Jacqueminot*. Albert Camilli's essential-oil factory, Laloue, located next door to the Chiris factory, was in bankruptcy. Their stock of rose essence was therefore unusually inexpensive. This, along with his grandmother's financial help, made it possible for François to work on a rose perfume. He sought a new and different effect from the rose, a classic aroma that had enticed humanity for 3,000 years. Homer had written of the rose oil that Aphrodite smoothed over Hector's body. Homer also specified that macerating rose petals in olive oil created the liquid. Rose essence, popular for its uniquely lasting aroma, had been widely sold for eons, since its introduction on the Greek and Trojan markets.

François would name his own light and quite feminine rose fragrance *La Rose Jacqueminot,* after the large *rosa centifolia,* deep crimson in color. First introduced in 1853, this particular rose had been named after Gen. Jean-François Jacqueminot, the popular commander of the Paris National Guard who had refused to give the order to fire upon his fellow Frenchmen during the 1848 uprisings. Jacqueminot's career was ruined by this decision. He was replaced, but he was always remembered as a hero by the French populace. François identified with Jacqueminot for the same reasons he related to Napoleon. Once he had selected the rose he wanted to work with and assured himself of its availability, he set off for Paris and for Yvonne.[3]

CHAPTER 5

Les Visionnaires

I knew I was to be a perfumer; it was a career made for me.

François Coty

François returned from Grasse to his bride and son in Paris, the mecca of fashion and art, late in 1902. Twenty-eight years old and five feet six inches tall, François radiated knowledge, energy, and determination. The family lived in a small apartment at 76, rue de la Boetie, near the Champs-Elysées. This area of bourgeois activity, both residential and commercial, suited the couple and their enterprise. Over time, artists overran rue de la Boetie. Pablo Picasso lived there with his first wife, Olga, the Russian dancer. Artist Paul Guillaumin moved into #108. Retail art galleries, including that of Paul Rosenburg at #21, replaced the pharmacies after World War I, and La Licorne Gallery, run by dentist-connoisseur Dr. Girardin, became a popular meeting place. By that time, François had moved on to become rich and famous.

François and Yvonne Coty were pioneering artists for the neighborhood, and their astounding success caused them to leave before this art colony became dense. Their little apartment on rue de la Boetie became their factory. François continued selling his *Cologne Coty* while inventing new products. The production of *La Rose Jacqueminot* was in the planning process for his envisioned "House of Coty." There was space for a tiny laboratory and a sewing room for Yvonne's perfume pouches. Their close friend, the pharmacist Raymond Goëry, dropped by to assist in the laboratory. François had asked him to join him in the business, but Goëry was hesitant since he had no money to invest.

To ensure that *La Rose Jacqueminot* was bottled attractively, François chose one of the most prestigious glassmakers in France, Baccarat, established in 1764 in Lorraine on the banks of the Meuse. The Baccarat bottles were expensive, and François needed more money; he convinced his grandmother to finance the endeavor.

François Coty, wearing his large diamond stickpin.
(Elizabeth Z. Coty Collection)

Using her training as a milliner, Yvonne fit the bottles with gold string and binding to make them more elegant. Working with François, who concerned himself with every detail, she sewed silk pouches, velvet ribbons, and satin trimmings. Yvonne's brothers, Henri and Paul, and her young uncle, Alphée, designed and engraved labels for the bottles.[1]

The widening popularity of perfume at the end of the nineteenth century coincided with new developments in advertising. In the early days, the contents of a bottle were its most valuable commercial asset, and the bottle itself was unimportant. The label covered most of the bottle, sometimes giving the history of the company. Immediately, François recognized that the fragrance itself was not the only consideration for the buyer. "A perfume needs to attract the eye as much as the nose. It is an object before being a scent," he said. He also wanted his labels to be more than an information center.

Toward the end of 1903, François was ready to launch *La Rose Jacqueminot*. He set off in his best suit to sell his perfume to the retailers of Paris. Trained on the wharves of Marseille, he proved within days that he was an outstanding salesman in Paris. He sought accounts from department stores and boutiques. His energy and charm also opened up new venues for his product, such as kiosks that had never before sold perfume or cologne. The aesthetic appeal of the bottles nestling in Yvonne's attractive pouches with their original, fancy labels inspired proprietors to make wholesale purchases from François on the spot.

With all the talk of Baccarat, Lalique, and other professional designers who eventually worked for François, Yvonne's role in the development of the Coty look must not be forgotten. She developed the first House of Coty packaging designs for the Baccarat flasks or bottles. Her concepts, acquired in part through her training with her mother as a milliner and her association with the engraving business, were instrumental to the initial success of Coty perfume. With her help and support and that of her brothers and uncle, Coty's perfume industry was able to expand quickly.

La Rose Jacqueminot was perfected in 1903 when François was twenty-nine years old, the year of his daughter's birth. His purchase of the Laloue factory inventory in Grasse made possible the rapid manufacture of *La Rose*. The money for production startup came from four sources: the Chiris family, François Carnot, the Dubois-Le Baron families, and Anna Maria Belone Spoturno in Marseille.

Convincing Villemessant to Sell La Rose

The family always told the story that when François attempted to see Henri de Villemessant, director of Les Grands Magasins du Louvre, Paris's most fashionable department store, he was left sitting in the reception room, ignored. Villemessant was on the board of Le Figaro, his family having founded the newspaper, and he associated socially with Arène, so François expected a warm welcome. The secretaries were unimpressed. Why should an unknown parfumeur be admitted to Villemessant's office when Eau de Lubin and Rigaud's Air Embaumé were already selling well?

Les Grands Magasins du Louvre in Paris was the department store where Coty sold his first scents. (Elizabeth Z. Coty Collection)

The story goes that after several days, when his patience expired, François tricked the director into smelling his fragrance. He dropped a bottle of La Rose Jacqueminot by the perfume counter at the gigantic store, then strolled away to await results. Customers inhaled the scent wafting toward them and swarmed to the counter, demanding bottles of the new scent by the dozens. The commotion was such that Monsieur Villemessant rushed to the floor to see what had happened. He was surprised to discover that the source of the disturbance was the young man who had been an aide to Arène. He had no idea that François had been warming a chair outside his office for several days, much less that he had transformed himself into a parfumeur.

This interesting story, so typical of the personality of François, may be exaggerated, but it is true that his mother-in-law, Virginie Dubois Le Baron, whom he loved dearly and who always helped him, had worked at the department store. Her influence may have given him entrée.

Immediately, *La Rose Jacqueminot* became the rage of Parisian shoppers. Villemessant presented a much-sought-after stall to François on the main floor. When it became evident that François's perfume was an unprecedented success and that capital for immediate expansion of production would be needed, Villemessant offered him revolving credit. At once, François established stalls in the six major department stores in Paris.

His success with *La Rose Jacqueminot* was so astounding that François was declared a millionaire in francs within months. He was by now not only a *parfumeur* but a successful marketer and businessman. On the other hand, he had to obtain more and more financing to meet the demand for more perfume at the same time that he had to work to create a second, third, and fourth scent. Yvonne managed the packaging operations, and bookkeeping was a constant demand on her time, too. The reported millions were needed for perfume supplies, bottles, and packaging.

Baccarat remained François's choice for containers in his first large production of *La Rose Jacqueminot*.[2] The firm eventually produced hundreds of thousands of the slim classic bottles that collectors associate with *La Rose Jacqueminot*. François introduced the marketing concept of attractive packaging to the perfume industry.

A larger, second run of *La Rose Jacqueminot* was released in 1904, and within a year Coty had created two new scents: *L'Origan* and *Ambre Antique*.[3] Coty Société Anonyme (Coty SA) was formally established in France, in 1905, when François brought out *L'Origan*. From then on, Coty's labels included an embossed date in Roman numerals: MCMV. He frantically continued work on four other fragrances: *Jasmin de Corse, De L'Ambréine,* and *La Violette Pourpre* were distributed in 1906 and *L'Effleurt* in 1907. His nose was not more important to his immediate and astounding success than was his natural business sense. His grandmother, in-laws, and mentors continued to be amazed by his talents, and they also continued to invest their francs in Coty SA.

François was able to afford a retail shop at 374, rue Saint-Honoré, in the heart of Paris's historic perfume district. He rented a display cabinet at the Hôtel Ritz, knowing that the most fashionable people in the world would see his products there. In 1906, he created his first boutique for the House of Coty, at 28, Place Vendôme. René Lalique, with his award-winning jewelry for the rich and famous, was across the street at 24, Place Vendôme.

François's Competition

The *parfumeurs* along rue Saint-Honoré and rue de la Paix represented a trend toward beauty, style, and decoration in feminine society. François cleverly set up his House of Coty near the Ritz and Meurice hotels. The manufacturers of the *objets de luxe* for which

Paris was famous, including dress designers, jewelers, and Louis Vuitton luggage, could be found near the new House of Coty.

Coty's competitors were nearby as well, some in their third generation. The patrons of the other *parfumeurs* included the czars and czarinas of Russia, French royals, and members of the British court. François studied this competition and sought to understand his potential clientele. He intuitively comprehended the dreams and longings of women, becoming more and more involved emotionally in women's femininity. Their new desires and needs, so evident at the beginning of the twentieth century, interested and attracted him. He conceived a plan to profile types of women and create specific perfumes and colognes for each type. François combined his own attraction to women with his developing business to become one of the architects of the new, freer concept of femininity in all social classes. He knew that he could attract to his House of Coty the chic, elite women of France, but he determined to create an entirely new clientele that would include all women, everywhere. He also expected to expand into another much-needed field, cosmetics for all women. It would not take long.

Houbigant, at 19, rue Saint-Honoré, had an especially long history, having been established in 1774. Napoleon and his generals had gone into battle perfumed by Houbigant. The bottles were stored in campaign chests, guarded by aides in the tents of Napoleon's leaders. That company had been continued by Houbigant's son. Then it was owned by Chardin, Magny and Gabillot, until Javal and Parquet bought the firm to become the suppliers to most European courts by 1881.

Guerlain, at 15, rue de la Paix, opened in 1828 under Pierre-François Pascal Guerlain. The second generation, under Aimé Guerlain, created the famous *Jicky* in 1889. François had studied *Jicky,* with its natural notes of lavender, bergamot, and oak moss, and determined to design a perfume that surpassed its excellence. Many Guerlains—brothers, sons, nephews, and grandsons of the founder—continued the firm, but their signature perfume, *Shalimar,* did not appear until 1925, when Coty perfume was at the height of its popularity.

L. T. Piver, at 23, boulevard des Italiens, had started as a perfumed-glove shop in 1769 under Michel Adam. His family members succeeded him and renamed the firm L. T. Piver after Louis-Toussaint Piver, who took over in 1813. During the time that the House of Coty was on Place Vendôme, L. T. Piver moved across the street, next door to Lalique.

François did not feel threatened by these distinguished, multigenerational firms that supplied luxury scents to the nobility and nouveaux riches of Europe and America. In his eyes, they merely spurred him on to his own eventual victory. He studied their fragrances and their marketing. Then he applied his own energy, artistic vision, and business acumen and strived to exceed them as no one had before.

Within a few years, the czsarinas of Russia used only Coty perfumes. François had been prescient, setting up retail outlets in Russia as his first foreign endeavor. In their teens, the four Romanov princesses stopped taking cold baths in the morning and began taking warm baths at night with perfumed water. Olga preferred La Rose; *Tatiana favored* Jasmin de Corse; *Anastasia stayed faithfully with* Violette. *Marie, who tried many scents, always came back to* Lilac, *always Coty.*[4]

The Russian people seemed infatuated with Coty's perfumes. François was selling his fragrances in the boutique at Place Vendôme when three imperial Russian Cossacks purchased several bottles and emptied the contents on their uniforms. After they left, François laughed heartily and wondered whether the men wanted to attract women or each other.

Russia was François's earliest and most successful foreign conquest. François Carnot had returned to Paris from one of his yearly rail trips to Russia, on behalf of the Rallet fragrance factories in which he was financially involved through his wife, a Chiris. Rallet factories had been in production in czarist Russia for years. His information about the great market potential of Russia fascinated François. The two friends traveled there the following year, and François consigned to Rallet a few of his most popular products. Their immediate success among the nobility and the elite of Moscow and St. Petersburg gave the audacious Corsican all the encouragement he needed. He opened his first subsidiary company at 33 passage Djamagoroff in Moscow in 1905 and set up another in 1910. Russia and France were political allies at that time, and it was important to François to succeed in business where his idol Napoleon had failed in war, and where his ancestor, François-Joseph Spoturno, had been killed.

Longchamp

François needed a place to research and develop all aspects of his expanding business: perfume, bottles, flagons, labels, packaging, advertisement, promotion, and delivery. Remembering his time with Arène at the celebrated racetrack behind the Bois de Boulogne, and recalling the Château de Longchamp beside it, he acquired the château—his first—in 1906 in a ninety-nine-year lease from the City of Paris. It was situated a short distance from the Seine River and Suresnes on the opposite bank. The history of the place impressed him.

After Napoleon III had presented the entire Bois de Boulogne to the City of Paris in 1852, he had given the Château de Longchamp to Georges Eugène Haussmann in thanks for his work in restructuring Paris's urban plan. The post-French Revolution *maison de plaisance* incorporated part of a medieval abbey. Haussmann established ornamental lakes and ponds with winding paths and opened the Longchamp racecourse with its restaurants, kiosks, and pavilions in about 1857. After Haussmann's departure, the City of Paris had lodged its conservators at the château.

Coty worked to restore and alter Longchamp for both residential and commercial use, installing a state-of-the-art apartment for Yvonne and the children. After extensive renovations and rebuilding, including a glass dome by René Lalique and the fitting out of a stone tower with walnut trim by Gustave Eiffel, Coty added Longchamp to his letterhead. He identified it as an office and laboratory for his perfume research and development.

In renovating the building, Coty gave full rein to his engineering proclivities and his fertile imagination. White ceramic tile was laid in profusion, and every detail was attended to with painstaking craftsmanship and panache. He retained the exterior features and repaired and extended the wall around the property. The first indoor swimming pool in the Paris area was installed in the cave below the first floor. At Longchamp, Coty indulged himself for the first time, outdoing Haussmann with a beautiful and impressive garden like those he later established at his landmark residences throughout France. This was the couple's first elegant residence and a preview of what was to come—purchases and renovations of huge swathes of real estate across France.

Le Centre International de l'Enfance, a foundation established by Dr. Robert Debré, a noted pediatrician from Alsace and head of the Paris region medical services in World War I, occupied the château for a number of years after Coty gave up the lease. Now the City of Paris administrates the sadly vacant property. Destruction in mammoth proportions, through neglect and vandalism, has occurred. René Lalique's ceiling dome has been smashed, and tile floors have been crushed. It is not too late, though, to rescue this historic landmark, once its future use is established.

Marly

At the same time he was renovating Longchamp, François bought the house he and the family called Marly. In the village

Yvonne Coty, about 1904. (Elizabeth Z. Coty Collection)

of Marly, near Versailles, on the charming rue de Montval, was a stone cottage that François bought for Yvonne because of its proximity to the Marly golf course. Yvonne said, "We never slept there but used it for changing our outfits after playing golf." How soon after they acquired their first wealth did François and

Gustave Eiffel designed the interior staircase of the tower
at Longchamp for Coty. (Elizabeth Z. Coty Collection)

*Yvonne take on the trappings of fortune—golf, horses, travel,
designer clothes, an entourage—everything. After François's
death, many family members found the cottage useful as a
temporary residence. Antoinette Mouchet-Coty, Roland's second
wife, and her young son, Yvon, lived there until she moved to her
own apartment after she and Roland were formally separated,
though never divorced. She felt at home in Marly, having been
born in nearby Versailles. The duke of Châtres, Christian, son of
François Coty and his mistress Henriette, found it convenient to*

house his young family there, at Antoinette's suggestion, when his finances were poor.

La Namouna

The Villa Namouna, in Beaulieu-sur-mer, which belonged to Gordon Bennett, publisher of the Paris Herald and a string of other newspapers, became a Coty property in 1910. Bennett's "white fortress," surrounded by waving green fronds of palm trees on a wide boulevard lined with stately homes, became a private retreat for François and for his attorney, Justinius.

Between 1910 and 1920, François continued to buy estates of the rich and famous, and parallels began to emerge between Bennett and François. Bennett conducted business from his 314-foot yacht, Lysistrata, with a 100-man crew. Besides a Turkish bath, the yacht featured an Alderney cow that lived in a padded stall. François was not to be bested by anyone, so, not long before his death, he bought the second-largest privately owned yacht in the world from the former caliph of Turkey. Bennett was an avid polo player from 1905, and Roland Coty later took up this sport.

The similarities in interests and excesses between Bennett and Coty are notable, from the newspapers each owned to the numerous manor houses and châteaux. The two men had enormous energy and pursued projects that were considered unusual and unnecessary. Bennett is remembered as the man who sent reporter Henry Morton Stanley to Africa to find the Scottish missionary. The world was amazed when Stanley reported his discovery along a trail in darkest Africa, with the comment, "Dr. Livingstone, I presume." François sponsored flights by Frenchmen around the world and designed and financed their aircraft.

Coty and Lalique

François had seen the elite and wealthy, dressed in their finery, parade through Lalique's door across the street from his own Place Vendôme shop. The celebrated actress Sarah Bernhardt wore only Lalique jewelry. That was enough for François. He thought that if the noble and socially prominent women of Paris flocked to René Lalique for their adornments, they would come to the House of Coty if Lalique designed his perfume containers.

François initiated a longtime, crucially important business relationship with René Lalique, whom he had known since 1900 through his Chiris and Carnot connections. When Carnot had introduced François to Lalique, René Lalique was known best internationally as a prizewinning art nouveau jeweler. François also knew that Lalique had begun to dabble in glass sculpture. The charming and energetic François Coty not only formed a fast friendship with Lalique, but also with the Lalique family, and he convinced the distinguished jewelry designer to help him with his perfume flasks.

Lalique and Coty united talents, creating even broader appeal for the fragrances through the development of exquisite flasks and packaging. Although François had purchased his first *La Rose Jacqueminot* bottles from Baccarat, he realized that a number of well-established perfume companies used Baccarat flasks. He wanted to be unique in all aspects of his business. At François's insistence, the bottles and flagons Lalique would design for Coty perfume would be works of art and produced for Coty alone.

Their relationship began with gold-embossed labels ordered from Lalique. François's need for labels had surpassed the production capabilities of his Le Baron in-laws. He and Lalique then began to design bottles, bottle stoppers, and molded-glass flagons. The first of the Lalique flasks designed for Coty were intended for mass production. They were produced at the glassworks of Legras and Company, a large firm in Saint Denis, near Paris.[5] These initial bottles were unsigned and relatively simple rectangular or square flasks. As money rolled in, François raised his standards since he considered himself an artist, and he participated in every level of design. The results were Lalique's etched-glass flasks, embossed with golden labels, each featuring an exquisite stopper. These bottle stoppers were honed to fit only one flask. Each stopper was engraved with its own discrete serial number, as if it were a print or lithograph.

Jean-Jacques Vignault, who began his career as a young driver for François and became a Coty officer and family friend, described the process of creating the bottle:

> In 1910, [Lalique and Coty] together created delicately cut bottles with an emery-cut stopper. In this system, the crystal stopper was cut to fit to one and only one bottle. At the time, the bottom of the stopper and the bottle were both numbered. Each was hand-cut glass of very high quality. Stopping of the bottles was completed by a seal that surrounded the stopper and terminated with interlaced gold threads and ribbons.[6]

The two men, Coty and Lalique, changed the look and meaning of perfume. At first, the engraved and embossed labels were very small. Then Lalique, designing both the label and the flask, integrated the label into the design of the frosted incised or repoussé bottle.

Sometimes the name of the perfume became part of the bottle and stopper design. At times, these innovations obviated the need for paper or gold-leaf labels.

Coty and Lalique introduced the then new concept of coordinated package design into the Coty company production plan. The two were the first to unify the design motifs of bottle, stopper, label, and container into original creations accepted as works of art. The collaboration produced the most sophisticated and original of Lalique's fragrance-flask designs. He designed at least sixteen bottles working closely with François.[7] Later, much to Coty's chagrin, Lalique produced designs for Worth, d'Orsay, Houbigant, Guerlain, Molinard, Roger & Gallet, and, after his death, Nina Ricci.

Once it was thought that the bottle Lalique designed for Coty's *Cyclamen* in 1909 launched their official partnership, but they had collaborated as early as 1906. Some consider the flask for *Ambre Antique* (1907) the finest product of their collaboration. Others argue that Lalique's best flask for Coty was for *Au Coeur des Calices,* created in 1912, with its luminescent light-blue glass, molded inside the container to recall the rounded center of a flower. The stopper of that bottle is particularly striking. An unopened bottle in the original presentation box has sold for over six thousand dollars to collectors.

The Lalique bottle for *L'Effleurt de Coty,* dating from 1908-10, has a rectangular body and is molded on the front with a frosted and brown-stained panel. The panel displays a sinuous female nude emerging long-limbed from the attenuated petals of a flower and billowing up into an ethereal sky. The words *L'Effleurt de Coty* are molded along the bottom of the image. The tall stopper is a stylization of an Egyptian scarab. This bottle represents the apex of the Coty-Lalique concept.

One side of Lalique's bottle for *L'Entraînement* displays a male and female figure walking together. The reverse shows the couple kissing. The figures are surrounded by a bas-relief, beribboned, floral cartouche.[8] These are just a soupçon of Coty's original endeavors with Lalique.

In 1913, Coty commissioned Lalique to design an etched-glass facade for Coty's New York boutique at 714 Fifth Avenue. Lalique decorated the glass front with acid-frosted poppies and other incised and embossed work. The unique Lalique facade eventually was covered over, but it was rediscovered, largely intact, in 1985 and returned to use at Henri Bendel.

Lalique created many other larger pieces for Coty, designing entire store entrances and chandeliers for both retail establishments and François's many private residences. He designed repoussé logos for use in Coty factory facades across Europe and balusters and stair rails for François's homes and offices. Lalique created Coty's glass-fronted display cases, in addition to Coty installations for passenger ships and fairs worldwide. Eventually Lalique even provided architectural detail for the Coty yacht, the *Alphée*.[9]

One of the most handsome *objets de luxe* that Lalique created, about 1910, for Coty was a tester for twelve perfumes presented in a fitted box. Affixed to the interior of the lid is a bronze plaque representing three art-nouveau-style female nudes cavorting with one another. Over their heads waft the stylized words *Les Parfums de Coty*. This advertising plaque in bronze or copper gilt with the three dancing nudes became the Coty SA logo throughout François's life. The easily recognizable design was also used as Coty's business letterhead and appears, in one or another creatively manipulated form, in raised stone and marble wall designs and frescoes that were installed in François's various factories, shops, and châteaux.

François Coty should have added architect to the extensive list of vocations on his business card, and buildings should have appeared on his logo. Real-estate purchase, the reestablishment of residences, ancillary buildings, and gardens, as well as the design and construction of his dozens of factories gave him real enjoyment. Not even perfume creation and a worldwide business fulfilled him after he became wealthy. Working on his own properties with draftsmen, architects, craftsmen, and landscape specialists presented a private pleasure and a creative vent.

He determined to buy Chambord, the sixteenth-century residence of King François I and France's largest château. Coty wanted to restore its 400 rooms, 100 staircases, and 105-foot-high tower, which began to fall into disrepair as soon as François I died. Although it had been stripped to its shell over the centuries, Coty envisioned it as his international fragrance and cosmetics headquarters.

He was surprised that he could not achieve his desires, but Monsieur Persil, an associate of Premier Alexandre Millerand, opposed the purchase at any price. As a result, Coty developed a lasting hatred of Millerand, slated to become president of the Republic. Not only did Coty personalize his politics, he also acted vengefully toward those who crossed him. Unable to obtain Chambord from the state, he held a grudge.

Château d'Artigny

Unable to acquire Chambord, François embarked on an extended and frenetic search until, in 1912, he bought the d'Artigny estate and château in the Indre Valley of the Touraine province near Montbazon.

His Ornano cousins, originally from Corsica but long resident in the Tours area, alerted him to the availability of the estate. The Puy d'Artigny had been the fortified bastion of the nearby château of Montbazon, built between 1360 and 1380 during the Hundred Years War. It was part of a military system established along the River Indre to defend the city of Tours against the English army. Coty paid Raymond Bacot 600,000 francs for the old estate: 600 hectares of farmland, two mills that Bacot had established, and all the buildings that had been added to and altered from the original medieval group.

Jean d'Artannes, captain-governor of Montbazon, after whom a nearby village is named, owned it in the fifteenth century. The name d'Artannes became, over the centuries, d'Artigny. René Testard de Bournais, treasurer of the Tours mint, had the old fortification razed and rebuilt in 1769, using a medieval look on the exterior. When Coty surveyed the property, he saw a mixture of neo-Gothic towers and pseudo-Renaissance wings built around the old manor house. They did not suit him, and he demolished the manor house.

On the site of the former *puy,* an old Gallic word meaning "hill," overlooking the valley of the River Indre, Coty created a facade that is almost a replica of the Château de Champlâtreux in the Val-d'Oise, which belonged to the venerable Noailles family. Coty, though, utilized materials brought in from Corsica and all the places in which he held an architectural or sentimental interest. In his usual grandiose fashion,

François Coty's Château d'Artigny sits on a hill above an original outbuilding of the property on the River Indre near Tours. (Elizabeth Z. Coty Collection)

Coty made his own château larger than the Noailles family's original.

The Château d'Artigny became his lifelong hobby. Emmanuel Pontremoli was just one of the architects, who, along with many draftsmen, was subjected to Coty's active participation in every aspect of the plans and their execution. Over one hundred workers labored for twelve years, and still the new château was not finished. Coty's demands and whims were unparalleled, both outside and within the château.

When World War I came, a skeleton crew toiled on, and Coty had them convert the as-yet-uninhabited château into a hospital for wounded French soldiers. He had been brought into wartime philanthropy through his association with François Carnot. Both men were horrified and distressed by the thousands of badly mutilated Frenchmen sent to Paris from the trenches.

The château would take twenty-one years to complete. The facades and basements are finished in the Comblachien stone common to the Côte d'Or and reputed for its quality. Coty brought in stones from the quarry at nearby Evreux, and he considered himself the engineer in chief. As emperor of his new estate, he introduced a number of innovations, such as electric gates and an air-conditioned cellar. The conveniences of the castle became grandiose, and excess, so typical of the owner, abounded at every level. An ice-production plant was housed in the basement, and pipes delivered ice water to rooms. The three-boiler system that provided hot-air heating could also send cool air when needed. Multicolored Carrara marble covered the kitchen floor, and the pastry kitchen, complete with copper sinks, was decorated with pink and green marble.

Another kitchen was built upstairs for Yvonne's pleasure in creating special dishes if she were hungry in the middle of the night. A talented gourmand, she practiced guessing the ingredients of the dishes that her various chefs presented at all her residences. As hostess of the house, she frequently taught the chefs. One couple, trained at the Coty household, was snatched away by the maître d'hôtel of Buckingham Palace. Guests who arrived by rail from Paris at Saint-Pierre-des-Corps station were brought to d'Artigny in a chauffeur-driven Rolls Royce or in Coty's unique Renault.

For everything from custom-built kitchens to linen closets, Coty made original and highly detailed demands on his craftsmen. Today, the wardrobe still has two floors, with 140 cupboards made of fruitwood with mother-of-pearl and inlaid ebony that can hold up to two thousand articles of clothing. Large closets in the air-conditioned basement kept Yvonne's and guests' many furs cool. Small closets were divided into sections for hats, muffs, and gloves.

D'Artigny was also the perfect showcase for Coty's growing art collection, with pieces by Boucher, Greuze, Fragonard, Watteau, Reynolds, and Gainsborough. In the antique manner, he had artworks installed as panels with lavish moldings enclosing them above doors and on walls. Aubusson and Göbelin tapestries vied for space. The art and the hangings are gone now, but the exquisite moldings, built into the walls, remain in place.

The ballroom floor of inlaid fruitwood was installed and then relaid eight times, after François determined that his billiard ball had rolled from the center to a corner. He was not satisfied until the ball remained in the middle of the room. François was adamant that the floor be perfectly level for ballroom dancing.

Remember that François and Yvonne had each residence outfitted with everything for year-round living, from food to clothes, so that they could drop in at any time with just twenty-four hours' notice to the permanent employees and caretakers. This was Yvonne's rule. Of course, there was a resident tailor at d'Artigny. François insisted on having his clothes altered with every change of weight, no matter how small. A shoemaker and a hairdresser were also on hand for him, and all the staff was expected to assist guests. There was even a resident doctor, paid 300,000 francs a year. And, of course, the chef had to be the best in France. Coty lured the Russian chef Sipiaguine away from the Hotel Royale in Evian, paying the breach-of-contract money.

Charles Hoffbauer, winner of the Prix de Rome in 1924, painted a fresco in the rotunda of the new château, depicting himself; François and Yvonne; Roland Coty and his eldest son, Henri; the Cotys' daughter, Christiane, with her daughter, Rolande; and a number of friends and protégés. Among them are the Aga Khan; Guy, Baron de Rothschild; and the baroness. The theme is a masquerade ball, each section featuring life-size figures standing by a wrought-iron railing. In the small ovals in between are vignettes with individual portraits.

Three of François's mistresses, Edwige Feuillère, Cécile Sorel, and Marie Marquet, are included in the trompe l'oeil ceiling as Harlequins and Colombines, stock characters from comedic theater. They are not far from the rendering of Yvonne, masked and standing beside Coty, who is presented in a swaggering pose in a black cloak. The two of them are greeting the actress Colette Darjac. Coty's protégé, the Japanese painter and printmaker Tsuguharu Foujita, is also included. Since Coty financed the Ballets Russes and helped Sergei Diaghilev and Serge Lifar, they too appear in the mural.

Building the château and all the outbuildings was not enough for François. He reconstructed four nearby mills: the Moulin de la Braye à Montbazon, the Moulin de la Bouchère à Veigné, the Moulin de la

Fresnaye à Monts, and a mill adjacent to the Manoir de Beaupré à Veigné. This was a great act of conservation, but, unfortunately, some are crumbling today.

François lived at d'Artigny during the time that his grandchildren were raised in a nearby country château, the Château de Vaux, not far from Azay le Rideau. Coty lore abounds in the nearby towns, where so many of the inhabitants worked for François or Roland.

One well-remembered incident concerns a local doctor who was called when François's doctor was away. Their dialogue, as Yvonne reported it, reveals François's high metabolism and unwise eating habits, considering his tiny frame. François announced to the physician that he ate at least five pork chops at each meal. When asked about his consumption of eggs, Coty explained that he raised hens and ate at least one thousand eggs a year. The doctor told François not to be surprised if he had health problems.

Bodyguard stories abound, as well. Coty had six round-the-clock bodyguards. His daughter, Christiane, remembered their constant presence because of their willingness to push the numerous swings her father had bought on shopping sprees the two enjoyed in Tours. Each of the swings had a different cushion to match the child's dresses.

Years later, the Morelos boys, grandsons of François Coty and Henriette Dieudé, recalled their mother, France (Françoise), talking about her trips to d'Artigny as a child. France, the eldest child of Henriette and François, had married a Mexican count, Lorenzo de Morelos, whose ancestor was governor of Jalisco, Mexico. Coty's entire illegitimate clan, according to France, was brought to d'Artigny when Yvonne was not there. Since Roland and his wife and children lived nearby, his family and others must have been aware of François's illegitimate family. He never tried to hide them; he loved all of his families.

After Coty's death, the Château d'Artigny was sequestered at the demand of his many creditors, since his estate could not be settled. Yvonne's divorce had claimed most of his wealth—billions of francs over the last four years of his life. D'Artigny was occupied in June 1940 as the headquarters of the Naval Ministry under Pétainist admiral François Darlan. Later in the war, German troops held it. It became an annex to the Tours General Hospital, then a shelter for the evacuated inhabitants of Lorient in Brittany, which had been bombed. Then, until 1946, it served as a maternity ward.

Finally, in 1947, Christiane and Roland Coty inherited the vacant property. Twelve years later, they sold it to René Traversac, whose goal was to make d'Artigny "the finest hotel in France." In 1960,

Michel and I were able to spend a last lovely time there before it became a hotel, which opened in September 1961 with fifty-three rooms and suites. The last château to be built in France is now a luxurious five-star hotel.

Throughout the years of the war and German occupation, François's personal wine cellar with 50,000 bottles, said to be the best collection in France for the period, remained hidden and intact. Today, the château holds the annual convention by the Wine Tasting Institute to judge the new vintage.

CHAPTER 6

La Cité des Parfums

François Coty: Industrialist, Artist, Technician, Economist, Financier, Social Scientist.

Calling card of François Coty

Coty's perfume business was so successful that he needed new production facilities soon after he leased the Château de Longchamp. By 1907, he had a facility at rue Perronet in Neuilly, where his two children, Christiane and Roland, attended school. In 1908, François and Yvonne bought a fishmonger's warehouse on rue de Saint Cloud to store bottles and equipment. They also rented a barn from a bicycle seller named Malraux, where they set up a factory.

Near Longchamp on the other side of the Seine was the village of Suresnes, a place long associated with the fragrance business, beginning with Fargeon, *parfumeur* to Marie-Antoinette. Fargeon manufactured his court perfumes there. His vats still sat in the barn of a house near Villa La Source when it later belonged to the Gondi family.[1] In 1909, Coty bought Villa La Source. He and Yvonne created a penthouse there where they sometimes lived, multiplying the number of their residences by four in as many years.

François then settled on Suresnes as the main site of his rapidly growing perfume industry, partly because of its location less than a mile from Longchamp, where he already had a home, business offices, and a personal laboratory installed in the château. Suresnes's Napoleonic history also appealed to him.[2] In addition, for a sports enthusiast such as François, Suresnes offered another pleasure. It was a passing point for serious cyclists. Though the chic cyclists went by the Bois de Boulogne, on any given Sunday fifteen to twenty thousand wheels circled Suresnes. One could see much of this action from Café Picqué.[3]

While François was expanding his facilities, René Lalique invested in the glass business, renting in the fall of 1908 the glassworks at Combs-la-Ville on the Seine, for which he acquired a staff of over fifty. The personal friendship and partnership between Coty and Lalique grew along with the fortunes both were making in the perfume business. In 1909, Lalique developed and patented new glass-casting methods, using iron molds. Again, in 1911 and 1912, he registered patents for glass blowing into a two-part cast. Lalique became widely known for his artistic manipulation of the glass surface, including acid frosting and the felt wheel polishing that crowned his blowing and casting processes. All of these techniques were used in the glass Lalique designed and produced for Coty. Lalique's designs had to be mass produced and functional, but at the same time works of art; he succeeded with élan.

World War I

At the outbreak of World War I, Coty's life changed forever. French patriotism consumed him. Coty went to the front for a short time in 1914, with the Nineteenth Infantry Regiment of Ajaccio. Forty years old, with a stationary eye, he was released almost immediately and returned to Paris. Public records in Ajaccio's Notarial Archives refer to his discharge. He had "atrophy of the pupil" in the right eye and "thrombosis of the central vein of the retina with 60% vision, and astigmatism in the left eye." Detractors have said that he paid for the medical report that caused his dismissal from military service. However, his visual problem is documented and also discernible in photographs of François. His fixed gaze in the right eye is obvious from youth.

After his release from the military, François returned to Longchamp and Suresnes, throwing himself into his perfume business. At Suresnes, he continued to design and build his large factories and ateliers, or workshops, for all aspects of his perfume industry. While the buildings were going up, François was working feverishly with Yvonne at Longchamp and Villa La Source at Suresnes. Both places had work and living quarters, so that François could work whenever an idea struck him, which was often in the middle of the night or just before dawn.

As a whole, the perfume industry up to that time had lacked François's essential ingredient: his astute powers of observation. He succeeded by presenting to the women of the new century something they longed for—affordable but tasteful feminine products in the world of fragrance and cosmetics. When François's career began, the cosmetics industry was developing, but with little of the vision, glamor, or variety that marked the products he developed. Nor had the other companies begun to target middle-class or working women, even though these potential customers were more numerous than any other groups. Over time, François, while keeping his luxury market in perfume, would provide affordable perfumes as well as powder and other beauty products for all women.

Air Spun Face Powder

It all began with face powder. François was walking along the street one day when he noticed the breeze blowing dirt into a corner of the curb. In a short time, the heavy particles sank and the light ones remained on top. This natural process of separating large and small particles impressed François. He reasoned that a similar process

Air-Spun powder was Coty's own formula and a bestseller among his cosmetics. This Coty Inc. advertisement is from 1960. (Elizabeth Z. Coty Collection)

could be used to create a lighter face powder. Returning to his factory with this idea in mind, he invented a centrifugal-force machine that sifted out the lighter powder particles. "Air Spun" face powder was born. François patented the process, which created the world's most refined face powder. Previous powders had remained on the skin surface; his formula was absorbed smoothly into the skin. He soon found he could sell more Air Spun powder than fragrance. It became the most famous and rewarding product he produced, achieving the largest volume of sales of any cosmetic product worldwide. Coty sold ten million boxes in the first shipment to Asia. Soon thereafter, he created "Rachel," an Air Spun powder specially designed for golden Asian skin tones. This was a first in the industry, since no one had thought of the enormous population of the Far East. Chinese sales alone brought in millions of francs a year.

An article from this time, "A Factory That Is Pleasant to Work In," describes the Air Spun section of the plant.

> The most impressive workshop is, without contest, that in which the Air Spun powder is studied. The classic methods of grinding and sifting are replaced by "micronization," a patented process exclusive to Coty. Its principle is the pulverization of powder particles by cold air, dry and strongly compressed, that is produced by two compressors. . . . The powder molecules are held in the micronization "drum" and spun at a speed in excess of 30,000 RPM. The particles crash into each other because of the jets of compressed air and are reduced to extremely fine particles.

Air Spun powder's exclusive production process revolutionized the art of self-beautification.

About the same time, François introduced natural ingredients into his cosmetics products: he added vitamin-rich avocado to his hydrating cream and beauty milk. These avocado-based items developed into a major line of expensive cosmetics. Coty's twenty-four-hour lipstick was, like all other lip rouges of the period, tar based, but François used natural additives to make his product last longer than those of his competitors.

Coty coordinated his new cosmetic products by scent, including makeup, powder, lipstick, and other beauty aids, to match each of the perfumes and colognes. To ensure affordability for the middle and working class, the products making up a set were bottled and boxed in small amounts. No matter the price or amount of the contents, the packaging remained a priority. Coty never skimped on quality or aesthetics.

In a short time, Coty cosmetics became as profitable as the

perfumes. Eventually all Coty production centered in the Suresnes area, with laboratories and ateliers for everything from soap production and flask filling to the range of articles based on alcohol. The finished products were stored in a huge central warehouse. Coty was designing and building at Suresnes constantly—places for the development, manufacture, and shipment of his products. If he was not using his creative mind to design new buildings for his plant or to develop new ways to efficiently produce and distribute perfume and cosmetics, he was dreaming up new products.

François sought a packager with a talent that matched Lalique's designs for his glass. He chose Léon Bakst, then designing stage settings and costumes for the Ballets Russes. The choreographer-producer Sergei Diaghilev, whom François and Yvonne had sponsored at the Paris Opera, introduced François to Bakst, who created Coty's first powder box as a novel artistic exercise. The Moroccan leather boxes he designed had genuine gold-leaf embossing. At the time, each box cost an equivalent of two dollars to make, or forty-five dollars today. The design of the boxes and the gold powder puffs, marked with the Coty name, was registered as a trademark on February 7, 1922, long after it had begun to be used.

The Air Spun face powder packaged in these lovely boxes became the best-selling powder in the world. Coty, always thinking of profit, paid customers to return their empty powder boxes; he sent them to Japan, where workers scraped off the gold leaf from the leather so that it could be used again. It is almost inconceivable that a man of such wealth would set up a department for his employees to painstakingly remove the gold from empty boxes, and maybe even more inconceivable that he would make a profit doing it. Later, François's commercial artist, Georges Draeger, adapted Bakst's powder-box design into a less expensive version that is used even today.

With the Lalique-designed Coty flasks, and Bakst-designed powder boxes, François now searched for the perfect graphic artist to realize his ideas for the promotion and advertisement of his cosmetics. Georges Draeger from Montrouge was his solution. Georges's father, Charles Draeger, founded the family graphic-art firm in 1886. His sons Georges, Maurice, and Robert succeeded him. In 1914, Georges Draeger began creating boxes and other packaging presentations for Coty. He was the first of a series of fine graphic artists and designers Coty employed in France, eventually raising the standards of advertising and window displays around the globe.

Because of the difficulties of keeping up with the demand for Coty products, François doubled his industrial domain with a new factory that occupied Ile de Puteaux, adjacent to Suresnes. At one atelier, workers stamped the powder boxes and perfume presentation boxes with metal. They stamped lipstick tubes and covers for talc. In separate facilities, workers performed electrolysis, gold and nickel plating, engraving of flasks, and mass production of emery boards. Printing and copper engraving occupied separate, specially designed ateliers.

After the war, François added to his means of production by establishing a boxing factory at Neuilly. It produced boxes for the powder, packaging boxes, and presentation boxes in cardboard and in Moroccan leather. In 1920, at Pantin, he created his own glassworks (*cristallerie*). This addition assured a complete supply of flagons, over 250,000 a day, as Lalique no longer met the demand and Coty was prepared to take over the glass production.

Lalique's Glass Production Falls Behind

The reported break between François Coty and René Lalique that resulted from this development has been overblown (no pun intended). Coty's vast production needs exceeded the Lalique plant's ability to produce, and, as always, Lalique was more interested in design than production. After a 1920 court case between François and René, a case that Lalique won, René continued to design for Coty, but he did not manufacture. As gentlemen of the time were known to do, the two men continued to collaborate amicably on design issues throughout the lawsuit and afterward.

Coty employed a staff lawyer, a Monsieur Wascat who called himself Justinius. His sole occupation was initiating lawsuits against the companies and individuals all over the world who tried to copy François's scents, bottles, and, above all, powder boxes. François was adamant about protecting all of his creations.

Vincent Roubert supervised new production at Suresnes from 1923. A young *parfumeur* from Grasse, he had trained at the Rallet factories, which had relocated from Russia to Grasse. Hugo Firmenich, a Geneva firm, and de Laire were the large extracting companies that competed to supply Coty's perfume business with wholesale ingredients. François was especially loyal to Frederick Firmenich, who had supplied him with ingredients on credit for *La Rose Jacqueminot*. Sales representatives from the extracting companies swarmed to Suresnes, and François became their most important client.

An early 1920s Coty pamphlet states:

> In their [Coty] laboratories, teams of specialized chemists engage in their research without cease, striving to create new

perfumes and products. Innumerable base materials, natural and synthetic and the entire gamut of colors are studied and tried. Beauty products and makeup are the subject of most of their studies, in the biological area.

Alcoholic products: perfumes, eau de cologne, eau de toilette, etc. form a very important place in the factory. An immense cistern of 15,000 liters of pure alcohol are turned into "freezes" in which specific scents are created; by immense pipes the liquids are sent to freezing chambers and filter apparatus.

Automatic production lines ensure the filling of perfumes, eau de cologne, the conditioning of lipsticks, creams, etc. . . . by the best possible processes of rapidity and hygiene.

The activities of the factory not only consist of manufacturing products and inventing new ones, but also in creating impeccable presentations for these products: large workshops are devoted to the decoration and the fabrication of cartons by machine and the most modern techniques.

More than 1000 people treat, transform, pack, and send more than 6,000,000 articles, 300,000 liters of alcohol, 300 tons of glass, 400 tons of cardboard, etc.

In 1921, Gabrielle (Coco) Chanel—who had about three thousand employees at her rue Cambon residence and couture house and her boutiques in Deauville, Cannes, and Biarritz—introduced Chanel No. 5, reportedly designed by her perfumer and friend Ernest Beaux, who by then had arrived in Paris from Russia. I was always told by Yvonne, my grandmother-in-law, that the perfume was named after a station in Coty's laboratory at either Suresnes or at the Rallet factory in the south of France at that time. Others say it was Beaux's fifth attempt at creating the aroma she wanted. François had known Gabrielle Chanel since the early days in Paris when Arène had introduced them at the Longchamp races. Later Coco became a friend of Yvonne Coty. I was told that François had offered his factory facilities to experiment in the creation of her first fragrance, one of the first couturier-sponsored perfumes. Coty billed Chanel for the work. The original bill was presented on old brown paper with the company watermark. Monsieur Greilsamer [Raymond-Charles, the manager] showed the bill to me in 1960 in the "morgue," as they called the place for junk and old records in the basement when I first visited Suresnes.

François himself later commented that it was a sad mistake to help create a fragrance for Chanel to name after herself. "Now every designer in Paris will want their own fragrance in his name," he said, according to Yvonne. In the end, though, the Coty company went on to produce perfume for Lentheric, Lancôme, Nina Ricci, and other fashion houses. François commented that he was sorry he had started a service that would give his own company more competition. Having started it, though, he went about building on the new custom, making ever more millions.

Designer Paul Poiret was the first to associate perfume with the fashion business when he established *Les Parfums de Rosine* in 1911 and in 1913 produced *Nuit de Chine.* Poiret tells a story in his autobiography that indicates that François did not neglect opportunities to expand the perfume business in Paris by creating perfumes for fashion houses or producing and distributing perfumes that the fashion houses created with their own *parfumeurs.*

> I was with Rousseau [the chief bookkeeper] in my office, when one morning I saw arrive M. Coty, small and mild mannered, laced into a pale grey suit, with a little straw hat on his head. I didn't know him. A song of my youth came to my lips: *He was a little man / All dressed in grey / Hey, hey . . .*
>
> He seated himself with assurance in an armchair and made me the following declaration:
>
> 'I have come to buy your perfumery business.'
>
> 'But,' I told him, 'it is not for sale.'
>
> 'If you continue as you are doing,' he answered, 'you will take fifteen years before you reach any great importance. If you come with me, you will profit from my management, and in two years you will be worth as much as I am.'
>
> 'Quite so, but in two years my business would be yours, while in the contrary case, in fifteen years it would still be my own property.'
>
> 'You understand nothing about business, Monsieur,' he replied, rising brusquely, and squashing his boater on his little head, he departed raging.
>
> Silently we watched him go; M. Coty had the dimensions of Bonaparte.[4]

Coty's appetite for acclaim and recognition drove him faster and faster; no rejection could stop him. Jean-Jacques Vignault, who became president of Coty Inc., related in the in-house magazine, *Coty Review*: "One day in 1922, François Coty decided to invite Fernand Javal to the Château de Longchamp. Javal was the proprietor of the House of Houbigant. During the meal, Coty proposed: 'Between us, we have cornered almost the entire perfume market. Why not combine our production while maintaining our individual brand identity and distribution networks?' Monsieur Javal was incensed, and stormed out of Coty's château." After all, Houbigant had been in business for centuries. Before Coty was born, the company had been official suppliers to courts of Europe. Coty tried to take over anything he found to his liking.

Other Perfumers in Suresnes

At Suresnes, François's perfume-related plant, the most complex ever conceived, attracted other *parfumeurs*. His handsome, functional buildings reflected in the beautiful Seine across from his offices at Longchamp. He named the complex La Cité des Parfums, in his usual audacious fashion, but he did not expect that his presence would draw most of the great perfumers and perfume manufacturers of the period to Suresnes. Jean-Philippe Worth, Volnay, René Sordes, Richard Hudnut, and others followed Coty to the little town. Suresnes soon became the world capital of the wholesale perfume business.

The celebrated Parisian *parfumeur* Hugues Guerlain brought his production to Suresnes in 1919. Maurice Blanchet joined him in 1921. In 1922, Jean-Philippe Worth had his offices in the square bounded by rue Chevreul and rue Dupont, facing rue de Saint-Cloud. Worth perfumes sold worldwide from 1932 until 1939, when the

Cité des Parfums, Suresnes. (Société Historique et Artistique de Suresnes, Archives)

Workers manufacture rouge makeup at Coty's *Cité des Parfums*.
(Société Historique et Artistique de Suresnes, Archives)

Second World War closed down production.[5] Not so with Coty, who continued to produce throughout the war.

René Duval (1887-1936), a Coty employee trained by François, established his own business and became an important figure in other perfume or cosmetic businesses. He became one of Coty's first seven market representatives in 1906. Soon thereafter, Coty appointed him commercial director. In 1919, Duval created his own enterprise, naming it Volnay. He installed his offices and processing unit in a villa on the hills of Mont-Valérien near Coty, purchased from the family of the actress Gabrielle Dorziat. Duval capitalized on this connection with the actress by creating *Le Parfum de Gabrielle Dorziat* and advertising in the theaters where she performed. Naming perfumes after stars is not new after all.

The corporation of René Sordes was established at 11, rue Jules Ferry in Suresnes. It specialized in producing synthetic perfume ingredients, most notably ionones, with "notes" of iris and violet that are often used as modifiers of scents. The factory moved to the then newly named avenue Franklin Roosevelt in Suresnes before eventually relocating to Normandy in 1993.

Richard Hudnut came to Suresnes in 1920. Hudnut perfumes and cosmetics were fabricated on rue Pagès in Suresnes and carried a French label, but they were usually exported to the United States. The Hudnut Company remained in France until the end of the 1950s, when it moved to the United States.

The Architecture of Suresnes during Coty's Time

The buildings at Suresnes conceived by Coty and constructed under his careful supervision exhibited taste and quality. Coty became an artist-architect with these structures, designed in the early art-deco style. There is also evidence that François was influenced by the architectural concepts of Claude-Nicolas Ledoux (1736-1806), among whose many Parisian "city gates" was the one at Monceau, near François's Bois de Boulogne residence. In 1923, François purchased and began to rebuild the Pavillon de la Comtesse Du Barry at Louveciennes, between Paris and Marly. Ledoux had designed the pavilion, and François had an opportunity to study his work meticulously when he ordered his workers to relocate the building stone by stone and to replace or restore every architectural detail. Then, he amused himself with twentieth-century innovations, using modern technology and materials, fancying that he was improving upon Ledoux's original work.

Coty's Cité des Parfums bears similarities to Ledoux's Cité Idéale and Les Salines near Besançon. Wherever François's architectural ideas may have come from, he expanded them to include space for all the social services he provided. At his Cité des Parfums, Coty became a pioneer in the development of social services for thousands of employees, mostly women. His facilities at Suresnes and his other factories around the world became renowned for the amenities that enhanced the workplace for workers. A Coty pamphlet from the early 1920s, showing the Cité des Parfums, indicates that the complex provided not only technical, commercial, and administrative services but social services as well. These included medical services, a model infirmary, and an application process for receiving financial aid for further medical needs, as well as social security. Showers, a large dining hall, a waiting room, and a library were installed. François even provided a loan office so that his most enterprising employees might start businesses of their own. He thus became a private banker, one more illustration of the wide range of his interests and his creative genius in taking advantage of every possible opportunity.

In 1915, Henri Sellier, then president of the Office Départmental des Habitations à Bon Marché de la Seine, planned the construction of a Cité-Jardin (Garden City) at Suresnes. It was to be a gigantic public works project, and there is evidence that François Coty's Cité des Parfums had inspired this undertaking. In 1917, architect Alexandre Maistrasse was commissioned to design a plan where groups of four-story buildings would be adjacent to individual pavilions. This novel architectural ensemble was to welcome between eight thousand and ten thousand inhabitants of a growing modern town. The completed Cité-Jardin featured these buildings, as well as innovations such as a swimming pool, gymnasium,

Interior of Coty's factories at the Cité des Parfums in Suresnes. (Société Historique et Artistique de Suresnes, Archives)

residence for the aged, and hotel for bachelors. Henri Sellier became mayor of Suresnes in 1919, serving until 1943.

Sellier also aimed to improve the health of children by building schools and homes adapted to their physical conditions. In June of 1920, an outdoor school with a capacity for 100 children was installed at the ancient stud farm of Fouilleuse. All the amenities and learning facilities of Sellier's Suresnes paralleled the architectural and social work Coty had undertaken already at his Cité des Parfums. In 1934, Coty gave 1 million francs to the Bureaux de Bienfaisance of the towns of Suresnes, Puteaux, and Neuilly-sur-Seine. The generosity François bestowed on these towns where he had established his factories is another indication that Coty and Sellier worked together in Suresnes. Coty's last bequest in Suresnes directly financed Sellier's charity project there.

The Coty System

François developed the Coty system, later known as the vertical system of operating businesses, at the Cité des Parfums. A vast series of businesses, industries, and factories operated in a huge group of buildings and ateliers on the grounds at Suresnes, Pantin, and Puteaux, under a monolithic system of operations that François Coty himself devised and oversaw. He transferred this then-unique system to all his factories worldwide. The system at Cité integrated research, development, production, packaging, marketing, advertising, and exporting in an unprecedented way. Coty produced and owned every aspect of his perfume business, from the fields of flowers and herbs, glass blowing, chemical laboratories where Firmenich of Geneva delivered raw materials for processing, presentation and container boxes, and label design and production to the making of transport boxes. Transportation and delivery of all products to both wholesale and retail destinations were also part of the undertaking. Banking and bookkeeping were handled in-house as much as possible. As many as 100 accountants worked in one gigantic room, with François Coty exercising complete control over the whole system.

This determination to control everything and everyone around him became characteristic of François as he matured. He had become more and more wealthy and was now identified as France's richest man. His passion for control expanded into his real-estate purchases and construction projects. It was also evident in the political effort he launched in Corsica in 1919 and in his 1923 entry into the news business when he bought *Le Figaro*.

François's passion to control began to manifest itself in the acquisition of multiple mistresses. If he could not totally control his own wife and children, he could control women who participated in his growing sensual life. His money had come in fast, faster than any fortune in France. He found himself to be an important man, and he loved it. He adored wearing his personally designed wardrobe and his outrageous jewelry and acquiring art, houses, automobiles, airplanes, and women. This did not mean that he showed it all off, but he recognized his own wealth and importance. The more money he had, the more power he was able to wield, and he began to indulge his early interests in journalism and the exercise of power he had learned from Senator Arène. Evidence indicates that Yvonne adapted well at first to her husband's expanding ego. She could ignore his extramarital sexual life because he exhibited sincere love and affection for her and their children, showering them with gifts and attention when they found themselves together in his and her increasingly occupied lives.

Coty's Marketing Innovations

A man of enormous creative energy, Coty maintained an avid interest in the artistic aspects of perfume development, even as he showed genius in the business end of the empire he was building. No detail escaped him. Thinking of himself as an artist, he incorporated art into his program for sophisticated worldwide marketing of his French perfume business. A salesman as well as a seducer, he knew what a well-chosen phrase could do. Each perfume had its own advertising copy. *L'Or* of 1912 was for "pale-eyed blondes who will love the way this fragrance blends with the aroma of blond tobacco." *La Jacée* was "unobtrusive and subtle, a fresh spring fragrance for young girls," and *Chypre* was "captivating" and "mysterious" for "the brunette's charm."

Perfume "is a love affair with oneself," Coty claimed, and it became, because of Coty, an essential accessory for women, like stockings or gloves. From the time of his sales venture with the pony cart, his clients had included socialites and housewives, a first for a producer of perfumes and cosmetics. François Coty's special perfumes were among the most expensive in the world, and they were sought after and fought over by the rich and famous. In the company's records, there is a long list of Coty scents chosen by celebrities. Mme. Jacques Guerlain, wife of Coty's competitor, would wear only *L'Aimant* and *Emeraude,* both produced by Coty. Author Colette, whose bizarre conquests and social activities were a regular feature of the daily newspapers, favored *Jasmin de Corse.* When such preferences were publicized, Coty's sales soared.

Coty had a sense of the importance of perfume to women, and he understood the need of all women for something customized to them as individuals, no matter how rich or poor, beautiful or modest they may be. He wrote in 1905, "[My desire is] to give all women the ability to be beautiful by placing within their reach quality products conceived, manufactured and sold with this goal alone; such is the objective that I determined upon. Its realization will give birth to a new industry with dimensions unheard of anywhere in the world before now."

Working with his in-house designers or with Lalique, Coty devised innovative retail cases, lighting, and signage. He recommended his presentation concepts to the retail outlets that sold his products. As a brilliant marketer with aesthetic sensibilities, he created a new market for graphic artists, lithographers, engravers, and interior designers. François Coty perfected the aesthetics of presentation. His chief designer, Georges Delhomme, worked with Coty to invent a new display concept featuring only one product—a bottle of perfume, a box of powder, a glass jar of cream, or a powder puff—but dozens of units of that product placed side by side in the case. The rows and columns composed of multiple copies of a single perfect product fascinated window shoppers.

Delhomme then proceeded to attract customers with the opposite approach. On the steamship *Atlantic,* the Coty display case exhibited one exquisite bottle of perfume lit by an invisible projector, which had been designed especially for the display by Philips Engineers.[6] At the Grande Maison du Blanc in Paris, Delhomme created a display to suggest a waterfall: thousands of identical bottles of perfumes were arranged into serried, semicircular ranks. At the Grands Magasins du Louvre, Delhomme recreated the Place Vendôme shop of the House of Coty. The Galeries Lafayette's window exhibited hundreds of overlapping powder compacts, creating the visual effect of a deep-pile tapestry.

An innovator in the psychological strategies of marketing, Coty was the first to use his own products—the way they looked, smelled, and felt—as well as newspapers, posters, radio, and cinema for advertisement. Many of his publicity programs were both original and successful, and thereby influenced the development of subsequent marketing techniques by his competitors. Coty demonstrated a flair for timing when he released products. *L'Origan,* with its warm and intoxicating scent, came out in 1905, the year that the Fauvist painters became renowned. *Iris,* a bud-vase perfume, was created in 1913 at a time when the Russian ballets were taking Paris by storm.

A Coty delivery truck at the Cité des Parfums, bears the François Coty signature to advertise the company and its perfumes. (Société Historique et Artistique de Suresnes, Archives)

Coty realized that his own name could be used as a marketing tool. At Suresnes, the Coty signature was painted in gold on the sides of the black delivery vehicles. These vans and trucks left Suresnes to travel all over France, delivering similarly signed Coty products to ships sailing around the world. Coty's signature, printed on boxes, storefronts, and factory facades, became recognizable worldwide. Coty perfected the use of his name as a logo throughout the world. During his lifetime, his name was as important as the fragrance. He reveled in this.

Coty Inc. joins in the 100th anniversary celebration of Fifth Avenue, New York, in 1924. (Roulhac Toledano Collection)

CHAPTER 7

Perfuming the Globe

In business: François Coty, a great name in perfumery.
Memorial of Corsicans, Ajaccio

Sixteenth- and seventeenth-century fathers of the nobility wrote scripture-laden treatises for their sons on what to do and not to do in life. About 1600, Englishman Francis Osborne wrote one such epistle to his son, when the youth embarked on the Continental grand tour. His advice was that gloves and doublet should be ordered from a French tailor, but "Spanish perfumers are best." That dictum changed as the twentieth century began. Despite cologne's first development in Cologne, Germany, by Italian *parfumeurs,* France now led the Western world in the fabrication and marketing of fragrance. By the end of World War I, François Coty's French perfume and cosmetics industry exploded across the globe. Coty SA expanded exponentially in the creation, manufacture, and selling of perfumes and cosmetics on every continent.

Perfume permeated French life and literature in Coty's day. Women indulged in applying newly popular fragrance. Writers referred to perfume in their essays, memoirs, and novels. During *La Belle Epoque,* a plethora of scent-related poetry and prose appeared. Marcel Proust wrote, "Let a noise or a scent once heard or once smelt, be heard or smelt again . . . and the permanent and habitually concealed essence of things is liberated and our true self . . . is awakened and reanimated." To French poet Frédéric Mistral, Grasse, where the French perfume industry developed, was a "Valley of love, the promised land of Perfume." Architects, too, found that the perfume industry generated business for the design of factories and distinguished sales outlets. Molinard's distillation room in Grasse, for example, was designed by Gustave Eiffel, who designed the Eiffel Tower as well as the tower at Coty's château at Longchamp. Coty made it his goal to see that perfume and cosmetics became commercial giants from Europe to Asia and from North America to South America. His cosmetics became the subject of conversation and the object of purchase for women of every ethnic and economic group everywhere.

Innovator

François became the premier innovator in the history of perfume. Besides creating new scents using traditional, natural materials in fragrances such as *L'Ambre* and *Le Musc*, he was among the first to use synthetic ingredients on a worldwide scale. Not only new on the market, they were less expensive. More important, they could be produced more quickly. Coty perfumes and cosmetics had become so popular that he needed immediate delivery to his factories of vast quantities of raw materials year round. With aromatic chemicals or synthetics as the base of the fragrance, he could add just the right amount of the traditional natural products, and do so quickly and at a reasonable cost.

Among his most enduring achievements was the creation in 1917 of a perfume he called *Chypre*. His blending for this perfume was so popular and so successful that it became the principal fragrance in a family of its own. When fragrances since 1917 are a blend of chypre's variants, it is thanks to François Coty.[1]

As an industrial innovator, Coty understood, like automakers and media magnates, the essentials of modern business: mass consumption through effective marketing and presentation. These were as important to the business as the product itself. Cachet was another key: Coty had to devise a way to make his perfumes as necessary as attire. Through another innovation, he expanded market share through point-of-purchase price uniformity and control. He did this by establishing a price list and demanding that all his retailers bind themselves to it.

Coty developed his face powder into fifteen fragrances and twenty shades. Later, there were nineteen perfumes in production at once, all of which he had created or tested and altered personally. These perfumes were presented in flasks, large and small, making them affordable to most women. A lighter, less-expensive scent sold as eau de toilette in an atomizer.

Makeup matching his perfumes included Air Spun powder compressed in a compact along with rouge and lipstick. Talcs, soaps, bath salts and brilliantines were perfumed to match *L'Aimant*, *Emeraude*, *Paris*, *Chypre*, and *L'Origan*. Coty was one of the first to include vitamins such as A and D in a face and body cream. Coty

SA manufactured hand and nail cream, nail polish and remover, eye and lash color, and eyeliner. Beauty milk, conditioning cream for nighttime, foundation cream, and vitamin hydrating cream were developed along with foundation lotion, skin freshener, and special astringent. Coty led the way in the development of a vast array of beauty products. At the same time, he educated many of the founders of today's great perfume houses in his own plants and retail shops in Europe and North and South America.

While another provincial, Gabrielle (Coco) Chanel, was learning the names of the 1,200 families that made up the Parisian *beau monde,* a list that would help her in business, Coty was busy developing, for the first time in France, a clientele for perfume and cosmetics among the bourgeoisie and rural women. Coty's great success as *parfumeur* to royalty and nobility across the world while at the same time courting the middle class and even more modest classes with affordable prices created his popularity and wealth. The Coty name became a well-known brand to tens of millions of women. His company achieved the largest sales in the history of perfume in France and worldwide.

Historically, perfume had been a luxury for nobility and courtesans, the two extremes of society. The seventeenth-century noble Breton memoirist, Madame de Sevigné, traveled with her marquetry perfume casket filled with concentrates of jasmine, tuberose, ambergris, Turkish rose, and musk. Marie-Antoinette rushed her *parfumeur* to her boudoir before fleeing Versailles with Louis XVI and their entourage on her eventual journey to the guillotine. On May 17, 1815, a month before his defeat at Waterloo, Napoleon ordered perfumed gloves and other toiletries from his supplier, *"Houbigant-Maguy, Marchand Parfumeur, Grande rue du Faubourg Saint-Honoré."*

Perfume was essential for streetwalkers, too, no matter the cost. Because of this, pharmacists had concocted cheap heavy scents, filled with musk and packaged in medicinal bottles. It took François Coty, sensualist and notorious lover of the early 1900s, to open the world of fragrance beyond the women on both sides of this great divide to the largest group, the majority of women, in fact: middle-class and poor women. The time was ripe for this man, who could both create and market perfumes. François had immersed himself both in *parfumerie* in Grasse and in French society in Paris with Arène. He saw the opportunity "to go beyond the usual customers of the time, i.e., the women of the world and the demimondaines, to the bourgeoisie and even those who were not as well-to-do," recalled

Jean-Jacques Vignault.[2] Coty's theme was: "Give a woman the best product to be made, market it in the perfect flask, beautiful in its simplicity yet impeccable in taste, ask a reasonable price for it, and you will witness the birth of a business the size of which the world has never seen."

Coty considered himself impeccable in his own taste, exhibiting luxury and refinement simultaneously. He surrounded himself with beautiful things, and wrapped in his pocket he carried cut and uncut gemstones so that he could peruse their beauty and fine craftsmanship at any moment. Coty was a product of French culture at a time when its best-known characteristics were good taste and the good life.

Jean-Jacques Vignault wrote in the *Coty Review,* "François Coty had the passion for beauty, a need for luxury, a sure taste, an audacious 'nose,' and a great deal of audacity. But this impetuous man of rapid decisions knew also to develop the greatest patience, modifying without ceasing the composition of a perfume or the graphics of a decorator. He did not launch the fabrication of one of his products except after a long and creative period of personal testing and thinking about it."

As early as 1775, Jean-François Houbigant had opened a retail perfume shop on *rue du Faubourg Saint-Honoré,* bringing both Comtesse Du Barry, paramour of Louis XV, and Napoleon's Empress Josephine there as clients. Pauline Bonaparte, Napoleon's sister, preferred to frequent Jean-François Lubin, who opened Aux Armes de France in Paris in 1798. Lubin attracted a large, rich clientele, since, for the first time, he brought powders, lotions, smelling salts, and toilet accessories out of the pharmacy and into the boutique. Houbigant and Lubin paved the way for Coty, who foresaw the rise of cosmetics use worldwide.

Colette understood François Coty when she wrote of the importance of perfume to French culture and the economy: "The fashion designer is better placed than anyone else to know what women need and what suits them. Thanks to the designer-perfumer, perfume becomes more than a beauty treatment in the orchestration of elegance: it can be, it must, represent the direct expression of the tendencies and tastes of our era." She had been enamored with *Jasmin de Corse* since its release in 1906. She wrote that she wore it daily. Colette had known Coty from the turn of the century when he attended the fashionable salons with Arène and Carnot.

Perfume, then, is far more than an essence. Like the term itself, *essence,* it has been "essential" or integral to the development of French lifestyle and its luxury industry. The former French colonies also benefited from France's huge volume of perfume production, providing flowers and plants for the various scents. Plants that could not be transplanted well to France were grown for the perfume industry in Madagascar and Senegal. When France ruled scores of colonies around the world, Pondichéry in India and areas in Indochine had grown flowers for French perfume. Although geraniums from Réunion were the finest, lavender reigned supreme in Grasse. François Coty also took his perfumes and cosmetics to the colonies and former colonies. Both the French colonials and the well-to-do natives bought his products.

Wherever François went, he had all-consuming projects. These took him farther and farther away from Yvonne. While she and the children might join him in Corsica or America, there was seldom a moment's rest. The word *megalomaniac* appeared in reference to François in a Corsican newspaper before 1920, and his frantic activity isolated him from Yvonne. Their residences grew in number so fast that going from château to villa to *hôtel particulier* became oppressive to her. During the 1920s, they often crisscrossed France separately, staying among their different châteaux.

Premier Mistress

Shortly after returning from a trip to Corsica in 1919, Coty walked into his own boutique at Place Vendôme. He found himself looking at a new attendant, about the same age as his daughter. She was Henriette Dieudé, born in 1902 in Paris's fourteenth arrondissement. While strongly attracted to her, he probably did not realize that she would become one of the major players in the drama that was his life. At the beginning of their relationship, Henriette was just one of the many young girls that Coty took to the Hotel Astoria. Soon she was pregnant. Coty set up an elegant Paris flat for her. For the next ten years, his affair with Henriette, who achieved the status of premier mistress, and her growing brood of children, eventually five, eroded the foundations of Coty's marriage and destroyed his relationships with numerous colleagues. Although this ongoing liaison was one of many, it was so notorious that it became an embarrassment and continual irritation for Yvonne. It was also one of the causes of a schism that developed between François and his daughter, Christiane.

Despite all these personal distractions and claims on him, François never wavered from his life's central, consuming passion: Coty SA. More and more he traveled to England and Eastern Europe to develop contacts, design and build factories, and market his cosmetics. When he undertook a business trip to Egypt, he brought Henriette with him. His aim was to create a new product for his expanding perfume clientele in Cairo. He knew that traditional Egyptian scents were embedded in a wax base that was shaped into little balls, then secured inside small containers that were worn on the wrist. He wanted to devise a new product: a small, round, enamel holder for scented wax.

François visited one of the flower fields he was buying. When he laid eyes on a breed of unusual white miniature donkeys there, he purchased 200 of them and ordered them shipped to d'Artigny. Their "fragrance" was astounding, but François loved them and could not be convinced to get rid of them. The Touraine countryside became imbued with a different Coty "scent," prompting Yvonne to say, "It is reason enough to give this absurd man a divorce." What might she have said had she known Henriette had accompanied François to Egypt. Roland's children, François's and Yvonne's grandchildren, grew up among the little animals.

Parenting

François was too immersed in his perfume, cultural, and financial interests as well as his own love life to focus attention on his and Yvonne's children. From time to time, he lavished gifts on them, just as he brought gifts to his much-publicized mistresses. Coty's largesse was not casual. He was generous by nature and at times impassioned about his family and friends. The wife of the aviator Maurice Bellonte, whose flights François had sponsored, had tuberculosis. François arranged the purchase of an entire wardrobe for her—"whatever pleases the lady"—for 50,000 francs.

Roland, Coty's only legitimate son, and his daughter, Christiane, grew up in Paris, first at Longchamp and then at Villa La Source at Suresnes. Francois's wealth had accumulated so quickly that, by the time the children started their education at Neuilly, both of their parents were often away, leaving the youngsters with a growing staff to look after their needs. François did sail with Yvonne and members of his extended family to the United States almost yearly before World War I. Such voyages resumed in 1922, after the war's end.

Roland spent his youth trying to get his father's attention. At age seventeen, he undertook one of his most hairbrained stunts in this endeavor. He attempted to fly his new single-engine biplane under seven of the bridges that span the Seine in the middle of Paris. He succeeded not only in interesting his father but also the gendarmerie. François confiscated the plane, scolded Roland severely, then provided his son with an advance on his allowance. This disciplinary style was typical of François. Yvonne did not scold. She could not help but find Roland amusing. Sadly, the desire of Roland's soul, to receive his parents' loving accolades, was never fulfilled. He became a dedicated, lifelong playboy, another charmer in the Spoturno-Coty line.

Roland had Suresnes as his playground and his father's huge staff and their children as playmates. The plants' accessibility meant that he wandered about the grounds, went through the ateliers, and kidded with the employees. He enjoyed the exercise courts with Francois's workers and looked on at the ball games. Playing card games with the Coty truck drivers and other staff was another of his pastimes. As a result, he was comfortable with the working class by the time he was a teenager. He did not, however, take any great interest in the perfume business.

Christiane married in 1920, when she was seventeen. Her marriage, to Paul Dubonnet of the well-known wine family, was considered appropriate, at least by the Coty family. François and Yvonne had known Paul's parents for years. In 1911, François and Yvonne Coty and Emile and Yvonne Dubonnet had sailed from France to New York, for both business and pleasure. Then in 1922, Paul and Christiane Dubonnet sailed to the United States on June 24, out of Le Havre on *Le France* with François and Yvonne, part of a series of lavish wedding gifts from François for his daughter. Paul immediately began to work in administration for Coty SA.

Marriage allowed Christiane to move out of the life of her sometimes frenetic, obsessive, and authoritarian father. She also left the realm of art, creativity, and passion that embraced all those around François Coty. Her efforts to escape her home, though, resulted in domination by another wealthy, powerful family. Paul Dubonnet also followed in the footsteps of his father-in-law and employer, initiating successive love affairs that upset Christiane. Christiane and Paul Dubonnet's only child, daughter Rolande Dubonnet, was born in 1923. By 1929, the couple was divorced.

François Coty and the Women's Market

Coty not only brought new cosmetic products to women everywhere. He also provided jobs to thousands of women. Indirectly, he promoted the recognition and appreciation of women in all societies. His political league, *Solidarité Française*, had a women's section, as did his newspaper, *L'Ami du Peuple*, which was geared toward a working-class readership. He was the first of France's influential magnates to favor the vote for women. Coty's interest in and understanding of women fit into the development and success of his perfume and cosmetics business.

Through his hiring practices and his development of women as purchasers of retail cosmetics, François Coty presaged the women's movement. In the early twentieth century, a new "seat law" in France allowed shop girls to sit down when no clients were in the shop. Another law, called the Emile Loubet law, permitted women to become lawyers. The Chamber of Deputies, however, had turned down women's suffrage twice by 1906. French women finally gained their suffrage in 1944. Coty, raised by widows, promoted women's rights in all his newspapers and was thoughtful of his female employees at Suresnes. He gave them maternity leave and provided a nursery as well as pensions. His fellow industrialist Louis Renault, the automobile magnate, was furious at this. Once, in Renault's office, the two grabbed each other by their ties because Renault reproached Coty for his tendency to indulge his employees, especially at the factories in Suresnes. Renault outlived Coty, and during World War II he found himself labeled a Nazi collaborator. His automobile holdings were nationalized.

Christiane said her father called Renault a dandy, an odd choice of words because Coty must have known that he himself was France's most famous dandy. Coming from Coty, this should hardly have been an insult. Therein lies the story: Coty's perception of himself was often skewed. For one thing, he saw himself as a friend of the working class when it behooved him. This was not Socialism but the widespread paternalism practiced by some other French business magnates between the wars. Coty also wrote in *L'Ami du Peuple* in 1933, "Through the support of good friends, I found refuge at a desk that I have not left since." If the metaphor meant that he worked hard, that may be so, but he was seldom seen at a desk. He was constantly on the go around the world.

Coty began giving heavy financial support to the right-wing leagues that attracted so many of France's business magnates after World War I. Among his first large donations was 1 million francs in 1919 to Charles Maurras's Action Française. In Maurras, he found a strong and irascible character who would not allow Coty, no matter his millions, to influence him or his organization. Coty moved on to other leagues, providing money to many of them at the same time.

As an artist and a stickler for details, with unerring taste, he wrote:

> An object, a model, however beautiful or magnificent, is always open to criticism. I keep it in front of me for six months. It follows me everywhere. I look at it constantly. I turn on the light at night to

contemplate it more. If, at the end of six months it never displeases me, or I like it as much as the first day, I know that it will please everyone, everywhere—that it is in good taste, indisputable. In that case, I have confidence in it and I introduce it.

Coty's vellum stationery carried the watermark *Arches* and the signature of the artist, Draeger. Other letters have the name Lalique embedded in the paper. One letter reads:

Monsieur and dear client,

I have the honor of sending you with this letter the new list of prices imposed by the sale in detail of my Specialties. These prices are applicable from the 15th of January, 1920.

I hope that you will want to read attentively the letter and the General Conditions that precede the Tarif. The indications that they contain cannot fail to interest you. The confidential discount that will be made to you over the amount of each, deluxe tax and rights deducted, is from:

80% on l'Eau de Coty, ex-eau de cologne Cordon Rouge, creation, 1909.

35% on the perfumes, eaux de toilette, lotions, brilliantines, sachets, coffrets [small boxes].

40% on the Rice Powders.

The freight, the packaging and the insurance, charged until now to you will be charged to my company for all the orders above 200 francs.

I have the pleasure of informing you that from February on, I will put on sale a certain number of specialties and new perfumes conceived by me in the course of the last two years; they have not been fabricated until now because of the lack of certain primary materials and notably the bottling. In spite of the promises a hundred times renewed, my furnishers of bottles have ended by confessing their incompetence and I have been given the responsibility of organizing two factories, so important to give satisfaction from now on to all my clients. You will appreciate, yourselves, the quality of these new flasks when comparing them to the old ones.

I have also doubled my *Ateliers de Cartonnage* [packing] and those affected by impressions of Art. In this that concerns perfumes, I am myself composing new, perfectly original aromas. Their quality, from all points of view, marks real progress over my old creations. I do not believe that it would be possible to do better in the actual state of the chemistry of perfumes. The old specialties have been reviewed with the greatest care, and their presentation has reached important new heights with the objective of conserving a character of impeccable originality. All these new models have been the objects of registration at the Tribunal de Commerce of France [Copyright Office].

Hoping that you will know to appreciate my multiple efforts, I beg you to agree, my dear client, in the expression of my very distinguished sentiments.

Signed with the Coty logo, the letter reeks of François Coty's ideas, methods, and personality. It ranges from art to business to taxes to sales and back to art, with a purposeful slap at Lalique, who could not supply bottles fast enough to fulfill François's demand. Determined to succeed and to respond to the demand for his products, Coty could be ruthless to friends, as indicated in the letter. This blatant need to be the best in whatever he did was a characteristic of Coty that transferred from perfumery and business to all his activities: real estate, the press, politics, and even his philanthropy. He never gave up.

The letter cited above provides an inkling of another characteristic: François Coty completely controlled all his interests and involvements. He shaped women, châteaux, and newspapers to his specifications, and he tried to do the same thing with the governments of Corsica and France. This would prove to be his downfall. In the letter, François is setting up a defense of the lawsuit that Lalique brought against Coty SA for breaking their bottling contract. Although Coty SA lost the lawsuit, that did not keep François from garnering millions over the next years, producing bottles at his own glassworks. François loved to design bottles personally, using ideas from his growing art and decorative-art collections installed at his various *châteaux* and *hôtels particuliers* across France.

Over the years, Coty bought properties for growing flowers at Grasse, near Sartène and Ajaccio in Corsica, at Fondi, Italy, and south of Rome in the province of Latina. However, the perfumes and cosmetics were prepared in Suresnes. The glassworks that had replaced those of Lalique were producing 250,000 bottles a day down the road at Puteaux, a busy place where, in addition to bottle making, lipstick and cream tubes and jars were stamped while printing presses ran, sometimes round the clock. The packaging plant at nearby Neuilly produced the containers for Coty products as well as the shipping crates.

Coty's perfume *L'Or* was the most expensive in the world—$100 U.S. per flask in 1910, when the U.S. was still on the gold standard. That same year, *Styx* came out. In 1910, when the Ballets Russes stormed Paris with productions having music composed by Igor Stravinsky, directed by Sergei Diaghilev, and starring Vaslav Nijinsky, Coty became their patron. The stars visited him and

Yvonne at their various residences and occasionally performed. This, in turn, helped to make his fragrances popular with this émigré population.

In 1912, Coty opened retail shops and factories in England. His 1912 British catalogue listed twenty-two "handkerchief" perfumes. He launched *L'Entraînement, Cyclamen, Le Lilas Pourpre, La Violette Ambrée, Oeillet, France,* and *Jacinthe* between 1912 and 1917. When he established Coty England, Ltd. in 1923, François called on his old Corsican relations. Jean-Baptiste Ornano ran the company from London before establishing his own companies, Orlane among them. Coty sold huge amounts of his products in the British Isles. He expanded his factories in England to supply the endless demand for *Paris*, his best-selling perfume there, and his other products. One factory was at Brentford, set up in one of Coty's signature art-deco buildings and replete with the distinctive logo and a sign proclaiming *Parfums de Luxe*. The House of Coty retail shop filled a Regency-style townhouse at London's Strasford Place.

After Monsieur Ornano left his post to launch other perfume companies, the English firm was run by the Munday family, father and son. Their manicure sets, which hit the market in 1930, made millions for the business.

Coty continued his relationship with Antoine Chiris's sons, using Chiris as his materials supplier in France and Russia. Then François bought the Rallet factories near Moscow from Chiris. Coty used the facilities to develop special perfumes for many of the Eastern European fashion houses. He kept them until their confiscation by the Bolsheviks. Coty reestablished the facilities in Provence, bringing the French workers home from Russia at great expense. Ernest Beaux, of the great dynasty of perfumers who created French perfumes in Russia, was the director and chief of the Rallet laboratory from 1896 until 1911. When Coty brought his employees back to France, Beaux found himself in the land of his ancestors. He was the *parfumeur* credited with creating Gabrielle (Coco) Chanel's No. 5, one of the first blendings of natural fragrance and synthetic substances, in 1921, after Coty brought Rallet to France.

Benjamin Levy, an American reportedly of French background, had become the sole agent for Coty in the United States as early as 1910. He worked for years with Virginie Dubois Le Baron, Coty's talented and energetic mother-in-law, who came to the United States on behalf of Coty multiple times each year "with her parrot on her shoulder." Yvonne's mother represented the Coty family in the

United States between 1913 and 1923. Levy's relationship with Coty Inc. and the Coty family lasted beyond World War II. He supervised setting up Coty Inc. in Delaware in 1913 as an American corporation. Coty's grandmother, Anna Maria Spoturno, was listed as a member of the board of directors of the United States company. While Coty was briefly in uniform during World War I, Anna Maria Spoturno was supervising the building of his vast plant in Suresnes or helping to develop new products.

Expansion

After an astronomical artistic, fragrance, and financial success in Paris by 1910, with *Ambre Antique* (1905), *Jasmin de Corse* (1906), and *L'Effleurt* (1907) being huge sellers in France and *Cordon Vert and Cordon Rouge* colognes (1909) being bestsellers in Russia, Coty had moved across France to establish boutiques in the provinces. He put together a group of representatives who sold his products all over France, first to the great department stores and then to select retailers, or *parfumeurs détaillants*. He opened shops in Nice, Bordeaux, and the French colony in Algeria in addition to his exquisite boutique at 28, Place Vendôme. By 1910, he had expanded not only to Russia but to the United States as well. Soon, he extended his activities to other foreign countries, with representatives in England, Switzerland, Spain, and Scandinavia. By the late 1920s, François's French company, Coty SA, had subsidiaries in Armenia; Milan, Italy; Mainz, Germany; Buenos Aires, Argentina; Rio de Janeiro, Brazil; Montreal, Canada; Sydney, Australia; and Johannesburg, South Africa. Twenty-three agencies had factories. There were seventy-two agencies for distribution. Investment on five continents made Coty the largest worldwide organization for fragrance products.

After World War I, disgusted with his losses in Russia, Coty took the opportunity to develop cosmetics sales for women in Eastern Europe. He founded La Société Coty Roumaine in 1927, strengthening his presence in Romania. Already he had achieved enormous success in both his Romanian and Hungarian retail outlets. That year he also set up La Société des Cultures Florales Méditerranéennes, for the cultivation of flowers in France and Italy for perfume making.

Coty Helps His Staff

François Coty himself launched the careers of a number of notable executives in the perfume business. He mentored some of these individuals, and others he learned from, especially Alphée Dubois, Jr., Yvonne's young uncle. Always close to Alphée, François came to depend upon him more and more over time. Alphée held positions in various Coty's projects, providing acute intelligence and acumen. At Coty SA, he was director of production and technical director. Guillaume Ornano, Coty's Corsican cousin living in the Touraine, was appointed commercial director of Coty SA. Raymond Goëry, who discovered Coty's nose, decided to join Coty SA, running the departments for makeup—rouges, powders, lipsticks, and creams.

Jean Despres also numbered among Coty's protégés. His father was a professor who taught Roland Coty mathematics at Neuilly. With his usual largesse and enthusiasm, Coty hired the professor's son. After training in France and England at Coty, Despres sailed to America on the liner *France* to work for Benjamin Levy. Despres started as a salesman in the Midwest, advancing to assistant sales manager and, in 1932, to national sales manager. After Coty's death, he became executive vice president of Coty. He married Lilly Daché, designer of glamorous hats and fashions popular in the United States. When Bernard D. Lee, the publicist of Coty Inc., interviewed Jean Despres for his May 1983 article, "Days of Perfume and Roses," Despres described Coty as the originator of the perfume industry, and he remembered Coty as the supreme *parfumeur*: "I still recall our weekly 'wettings' [at Suresnes] when François would test the latest productions, and call for more bergamot, more patchouli. He was, without doubt, the world's greatest *parfumeur*." Because of his training with Coty, Despres knew that fragrance "was more than just a business." He declared, "It was a personal devotion to the taste and glamor that perfume typified—the ultimate tribute to the women who loved and wore it."

A number of Coty's trainees established their own businesses or became major factors in other cosmetics houses. Lancôme owes everything to Coty, since one of its founders, Armand Petitjean, began his career with Coty as an agent in Brazil. While Petitjean created perfumes in his own name, they carried the Coty hallmark. Later, with the Ornanos, Petitjean founded Lancôme, named after Le Château de Lancosme, where he he had seen a profusion of roses. At first, he was in partnership with Coty, using Coty money and hiring Georges Delhomme from Coty as chief designer. Serge Heftler-Louiche was Coty's personal and financial secretary, then managing director of Coty in France, before leading the establishment of Christian Dior after World War II. Among other Coty "babies" were Lentheric and

Charles of the Ritz, established largely by Benjamin Levy. Thus, Coty did his part in training and developing new leadership for the worldwide cosmetics industry.

Profit-sharing programs and contingency funds were available to Coty employees. He gave exit passes for mothers to nurse at home, and there were baby beds in all factory buildings. When he offered eight days of paid holiday, he was ahead of his time. He even instituted sports fields and football clubs for his employees long before such programs were common in the corporate world.

Although François had multiple interests worldwide, making fragrances gave him pleasure and energized him throughout his entire adult life. For example, six months before his death in 1934, François Coty worked with an employee, Vincent Roubert, to create a new scent, *A'Suma*. Roubert, who had created *L'Aimant* in 1927, called his employer a matinee idol and in 1947 wrote an account of their work together, saying, "As well as doing his own work [Coty] would help and encourage me with mine, some of which bore commercial fruit. It was a meeting of minds, a dedicated and sometimes exhausting collaboration, and I am proud of the results."

That same year, 1934, before he died in July, Coty employed Pierre Camin. More than seventy years later, recollection of their partnership had lost none of its sparkle for Camin:

> My meeting with him was arranged to take place at the Château d'Artigny, where Coty summoned all his business partners. I made my way there by train. A chauffeur in a Rolls Royce was waiting at Saint-Pierre-des-Corps station to pick me up. I was expecting to be received in some sumptuous office, but I was welcomed by the master of the house, dressed in a silk brocade dressing gown. He examined my drawings and kept one of them. After a three-hour interview, I let it slip that I knew very little about bottles. He said, "A bottle is for wine. Flask is the word we use here." Then Coty put me to the ultimate test. He showed me the small sphere destined to hold *A'Suma* and asked me what I thought. I replied that it needed a pedestal. He was of the same opinion, and so I was employed.

Pierre Camin described Coty's total involvement in his *parfumerie* design processes not long before his death:

> He summoned me at any time of the day or night, whenever an idea came into his head, and I was expected to rush down [to Château d'Artigny]. Sundays and holidays did not exist for him. It was nonstop creativity. I accepted these constraints, because the

pleasure of working for him outweighed the negative aspects. His judgment was infallible. I would submit some fifty drawings and he would immediately single one out, instructing me to "work on it." . . . But the most extraordinary thing about him was his creative ability.[3]

Coty's artistic talents remained in full force until his death.

CHAPTER 8

The Corsican Initiative

This realistic industrialist [Coty] was romantic about government.
He was driven to madness by toadies. He was, however, gifted and
capable of making his mark on history.

Paul Reboux

Clan Coty—François, Yvonne, Roland, Christiane, and their
friends and usual retinue of assistants—descended upon Corsica
in 1919 to begin François's great project of beneficence for the
place of his birth. In a short time, the aim of Coty's charity became
political. The family and their retinue first stayed at the Grand
Hotel d'Ajaccio, until François began his usual spate of property
purchases and renovations.

Barbicaja and Le Scudo

It did not take long to find multiple beautiful sites and buildings
available in depressed Ajaccio. One estate had belonged to Coty's
own family, and he felt vindicated in reacquiring it. Barbicaja, on
the beautiful seaside road that leads to Bay des Sanguinaires, had
been a well-known Spoturno family holding. François's grandfather,
Domenico, disowned by his own father, Mayor Jean-Baptiste
Spoturno, lost his portion of the inheritance of Barbicaja to his
brother Philippe-Gabriel. Philippe sold the family land in 1877 to an
Englishman. Reclaiming this vaunted property north of Ajaccio was
first on his to-do list when François returned as a billionaire to his
birthplace. He bought it in 1921 from Dominique Pugliesi-Conti and
built a new house on the cliff above the sea, planting the hills with
roses, carnations, and jasmine, hoping to improve Corsica's economy
through the production of ingredients needed for perfumes. The house
remains today under private ownership; below it is a greenhouse that
once was part of the Coty project for Corsica.

François's great uncle Philippe was the proprietor of Barbicaja when its oranges won the prize at the *Exposition générale de Corse* on May 15, 1865. Philippe Spoturno wrote:

> [I have] four hectares, planted in vine, olives, a market garden, oranges, citrus, pomegranates, apricots and figs from Barbary. I received first honor of plantations, a sum of one thousand francs, and I received a medal given by Prince Napoleon. This prize was for the best property of all Corsica, the most beautiful, the best maintained, and in full yield. The property is so highly spoken of that foreigners are envious. We need expenses for improvements, but this land is the future and the renown of our family.

A postscript to Philippe's pride in the Spoturno family property was his discovery one sunny spring day of a bearded fellow sleeping in the shade of an orange tree. It was Alphonse Daudet, whose son Léon, like François, became a nationalist politician, anti-Semite, and writer. Alphonse (1840-97) wrote about that day on the Spoturno property in his little book, *Les Lettres de Mon Moulin:*

> My finest remembrance of oranges comes to me still from Barbicaja, a great garden near Ajaccio, where I went for a siesta during the hot hours of the day. What fine hours I passed there. On top of my head, the orange trees in flower and in fruit burned their perfumes and aromas. The fruit was superb, of a reddish purple on the interior. They seemed to me exquisite and the horizon was as beautiful.[1]

Anatole France also wrote about Barbicaja.

Among Coty's architectural feats in Ajaccio was Le Scudo, a villa not far from Barbicaja. A remnant of Coty's coat of arms may be seen on an exterior wall of the house. The poet Valentine de Saint-Point, grandniece of author Alphonse de Lamartine (1790-1869), lived in Le Scudo as a guest of François Coty. As his mistress, she and Coty shared more than political views. Another famous Ajaccian, the singer Tino Rossi (born 1906), also descended from one of the ancient first families, would purchase the house from the Coty estate. It is now associated with the name of Tino Rossi, Corsica's most celebrated *chanteur.*

François bought a building at 14, cours Grandval in Ajaccio, which he owned from 1922 to 1931. There he set up the publication and administration of his newspaper *L'Eveil de la Corse.*. The mystery is why he never bought the family *hôtel particulier* in downtown Ajaccio, seat of the Spoturnos since the early eighteenth century. Perhaps he remembered how his grandmother Anna Maria was not welcome there.

Coty had decided that Corsica should enjoy economic equality with mainland France. His central animating force was dangerously close to that of his hero and relative, Napoleon. Their resemblance was more than physical. Both were small handsome men, always trying to look and be larger than life. Coty enjoyed an easy intelligence compared to his famous relative, who had studied incessantly in military school. Napoleon suffered more from taunts for being a Corsican than did Coty; after all, Napoleon had already elevated Corsica with his accomplishments by the time Coty began his own career. Coty's benefaction to Corsica could, he realized, propel him to election to the Senate from Corsica, thereby launching a political career in France, like his ancestor.

Coty's "Initiative for Corsica" became a philanthropic endeavor that extended beyond his lifetime, since his daughter, Christiane, continued his projects there for decades, in his memory. Corsica became the perfect site for his contributions, because of its small size, isolation, and location. Coty energetically undertook projects that he could organize and supervise, reaping lasting publicity for himself. He also felt at home in Corsica and reveled in his return as a rich and powerful industrialist to the island of his birth, where some of his ancestors had arrived in the early 1500s.

Over a fifteen-year period, Coty showered Corsica with $72 million worth of improvements that he conceived, organized, and executed. His interest in the island was deeply sentimental. For example, when a movie being shot about Napoleon needed money, he paid the cast. So that the director, Albegaz, could finish the film, Coty fed the 2,000 extras who acted as soldiers.

Corsica had such a bad reputation for its corruption, bandits, vendettas, and assassinations after the fall of the Second Empire that Republican deputies in Paris sometimes demanded the separation of Corsica from France. An anti-Corsica broadside of 1870 advertised, with irony, the sale of Corsica. "For sale: France offers to the universe and whoever would want to buy Corsica, for one franc, cash."

The island desperately needed Coty's help. Twenty thousand young Corsicans, out of a population totaling less than 180,000, died in World War I, fighting with the French army. Even liberal Georges Clemenceau reported the island's misery to Pres. Armand Fallières. Young Corsicans had been emigrating to the mainland, to California, and even to poor Sicily for generations. The ships leaving Corsica were not only exporting sheep's milk and sheep's cheese but also providing a way out of the country for young men. One of these ships may have carried away Jean-Baptiste Spoturno, François's father.

As the 1920s began, François decided to try his luck in politics in Corsica. First, he spent 300,000 francs in an election to support Adolphe Landry, locally referred to as the boss of Ajaccio. When that did not procure a political base for François to become an elected official, he turned around and backed the Bonapartists, Landry's enemies. Coty contacted Antoine Gavini, a political activist of the right in Corsica. With his help, Coty became county councilor in Ajaccio in 1920, which he hoped would serve as a stepping stone to the Senate.

In 1920-21, Coty was included on the Paul Doumer-Antoine Gavini list as a senatorial candidate from Corse du Sud. By this time, Coty had acquired both friends and enemies, and charges flew back and forth in the Corsican manner. From the outset of his reappearance in Corsica as a wealthy native son, newspaper editors and politicians had labeled him a rich man trying to use the island for his own interests.

In defense of Coty, one "L. L." wrote in a lead article in the newspaper:

> M. Coty is a man enormously rich. He did not arrive at his fortune without the capacity for order, for work and with the aptitude for industrial specialization that are the strong guarantees of a clear vision and exercised in appreciation of the public interest. . . . M. Coty has subscribed 25,000 francs for the erection of a monument to those who died for the nation [in World War I] and has given substantial gifts to the poor. He has established, with the aid of well-known engineers, a plan for the culture of flowers [for perfume manufacture] and he promises his help for the establishment of an energy and electricity plant to cover over 250 kilometers, from the west side of Porto to Sartène. This energy will permit the creation of a line without rails for electrobus or tramways with a subsidy from the state. It will make possible the distribution of light industry over all this area. M. Coty has put at the disposition of the engineers charged with the study of this project a sum of 50,000 francs.
>
> The senatorial delegates will know then that M. Coty has already furnished serious security for his plans and views relative to the economic relief of Corsica, his little country.

In May 1920, the weekly *Le Combattant* printed a piece by Castigat Ridendo about Coty's project, "Plants for Perfumes," which stated in part: "We have already described the projects that our eminent compatriot M. Coty has conceived for the agricultural relief of our country. He expects to create in our island the floral culture for perfumes with a view toward the production of essence for distillation or extraction of perfumes by maceration or *enfleurage*. . . . Our own area would become a hub of production for the perfume industry. Until now the principal center of this lucrative industry is in Basse Provence, Grasse and its surroundings, in le Comté de Nice, in colonial Algeria and in the Riviera of Genoa."

Coty pursued his plan for the economic improvement of the Sartène area. He bought land and planted it with roses and other flowers useful to the perfume industry. In fact, some of the land he acquired was adjacent to land long owned by the Coti family. Using Grasse as a template, he financed and organized small agricultural cooperatives for growing flowers for fragrance. He employed women to work in plants he established to distill the essence from the acres of flowers. Envisioning Corsica as competition with Grasse in fragrances, he had marshes and swamps drained, to be transformed into flower fields bordered with mandarin trees. In this manner, he continued the Spoturno family tradition of growing citrus trees. At the same time, he pushed modernization, such as hydraulic power; he brought a power station by ship to Ajaccio. With a supply of electricity assured, he installed electric streetlights in Ajaccio, and his tramway went into operation.

Another article in *Le Combattant* of May 14, 1920, relates:

> Our excellent compatriot M. François Coty, after some fifteen days passed among us with his wife, his children and some friends, has departed, carrying with him from his short trip to Corsica the best impression, the most comforting, for the success of his great projects of floral culture that constitute truly the economic renovation of our dear country.
>
> On leaving Ajaccio, M. François Coty did not forget the poor of our village and has sent to the mayor the sum of 2000 francs to be distributed as bread for the poor. This is just one more new act of generosity among many others that we will not forget. With such amiability he has received all the people who came to solicit for works of general interest. He has welcomed us all, responding to the demand of each.

Despite his largesse, or even because of it, Coty was four votes short in the primary and two votes short in the second round for the Senate. The next year he stood again for election, and lost. All the while, he continuing to flood the island with money. The improvements were much needed, since the last big money the French government had spent in Corsica had been for the railroad between Bastia and Ajaccio. Coty became a substitute for the state, especially around Ajaccio.

Coty understood the unwritten rules of island politics—vote buying, contested elections, bandits of honor, even assassinations—and he had his confederates use most of them. Finally, on his third run for the Senate, he succeeded, reportedly winning by one vote in 1923. But the Parliament accused him of not only of buying votes but of trying to entice a noted Corsican bandit to threaten delegates. Nonce Romanetti, "the bandit chief, who is a sort of Robin Hood among a certain element of the people," reportedly refused Coty, who then resorted to the law. Coty convinced the police chief of Ajaccio to support a rumor of shadowy support among the bandits.

When his electoral victory was officially questioned, Coty put all effort into retaining it, making the rounds of ministers and powerful senators to lobby for his seat and even going so far as to appeal personally to Poincaré, previously the target of his fulminations in *Le Figaro.* When he appeared before the Senate in Paris to defend himself, the members insulted and degraded him. On April 11, 1924, the *New York Times* reported, "By a vote of 178 against 31, the [French] Senate annulled the election of François Coty. . . . This ends a long but amusing story of the kind that can be written about any election where the count is close. The technical reason for the annulment was the fact that the elections of certain delegates who voted for the perfume manufacturer were declared void after his election. As Coty had won by the vote of one delegate, his enemies fought hard to make the annulment of the delegates retroactive and succeeded."

Thus was Coty robbed of his greatest opportunity to steer the history of France. Sealed in his opinion of the Third Republic, he would now tirelessly pursue its downfall.

Showers of Money and Improvements

While he owned agricultural properties in three areas in Corsica, Coty concentrated on his birthplace, Ajaccio, where he bought property in and around the city for various projects. He personally administered all his undertakings, although he hired a staff to take care of the details. Plans were made for a hotel association, schools of commerce, and cooperatives called *Centrales de Corse.* He seemed determined to do more for Corsica than any other individual had, even Napoleon or Napoleon III.

Nothing was too large or too small for François's largesse. Twenty thousand francs established a vocational school. Remembering his youth when he sold point lace in Marseille, Coty donated 2,000 francs to the lace-making school. The poor received 25,000 francs, distributed by one of the political organizations that agreed to support him in his quest for a Senate seat. Although the projects were criticized by some as buying votes, they certainly helped the island. In 1921, he created and developed schools of commerce in Ajaccio, Bastia, and Corte and, by 1923, about six hundred students attended these schools. Each year he provided 27,000 francs for clothing and Christmas presents for poor children in Ajaccio.

A 12,000-franc donation made possible the continuation of work on the sports stadium in Ajaccio, which had been begun in 1910. Eventually, it was named Stade François Coty. The arena was enormous for the place and the period, with a capacity of 10,660. He also contributed a generous 124,000 francs to continue needed improvements at the grotto containing a statue of Napoleon.

Articles in the Corsican newspapers referred to Coty as "the great Mediterranean" because he promoted Mussolini's plan, "Latinity," that related the Mediterranean coast of France and its islands to Italy and the other Mediterranean countries of Europe and North Africa. To foster this concept of "Latinity," he established the Bank of the Mediterranean in Nice as a base for the development of a banking system in Corsica. He continued to shower the island with money and improvements. *Le Canard Enchaîné,* a mainland French newspaper known for its sarcasm, wrote that the *checcoti* (check-Coty) was the real currency of Corsica. The *Sartène Enchaîné* called him "Monsieur Midas-Coty."

Coty established and supported *A Muvra,* a Corsican-language newspaper. Pierre Rocca, the editor, had an office in Paris, where Coty wrote him on July 21, 1921, asking him to publish a letter to the minister of public works that stated: "All the future prosperity of Corsica depends upon the realization of the [hydraulic works]. Corsicans must know the efforts that go into attaining the end. You know the major importance of the use of hydraulic force in Corsica."

Perversely, the press berated and reviled Coty for his improvements. *Le Reveil Corse,* a weekly published in Marseille, printed on December 4, 1920, a sarcastic open letter "to Monsieur Midas-Coty." Another article on Coty was entitled "Megalomania." The lead article against the Coty-Doumer Bonapartist ticket, "Challenge to the Misery of Corsica," accused Coty of trying to buy a seat in the Senate. They used his own speeches to ridicule their native son who, they said, had forgotten Corsica until it became convenient to remember it.

Coty's response was printed in several Corsican newspapers: "I am grateful for my constant labor and unusual comprehension of affairs that elevated me to one of the premier industrial seats of the world. I have a considerable fortune, the highest colleagues and contacts as well as enormous authority. I intend to put all this at the disposition of my small abandoned country." And so he did.

L'Eveil de la Corse, owned by Coty, covered his every move, both as a philanthropist and politician. Although Coty supported the newspaper financially, its columnists did not hesitate to expose his love life for all Corsicans to relish. Coty had ensconced his mistress Henriette Dieudé and their children in a waterfront villa in Calvi. It was one thing to have a mistress or more in Corsica, but to travel openly with a mistress and their illegitimate children when a perfectly fine wife existed was not countenanced. Even though Coty's notorious sexual exploits were bruited about Paris, where they were fodder for sophisticated gossips, provincial Corsica, with its individualistic customs, was a more conservative milieu. In this land where family and blood loyalty were of prime importance, a man must be more loyal to his sister than to his wife, but that man was still expected to be more loyal to his wife than to his mistress. Coty had made an egregious error. Therefore, the publicity about his various mistresses spelled disaster for his political aspirations in Corsica.

Coty's soft touch for the island of his birth caused citizens to brag even as they gossiped. One newspaper claimed, "Everyone knows that whenever someone mentions France or Corsica to François Spoturno dit Coti, he takes out his wallet."[2] This loyalty to his birthplace continued even after his death. The *London Times* reported, on April 25, 1936, after his death, that Coty had bequeathed the following: 51.5 million francs to the Office Centrale des Oeuvrages de Bienfaisance; 25 million francs to the town of Ajaccio; 1 million francs to Coti-Chiavari, his maternal grandfather's ancestral town; 500,000 francs to the Bureau de Bienfaisance d'Ajaccio; and 500,000 francs to the Union Générale des Corses.

Yet today François Coty is all but forgotten except for the stadium that bears his name. For some unknown reason, Coty never bought back the Spoturno house adjacent to Napoleon's house in downtown Ajaccio. It would have been a worthy landmark to the Spoturno-Coty empire.

The longtime Ligurians of Ajaccio resented the change in the spelling of his name. After Coty's death, when a narrow street was named after the famous son of Corsica who had poured his millions into his natal city, they called it rue François Coti. Corsica accepted his millions with alacrity, but they could not accept François Coty.

So it happened that Coty had little chance of breaking into Corsican politics despite his largesse and efforts. He had left Corsica as a child; by the time he returned as a billionaire, there was no room

for him in the highly clannish political system—not that this deterred
the determined man. He could afford to play the game. However,
Corsica is small and tightly knit; its politicians, like Adolphe Landry,
the political boss of Ajaccio, were outraged at this "Frenchman's"
interference in the political affairs of the island, even though it was
his island, too. Coty was viewed negatively by the French as Corsican,
while the Corsicans saw him as having transformed himself into a
Frenchman. He never fully belonged to either country. For Coty, it
was an uphill battle at every turn, and he did not resolve the problem
before his death.

CHAPTER 9

The Billionaire Collects

What is History, but a fable agreed upon.

Napoleon

Coty's first billion came from the world of women and his own business acumen. He took most of the money immediately to the world of men—where politics and the press reigned. He also continued to expend vast amounts of his unlimited fortune on architecture and art, both to satisfy his acquisitive nature and to provide himself with creative outlets. François's obituary in the *New York Times* reported: "He bought a whole string of châteaux, including the historic Château de Louveciennes, which Louis XV presented to Mme Du Barry; Château de Puy d'Artigny and Château de Montbazon in Touraine, as well as two domains in Corsica. Some years ago, he bought the late James Gordon Bennett's villa, Namouna, on the Riviera." That barely begins to tell the story. What about the Pullman house, Le Camiset, not far from Deauville? All told, François bought, restored, or designed fourteen residences and châteaux, not counting the estates in America. Several of these major purchases were made in quick succession at the beginning of the 1920s.

24-26, Avenue Raphael

By 1921, Yvonne and François Coty found themselves with such wealth and influence that they needed a *hôtel particulier* for entertaining their international friends and colleagues who came to Paris. They purchased a stone mansion on a two-and-a-half-acre lot in the newest, most elegant subdivision of Paris: 24-26, avenue Raphael in the Bois de Boulogne. Architect Ernest Samson had designed the building in 1905.

The family called their home simply "Avenue Raphael," and François and Yvonne lived the last of their years together there. Of course, François redecorated and almost rebuilt the relatively new mansion. Noteworthy for its Lalique stair rail with etched-glass panels that ascended from the first to the second story, the house featured an equally impressive three-story entry hall crowned with a glass ceiling by Lalique. Magnificent architectural feats directed by François met the eye from every direction. Avenue Raphael, with its original Lalique glass ceilings alone, was valued at several million dollars in 1960.

A famous incident in the history of Avenue Raphael was the night when the Duchess of Windsor and Yvonne hosted simultaneous garden parties in the late 1930s. The properties of the two grandes dames backed upon one another, so the clashing sounds of their two orchestras became an unbearable and embarrassing dissonance. Amicably, the neighbors simply cut a passage in the high wall separating their gardens, inviting their guests to wander back and forth from party to party. With the orchestras taking turns, the pleased duke thought the impromptu combined fete a "jolly good idea."

François's penchant for art could be indulged in the grand spaces of Avenue Raphael, and he turned the house into a museum for his ever-growing collection, which included works by Carpaccio, Fragonard, Reynolds, Greuze, Canaletto, and Boucher.

Avenue Raphael became the principal residence of Yvonne Coty and Léon Cotnareanu after their 1929 marriage. In 1960, Léon told Yvonne

Garden of Coty's Avenue Raphael residence at the Bois de Boulogne, Paris. (Elizabeth Z. Coty Collection)

Dining room of Avenue Raphael. The home was used by the German High Command during World War II. (Elizabeth Z. Coty Collection)

to sell it. King Hassan II bought it in 1961 and it became the Moroccan Embassy. Whenever Yvonne sold property, Léon received his fee as agent, in this case 2 million francs for him and 1 million francs for his brother Philippe, their attorney. The interior ceilings, stair railings, and elegant glasswork were auctioned off by Jansy under a separate arrangement. Expecting that the mansion would be preserved as an embassy, the family was horrified to see rows of apartment buildings go up on the site. The main entrance and a portion of Yvonne's house remain hidden. It is now the Gabon Embassy.

Rond-Point des Champs-Elysées

An even more total obliteration awaited the Parisian properties that Coty acquired in 1925. He bought two buildings on the Rond-Point des Champs-Elysées: the Hôtel Bamberger, for 10 million francs, and another from the family of Toulouse-Lautrec. Against its will, the staff of *Le Figaro,* the Paris daily that François bought in 1922, was installed in the Hôtel Bamberger.

The two buildings stood near the Grand Palais in Paris, where the Coty family attended art exhibitions, dog shows, fairs, and fetes planned for the rich and famous. When Yvonne and Léon returned from the United States after World War II in 1945, these buildings, like

François Coty incensed all literary and boulevardier Paris by moving *Le Figaro* from its historic site on rue Drouet to the Rond-Point des Champs-Elysées in 1925. (Elizabeth Z. Coty Collection)

much of Paris, were in shambles. *Le Figaro* had been closed during the war because Yvonne would not produce a paper for German consumption. Upon her triumphal return to postwar Paris, she set out to create a five-story apartment in part of the empty buildings.

If one faces the Rond-Point, the Champs-Elysées is on the left, with a treelined park running down the side of the boulevard. Now, Avenue Franklin Roosevelt passes the place where the Coty residences once stood. Yvonne's complex was five stories high, with fashion designer Nina Ricci established on the first level. A bronze winding staircase led to the next two levels, where Yvonne resided. The fourth story was Christiane's apartment, and the top floor was reserved for Yvonne's grandchildren or guests.

Yvonne so loved urban life that she made this apartment building, called Douze Rond-Point, her postwar Paris home. She was delighted with her apartment, with its double-glass front windows on the third floor trimmed in gold-anodized aluminum, making them not only functional but attractive. These windows enabled her to watch all the action from her aerie above the trees without hearing any street noise. Yvonne could look down as her great-grandbaby, Patrice, my daughter, was pushed down the narrow footpath along the Champs-Elysées in her sumptuous folding pram.

The concierge and his tubby wife ruled the cobblestone courtyard with its massive wooden gates and huge bronze knockers. The courtyard was large, originally built to accommodate wagons and horses. A vast window in the corner of the second and third floors made it possible for the concierge or his wife to call down news when the family entered the courtyard. Madame Jacques was known to hang out of the window almost all the time, just to see what was going on. The couple was essential to the guests' entering, since they released the latch after the bronze bell was sounded by the buzzer outside of number 12.

Across the Champs-Elysées was the competing newspaper, Le Soir. When Christiane sold the property after her mother's death, the buildings were torn down. A shopping complex replaced them.

Château de Sainte-Hélène

In 1922, Coty bought a château on the west side of Nice, on a hill facing the Mediterranean, to provide his children with a place to stay when they wanted to visit the casinos. The residence came with a history. In the late nineteenth century, it had been a guesthouse set in a park of twenty-five hectares belonging to one Monsieur Grosso. At that time, the principal building was at the place called the Palais de Marbre, which became the Centre des Archives Municipales for Nice. In 1882, Monsieur Blanc, the founder of the Casino of Monte Carlo, bought the guesthouse and renamed it Villa Blanc. After a number of interim owners, François Coty bought the place and named it the Château de Sainte-Hélène, after the old road that passes under the railroad bridge by the Eglise Sainte-Hélène. His appearance there with his family for "the season" helped to make Nice, with its Hotel Negresco, the luxurious southern capital of France. Coty entertained the Aga Khan and other notables there.

As usual, François transformed his new real estate. He reorganized the park as a showcase for the scents of his most precious perfumes. Trees from Australia and elsewhere were imported to provide a sensual aroma, redolent of the perfumes François created. The trees, planted elegantly along the long winding driveway, seemed to grow without blemish or bug and were beautifully groomed, rounded with flattened tops. They led to the residence's massive entrance door centered between the tall white columns on the veranda.

Lalique's craftsmen arrived and went to work in the château: the entrance hall, bar, and ceilings were embellished with René's dramatic glass. Yvonne chose genuine leopard skin to line the walls of the bar. The top of the bar was mahogany with a solid brass rail, in the style of an English pub. She imported white Italian marble for a two-story staircase and hallways. François used a particular pattern on wrought-iron railings in several of his houses, but in Nice, everything was art deco to coordinate with the interior architecture of the vast dwelling.

One of the most unusual moments of my marriage to Michel Coty came when we visited Sainte-Hélène. During my first trip to see the family in France, around Christmas of 1960, Yvonne heard that Michel and I wanted to visit one of her houses, as I am a career interior designer. She had never allowed anyone in her houses when she was not in residence, other than selected household staff, but she was impressed by my sincere desire and said yes. Her staff was given twenty-four hours' notice. The maître d'hôtel took our bags upstairs, and Michel was amazed to hear that we would be staying in Madame's boudoir, where the view was superior.

We decided to have a "little libation" in the marvelous bar with its leopard skins, then began to ascend the spectacular staircase. Suddenly, on the landing, Michel stopped. Looking pale and startled, he said, "I don't know where my grandmother's room is. I have never been upstairs before! We children were not allowed above the landing. It was Léon's idea."

I realized he was serious. Until he was twenty-eight years old, he had never been free to go upstairs to see his grandmother, who raised him. It was so startling that I had tears in my eyes, and I saw that he was equally moved. That night we had a joyful pillow fight to make up for all the years of isolation.

Yvonne considered the art-deco château one of her most beloved residences, and she often went there with Léon and their guests. After World War II, she gave it to the City of Nice. It is now Le Musée d'Art Naïf, used to display primitive art. They have removed the plaster and glass stairway François designed, which would be too easily destroyed, in favor of a sturdier, wrought-iron rail.

Louveciennes

At Louveciennes, on the road to Versailles from Paris, Coty found the *pavillon* that Louis XV commissioned architect Claude-Nicolas Ledoux to build for his premier mistress, Comtesse Du Barry. Coty knew well the purposes of eighteenth-century *pavillons*. They were built by and for the courtiers and mistresses of Louis XIV and Louis XV to escape the stifling discipline and censorship of the royal court. Love, dining, conversations, and cards, as well as music and reading, were the *raison d'être* for Louveciennes's *pavillon,* for both the Comtesse

Du Barry and, later, for François Coty. He wanted to possess the place immediately because it was an eccentric, splendid extravagance that evoked sensuality. In 1923, it became his for the 27 million francs he paid to Monsieur Loucheur, former minister of armament.

The *Pavillon de Musique* that Coty acquired had been the home of Comtesse Du Barry after the death of her lover, Louis XV, until her death on the guillotine following her 1793 arrest. The *pavillon* was an adjunct to the small château just up the road, built about 1681 by Louis XIV for Arnold de Ville, the Liègois who had designed at nearby Marly a machine for pumping water to Louis XIV's fountains, both at Marly and Versailles. Not satisfied with the scope of the property, Comtesse Du Barry and Louis XV turned to the architect Ledoux to design a supplementary building, which became the Pavillon de Musique that Coty bought.

During the French Revolution, the *pavillon* began to deteriorate, which was not arrested until the banker Lafitte acquired it in 1818. As other owners succeeded Lafitte over the course of the nineteenth century, most of the original decoration disappeared. After his purchase of the property, François Coty employed architect Charles Mewes to restore the *pavillon* for Coty's own specific uses, according to his own carefully developed plans.

In 1929, Coty began excavations to install a kitchen, fur-storage rooms, servants' rooms, and a swimming pool. These excavations below the foundations of the eighteenth-century building caused it to begin to cave in. For about a million dollars, he had it rebuilt according to Ledoux's plan. All the fixtures were copied, but Mewes had to choose between making the rooms smaller to allow for modern heating and wiring or enlarging the building while keeping Ledoux's relative proportions. He chose the latter, so the building as we see it is a reconstruction, and the inside a replica with all the original decorations copied except in the entrance and dining room.[1]

A new foundation was composed of two levels of basements, used for laboratories. François selected sanitary white tiles for the walls, ceilings, shelving, and floor. The corners of the basement rooms are sealed with curved tiles so there are no cracks or joints for impurities to enter. The basement closest to the first level was vast, with ceilings of glass brick in the art-deco style that allowed the light from above-ground windows to flood in, making it a cheerful space.

A third level was added above the cornice of the pavillon for François's secret retreat, but François, like Thomas Jefferson, kept changing his plans. François ordered workmen to tear down what they had been working on for weeks or months if he happened to visit in one of his creative and manic moments.

Coty died in 1934 at the *pavillon* at Louveciennes. (Elizabeth Z. Coty Collection)

To Coty, the *pavillon* was simply "Louveciennes," the name of the small town around it, while locals called it "La Maison de Musique." Toward the end of his life, Coty became known as the "gentleman of Louveciennes." After his divorce, he spent more and more time there, living in the end as a recluse, locked in his partially finished third level, inaccessible because the stairway had not been completed. In the summer of 1934, Francois Coty died there.

Later, during World War II, "German officers lived [at Louveciennes] and the concierge, Madame Petit, saved what she could. After the war, it became a part of the American School in Paris, with its salon transformed into a cafeteria full of coat-racks and formica tables."[2]

The bizarre history in the 1980s of the *pavillon* and its nearby château matches the drama of the Coty ownership.[3] Kiko Nakahara, a Japanese heiress and developer, with her husband, Jean-Paul Renoir, used $5 million of her father's company's funds to buy them in 1989. This was just one of nine historic châteaux near Paris and in the Loire region bought by the company, which also owned part of the Empire State Building. Plans were under way to transform them into luxury hotels, but according to her lawyer, "funds dried up when her father was arrested in Japan" and "she had to fire the maintenance staff and sell furniture to raise funds to pay her bills." Because of her desecration of a piece of France's heritage, the heiress went to jail, not far from Louveciennes.

The Julienne Dumeste Foundation has acquired and arranged to restore the *pavillon* at Louveciennes as a museum in honor of Madame Dumeste, Comtesse Du Barry, and François Coty.

Filolie

Coty was prone to remark that, unlike his other real-estate acquisitions, Château de la Filolie, near the town of Thiviers in Périgord Vert in the Dordogne, was the only one of his properties that ever made any money. This fifteenth-century manor, in a setting near a picturesque village of stunning historical value, was another of the acquisitions Coty made in the 1920s. He grew tobacco on the estate.

Thiviers began as a Roman town called Tiberios. By 1365, it had evolved into one of the thirty-two walled towns of Périgord, a rest stop for pilgrims en route to Santiago de Compostela in Galicia, Spain. After the French Revolution, the medieval buildings and convent served as the town hall and a school. The chapel became a center for the sale of grain and foodstuffs. Yvonne's mother, Virginie Dubois Le Baron, settled at Filolie in 1940, and she died there.

Filolie, enclosed by low stone walls, had a thatched roof and tall, majestic wooden doorways. At the time of its construction, it was located behind a defensive line, protected by the châteaux of Vaucocourt and Banceil, each now restored. La Maison Familiale Rurale de Thiviers uses Filolie today, under contract with the Ministry of Agriculture. This association is now international, but it was established in the southwest of France in 1901 to provide education for rural individuals to move up in the social and professional world. François Coty would have supported its aims.

Fascination with Airplanes

However expensive François's real-estate purchases, however large his investment of time in transforming each of his newly acquired properties, a man with his diversity of interests and the wealth to support them could not be limited to any one field of endeavor. Only his lifelong identification and preoccupation with his perfume and cosmetics business trumped his focus on many other areas of activity. Of his many passions, one that he shared with his son, Roland, was aviation. When on May 20 to 21, 1927, Charles Lindbergh crossed the Atlantic from the United States and landed in Paris, François and Roland stayed abreast of developments on this historic thirty-three-hour flight. Two French pilots, Nungesser and Coli, had gone down in an attempt to cross the Atlantic earlier that same year.

Upon seeing Lindbergh's success and the excitement across France when he landed at Le Bourget airport, Coty determined to see that the French surpassed the American's feat. He decided to finance a transatlantic flight in the more difficult westward direction by the French aviators Dieudonné Costes and Maurice Bellonte.

This was not a frivolous decision. He was the richest man in France and among the richest in Europe. He could afford to do what he wanted to do. Advancing the glory of France would also benefit his public image. The *Literary Digest,* reporting on the richest people in the world in 1931, named Coty the "perfume king" to head the short list in France. "While the Rothschild fortune is tremendous, Baron Rothschild is probably not the richest man in France at present," relayed a United Press correspondent in Paris, "for the simple reason that the fortune is divided among a large family." Motorcar manufacturers André Citröen and Louis Renault had become tremendously wealthy since World War I. "But the wealthiest of them all in France . . . is the Corsican perfume manufacturer, François Coty," the correspondent continued. "Coty has been making perfumes [and] has built up a fortune of more than $50,000,000. He also owns several newspapers and has become a financial and political power."

Coty was even included on the short list of the richest Europeans. The ex-kaiser, Wilhelm Hohenzollern II, remained Germany's wealthiest person, worth about $60 million, but Fritz von Thyssen, the steel magnate, had retained his fortune while "the war had played havoc with many great German fortunes, including that of the Krupp family . . . the largest of all before the war." Eastern European tycoons, their fortunes soon to be confiscated, held their own on the list. François Coty knew these men, since his cosmetics business and factories provided employment and contributed much to the gross national product throughout Eastern Europe. In Hungary, the wealthiest man was the land-holding noble Prince Paul Esterhazy, who owned about one-sixtieth of the total area of the country. Alfred Potocki, another landowner, was Poland's aristocrat millionaire, just above Prince Janus Radziwill. Coty had dined with them all.

Coty celebrated his immense wealth by donating a Breguet Bidon aircraft named *Le Point d'Interrogation,* the *Question Mark,* to the two pilots. They took off from Paris for New York on September 1, 1930. In an unusual move, Coty proceeded anonymously with the project, paying for it behind the scenes, but it is hard to imagine that he did not insert himself into Costes's and Bellonte's triumphal return. They were decorated by the president of the Republic as well as featured on the November 1 cover of *Le Miroir du Monde* and in the society edition of *Petit Parisien*. The *New York Times* reported a triumphal tour of the aviators to the United States, where a crowd of 30,000 children met them in Salt Lake City. They proceeded to Virginia, where the governor insisted they stay at the governor's mansion designed by Thomas Jefferson, in the same bedroom where Lafayette had slept.

Bellonte announced during the tour, "President Hoover was happy to accept our offer of a silver replica of the airplane by a famous Parisian jeweler, which will be presented to the White House as a token of our appreciation for the memorable hospitality we received there." Coty had conceived, designed, and paid for this gift, anonymously.

An unexpected tribute by Major Costes to François Coty evoked prolonged cheering from his American listeners: "There seems to be an impression in some quarters . . . that I have failed to recognize the importance of the assistance Monsieur Coty gave to my ambition to fly from Paris to New York. As a matter of fact, at the moment when Monsieur Coty gave me the plane for the transatlantic flight my prospects were very dark, and I tell you frankly there is little likelihood the flight ever would have been made if it had not been for Monsieur Coty's aid."

Coty's outright gift of the plane was a particularly magnanimous act because "so many foolhardy and insufficiently prepared airmen had lost their lives in transatlantic attempts previous to that time that the idea of a Paris-New York flight had become not only unpopular with the public, but was officially frowned upon," the flyer asserted. "By making me proprietor of the machine, he made me my own master."

Coty's lifelong interest in machines and transportation fit into his philanthropic plans related to patriotic ideals. He wanted Frenchmen to surpass the recent achievement of Wiley Post of the United States, who flew around the world with fourteen stops in eight and a half days. When he heard that Lt. Joseph Le Brix and Marcel Doret planned to fly nonstop from Paris to Tokyo in 1931, Coty ordered a custom Dewoitine airplane, named *Trait d'Union* (*Hyphen*). He had the logo of *L'Ami du Peuple* painted on the fuselage and presented it personally, amidst fanfare, to Le Brix and Doret. Coty ordered the plane's Hispano-Suiza engine from the same firm that had supplied his custom-made touring automobile. With its 650-horsepower engine, the Dewoitine had a cruising speed of 110 miles an hour.

The flyers hoped to cover the distance of 6,750 miles in sixty-two hours and, if successful, would continue across the Pacific to

California, making the Paris-Tokyo hop the first leg of a round-the-world flight with only three landings before returning to Le Bourget airport. Characteristically, Coty had forwarded a new engine to Tokyo and another to New York so that the plane could be overhauled in both places.[4] A mechanic, René Mesmin, who had replaced Doret, was aboard the *Hyphen* with Le Brix when the plane crashed en route to Tokyo.

François often spoke with automobile and airplane manufacturers about their designs before investing in them. He believed that he was influential in the design of the two airplanes that brought fame and glory to French aviation pioneers. Coty's own private plane was a Dewoitine, whose engine he had helped design. He demanded nerve and staying power from his business colleagues, and as Coty's test of their personal qualities, many potential employees had to endure a plane ride in the Dewoitine, during which he ordered the pilot to flip the plane or dive toward the forest below. Those who flagged during the intense moment did not remain on the short list for the job. Some of these men were so shocked that they decided not to work for Coty no matter what the pay or the advantage.

Collector of Automobiles

Another expression of Coty's fascination with technology was his interest in automobiles. During the 1920s and 1930s, the Hispano-Suiza was considered the ultimate in cars, the preferred marque of those who sought speed, size, performance, mechanical excellence, and grandeur. It was also the most expensive vehicle on the road. Hispano-Suiza advertised: *L'Hispano-Suiza est Reine* (*The Hispano-Suiza is queen*).

In 1924, François purchased a Hispano H6C sports model, a newly introduced short-chassis open roadster featuring a long, narrow body based on designs from the company's racing machines. With this car, he could travel from Paris to Château d'Artigny in record time, regardless of road or weather conditions. However, its lack of certain amenities, such as a top, eventually caused his enthusiasm for the car to wane until its specially designed hard top arrived from the factory. Shortly before his death in 1934, François ordered a replacement body, which was a sports coupe with full weather protection. The manufacturer created a milestone, one-of-a-kind automobile, the most sophisticated on earth. This car remained in the Coty garage after its celebrated owner's death.

Yvonne ordered Coty's rebuilt Hispano upgraded again in 1937, this time with an entirely new chassis, called a Type K6, which had been recently introduced. This version of François's Hispano remained in the family for many years. It was kept garaged, meant only for occasional use. Eventually, it was sent across the Atlantic to begin a new life in North America. The Delahaye 135M coupe, a somewhat smaller car, but still the pinnacle of motoring, that Yvonne bought in 1937 became her and Léon's primary car.

Roland Coty and His Family

Roland Coty tried briefly to settle down by working in Coty SA. He was a persuasive promoter and salesman, but he did not excel as an executive. Unable to get along with the more mature and experienced officers of the company, Roland ended his working days at Coty when he was just twenty-eight.

He had a family by this time. He had met Germaine Marguerite Charlot in 1921 in a sports arena, it is said. She was twenty-two, a native of Brive-la-Gaillarde, Correze. Their first son, Henri Roland Coty, was born that same year. Roland settled his family in the Château de Vaux, near the d'Artigny property his father had bought in 1912, but he and Marguerite would not marry until September 10, 1931. François Alphée Coty, the couple's second son, arrived in 1926. Yves Michel Coty came along on June 7, 1931.

For some unknown reason, Yves Michel's birth was not registered until 1938, when his grandmother Yvonne appeared before a notary on rue Belvedere in Boulogne Billancourt and took care of the matter. I was saddened to find out that Michel's parents did not marry until after he was born. I suppose my Virginia upbringing influenced my feelings.

The marriage pleased François immensely, because he was thrilled to have three grandsons, and thus three heirs to the Spoturno-Coty name and fortune. At that time, the name Coty was known throughout the world because of his perfume and cosmetics. François himself did not realize how well known his name was inside France—for the wrong reasons—because of his journalistic and political forays.

Roland was not deterred from a career. He just chose one as an international playboy, dedicated to polo, automobile racing, and sailing. He had begun sailing to the United States with his father when he was just eleven years old. Thereafter, he returned often both for business and pleasure.

Roland spent much of his adulthood representing Coty SA in professional automobile races in France and Italy. He drove the *Coty Spécial,* a car produced by the Hispano-Suiza company after François's specific designs and redesigns. At Le Mans in 1924, he came in thirty-third in the *Grand Prix d'Endurance,* with Marcel

Marguerite Charlot Coty with Henri and François, at one of the Coty estates in France. (Elizabeth Z. Coty Collection)

Roland Coty and Marguerite Charlot with their custom-built automobile. (Elizabeth Z. Coty Collection)

Mongin as his partner. There he drove an Omega Six. In 1936, he raced in the World Drivers Championship and the National Drivers Championship, where he drove the *Coty Spécial* against Bugattis, Talbots, Austins, Amilcars, a Salmson, an Octo, a Bignan, a Delage 2 LCV, a Montier Ford driven by Ferdinand Montier, a Georges-Irat, a Corre-La Licorne, and a Panhard et Levassor. Marcel Violet competed in these races, driving his Sima-Violet.

When he wasn't behind the wheel of a racecar, Roland, like many rich internationals, played polo around the world and gambled heavily. Among his polo partners and opponents were the dictator of the Dominican Republic, Rafael Trujillo; Chilean champion Pedro Ezyaguirre; and Porfirio Rubirosa. However, he was also a fun-loving father who adored his sons. Roland took them around the bars of Paris to brag about their athletic achievements as well as his own. Irresponsible in an attractive kind of way, he was brave, sweet, generous, and thoughtful.

Within the family, Roland's role was that of manager of his father's automobiles and racing stables. His father, determined to have a hand in every activity that inured to the glory of France, had decided that French horses should lead in Europe. Coty bought Le Camiset, the George Pullman estate on the Normandy coast, where he embellished

Roland Coty on horseback, pulling his eldest son on snow skis. (Elizabeth Z. Coty Collection)

the stables and pursued his goal of breeding a winning line of horses. Of course, his purchase of another American millionaire's estate and his plans there made the newspapers.

Coty seemed unable to resist buying properties that had belonged to the wealthy and powerful—even Americans. This contrasted with his constant rebuilding of historic properties that had gone into decline. Le Camiset had floor-to-ceiling windows and great rooms with high ceilings that peaked under the pointed roof. Like many gamblers, Roland enjoyed horseracing, and Coty placed him in charge of a massive racing stable with over one hundred horses. After Coty's death, the horses were sold to pay his enormous debts. Yvonne moored the Alphée there for years after François's death.

François had special furniture designed for each of his properties. For Le Camiset, he had a huge cinnabar table built by Chinese craftsmen while he was in Peking setting up factories and assembly plants. Its chinoiserie top is eight feet in diameter, made of six-inch-thick teak lacquered again and again to accommodate the carved figures in the chosen story. The French-style base, which François designed in nine pieces, had a lacquered and carved brace in the center equally as beautiful as the top. The carved figures seem to walk paths defined by colors underneath, as the story unfolds. François returned eight years after placing the order to ship the table to Normandy.

Roland Coty jumps one of the dozens of horses François owned and stabled in Le Camiset, near Deauville. (Elizabeth Z. Coty Collection)

The piece remains in the family and, over the decades, this 700-pound table has been shipped across the globe four times, finally arriving in Charlottesville, Virginia, to be placed at the Long C farm of his grandson, Yves Michel. Out of the thousands of pieces of furniture purchased by François for specific places in his various properties, this table, remarkably, is one of the few still owned by a Coty, Patrice, my daughter.

Emile Buré, a former journalist for *Le Figaro*, had grown to hate Coty. All the same, Buré not only recognized François's love of country, but he understood that Coty's stable at Le Camiset was developed and maintained for the honor of France:

> M. François Coty, because of the popularity of horseracing these days, acquired a long established racing stable. Almost without preoccupying himself, he made himself the figure of a great proprietor, just as he had done before—in industry, commerce, journalism, automobile sports and aviation. M. François Coty only wants to owe his success to himself.
>
> It is he who, assisted by his son Roland, sportsman of *grande classe,* shod according to his father's tastes, will make the stable conform to his father's will. Coty also asked his compatriot, Roch Filippi, the well-known entertainer, to collaborate on this new field of activity. With an *animateur* like M. François Coty, how can one not succeed?

Be reassured that France, thanks to the stable of François Coty, will prevail victorious on the track against rival nations. Once again, in this new domain the founder of *L'Ami du Peuple* will have merited the praise of his country.[5]

When his father died, thirty-three-year-old Roland was of an age to take over the reins of the Coty empire. In this, he failed his mother, leaving her to turn to her second husband, Léon Cotnareanu. Roland instead became skipper of his mother's yacht, the Alphée. He sailed with her and Léon and their guests throughout the Mediterranean, Black, and Caspian seas. He arranged the details of their anchorages and automobile trips to places of historic interest along the way.

In 1939, when World War II loomed, Yvonne gave Roland the money to buy a British Lysander, which was just getting into production that year and was being used by the Royal Air Force. Naturally, being foolishly brave and an excellent pilot, Roland started the motor of his newest plane and said, grinning, "I will be a hero yet." The government confiscated the little beauty immediately but allowed him to pilot it, as trained men were almost nonexistent at that time. Soon after the war began and Paris fell, Roland was captured by the Germans but managed to escape within days. The family is silent about his activities throughout the rest of World War II, but it is known that his headquarters were in occupied Paris. His family found him after Yvonne's return to Paris in a hospital recovering from tuberculosis.

Coty: Collector of Mistresses

François reveled in women's adoration of him. The small, elegantly attired man, with an enormous sapphire shining on his index finger, presented himself in any one of his hundred-odd handmade suits, his hair tinted and marcelled. He wore a gigantic diamond stickpin that became his trademark, à la Diamond Jim Brady. His manners, his look, and his persona were geared toward attracting individual women at the same time that he rushed away from hordes of them on the streets as they clamored to speak with him.

His private floor at the Hotel Astoria was a well-known rendezvous, and his appearances there with any number of lovely women were publicized eagerly. Some women sought his sensuality; others desired his largesse; some were sent to him for political reasons. Quite simply, François loved the female sex, but he had his criteria. Young women under eighteen especially attracted him. A potential mistress had to meet standards that were probably only known to François subconsciously. If one analyzes his choice of mistresses, one recognizes similarities among them: cleverness, vivacity. He enjoyed those who were not outstanding in their own right but significant in what they might achieve with his help. Those he selected blossomed under his attention.

Yvonne is not known to have spoken of the way she felt about her husband's parade of mistresses. After his longtime number-one mistress, Henriette, had produced two children, François is reported to have asked Yvonne for a divorce. Wisely, no doubt, she refused. He was probably not disappointed. He recognized in Yvonne and her family a certain sophistication that he needed around him. Yvonne provided grounding and restraint to keep him from total excess— indeed, from making a fool of himself. His mother-in-law was an officer in the American Coty company and one of his greatest friends and supporters. Without the assistance of Yvonne's brothers and uncles, Coty SA might not have been launched.

Artist and Art Collector

On his calling card, Coty called himself an artist, among other vocational titles. The creation of a perfume as well as the design of the packaging were genuine arts to Coty. When a new idea came to him, he would make notes or produce it wherever he was. Once during lunch at the Ritz in Paris, he handed his menu to the maître d'hôtel and dictated a project that had popped into his mind. On another occasion, Christiane remembers him waking her late in the night to help record his ideas after he became inspired by an eleventh-century illuminated manuscript in his collection. Though he had Lalique and Baccarat as collaborators, Coty sometimes designed the company's bottles, stoppers, labels, and ensembles for the presentation of perfumes.

Later, when the money was pouring in, he sought out the finest designers and graphic artists available to create the elegant interiors of his offices and shops, but he participated at every level. Details that he supervised, such as the exterior relief carvings at his factories, illustrate his true interest in the arts. He loved to be a part of the work, and most of his employees appreciated his talent. He aggressively oversaw illustrations and copy for magazine and newspaper advertising. For example, his *Country Life* ads for perfume, talc, and cosmetics were carried out by his in-house artists, such as Georges Draeger, Georges Delhomme, Jacques Helleu, and others, but the copy and design reflected his input.

Georges Delhomme (1904-89), who started as a painter, made posters for Coty and served as artistic director of the firm from 1931

to 1934. Jacques Helleu also created many of Coty's advertising
posters. Pierre Camin, who joined the company in France not long
before Coty's death, attributed much of his success to what he learned
from François Coty. After Coty's death in 1934, Armand Petitjean left
Coty to establish Lancôme, and Georges Delhomme went with him as
art director, remaining with Lancôme until 1965. It can be said that
François Coty brought art to advertising through his own innovative
work and his insistence that his advertising be done by well-trained
and creative artists.

Coty was among the first Parisian collectors to befriend the
Japanese artist, printmaker, and interior designer Tsuguharu Foujita
(1886-1968), paying for his gallery showings and finding commissions
for him. The Japanese artist with the lanky black hair became, under
Coty's sponsorship, the rage of Paris. Born in Tokyo and dying in
Zurich, Foujita had left a potentially exciting career in Japan to go
to Paris in 1913. He knew Picasso; Soutine was his neighbor and
Modigliani his best friend. Coty sponsored Foujita's first show in
1917 at the Galerie Chéron. After exhibiting at the Salon d'Automne,
Foujita became a chevalier of the Legion of Honor. In 1926, the
French state bought Foujita's work *L'Amitié,* and in 1928, because
of Coty's influence, he was one of the decorators of the Odeon. He is
best known today for the eroticism of his nudes and for his woodcut
illustrations for prominent authors.

Coty bought the works of Auguste Rodin (1840-1917), yet it was
Yvonne Coty who kept his *Seven Days of the Week* statues all of her
life. Coty knew Maurice Utrillo as well as the artist's mother, Suzanne
Valladon, also an artist, who had a residence in Corsica. A segment
of the Coty's property at the Rond-Point des Champs-Elysées was
the townhouse of the family of Toulouse-Lautrec. Yvonne collected
Lautrec's works and those of Henri Martin (1860-1943), a pointillist
from Toulouse who had studied under Seurat. A painting by Martin
decorated the entrance wall of the bar at her Rond-Point residence
after 1950, and others hung at the Château de Sainte-Hélène in Nice.

Coty chose Charles Hoffbauer (1875-1957), whom he met in New
York, to paint the great mural for the rotunda at Château d'Artigny after
the First World War. Hoffbauer, a graduate of L'École des Beaux Arts,
had been a prizewinner at the 1906 Paris Salon. Though he studied
with Henri Matisse, Hoffbauer remained traditional in his approach
to subject matter and developed a painting style that worked well
on large-scale murals. He received a significant commission in the
United States in 1913 when the Confederate Memorial Association in
Richmond, Virginia asked him to paint the history of the Confederate

Army. When the Great War broke out, Hoffbauer interrupted his work to return to France to fight for his country. Later he returned to Richmond, where he began his project anew, his ideas of the American Civil War transformed by his own World War I experience in France.

The 1936 sale catalogue of the Coty Collection at the Jean Charpentier Gallery illustrates paintings that Yvonne and François Coty collected. Yvonne continued to collect works by the same artists later as Madame Léon Cotnareanu. Many of these works had never been shown when the catalogue came out for the sale on Monday, November 30, and Tuesday, December 1, 1936, at a Charpentier gallery auction in Paris.

CHAPTER 10

Napoleon of the Press, 1922

One commits and then looks.

Napoleon

From 1922 until he died in 1934, as fast as Coty made money in his worldwide cosmetics industries, he spent it to reform the State of France. If this meant buying Paris's oldest and finest newspapers, *Le Figaro* and *Le Gaulois*, he did it. It did not faze him to underwrite forty newspapers for over a decade. He had learned early in life, in Marseille and then in Paris, that newspapers controlled the minds of men, and he wanted to control the hearts and minds of all France. As he saw it, he was spending his money to help Frenchmen help themselves.

Georges Clemenceau's newspaper, *L'Homme libre,* made a difference in the political climate, convincing the French public that Germany was a threat. Coty realized that what he, a potential politician, had to have was a newspaper of his own. Clemenceau, who had studied at the École Normale in Nancy, was a politician, professor, and newspaper publisher who opposed almost everything François Coty represented. Their sole points of agreement were their anti-German sentiments and their interest in Corsica, for different reasons. Clemenceau added power and influence to his political base through his small newspaper; therefore Coty determined to acquire power through purchase of a large newspaper.

In 1922, Coty decided to buy *Le Figaro,* Paris's prestigious conservative and intellectual daily. Journalism had fascinated him since his youth. After working at a Marseille newspaper, he had learned far more about the fourth estate from his mentor, Arène. In fact, he had been introduced to *Le Figaro* by Arène, who had been a columnist for the elitist journal.

The newspaper, begun as a weekly in 1826, leaned toward literary and foreign-policy content. It had long been respected as the paper of the conservative and literary elite. By the 1920s, it was fighting both Bolshevism and socialism. The paper had signed on with the anti-Dreyfusards, opting to support the military and the government bureaucracy, as did most of the nobility and the wealthy businessmen in France.

Coty's first overtures to buy the newspaper were rebuffed. A revered former director, Gaston Calmette, who had been assassinated on the eve of World War I in his office at *Le Figaro,* had vowed never to sell it to a radical socialist, much less one like François Coty. His attitude still prevailed at the newspaper offices, where insiders seemed to ask about Coty, "Who is this parvenu billionaire, and a Corsican at that, who thinks that he can take over a 100-year-old bastion of conservative French intellectuals?"

Never one to give up a battle, Coty found a front man, Camille Aymard, to buy some of the paper's stock certificates. In an ironic twist, the latter accomplished this by obtaining for Coty 4,000 shares from Prince Napoleon, heir of Napoleon III. Aymard charged Coty ten times what he himself had paid for the shares, using the profit to launch his own newspaper with a liberal editorial policy. In his newspaper, which Coty had unknowingly paid for, Aymard promptly criticized Coty as a right-wing nobody.

The sideshow was irrelevant to Coty. He had gained his objective: he owned 90 percent of *Le Figaro* shares. Establishing control, however, was an even greater challenge than acquiring the newspaper. Robert de Flers and Alfred Capus ran the paper on a daily basis as coeditors. Capus covered politics and de Flers was literary director. Robert de Flers was always grateful to Coty because he was on the verge of being fired as an editor when Coty bought the newspaper. De Flers was a marquis descended from an ancient French family, a fact that impressed Coty. A conservative intellectual, he was not only sophisticated but a playwright, a member of the Académie Française, and a man considered representative of *l'esprit français.* At first, the relationship between Coty and de Flers went smoothly. However, Coty managed to press his largesse in gauche ways. He paid de Flers' debts and bought automobiles for a number of his staff, causing embarrassment and triggering resentment. Surprisingly, though, de Flers had some loyalty for Coty when his other friends and family had fled. De Flers accompanied Coty to his ultra-right-wing speech at the Salle Wagram in the spring of 1934. It was a different story with the entrenched directors. They criticized Coty for being politically "pink" if not red. He did too much for his workers at his Suresnes factories, they opined. A man who pursued such policies had no business owning *Le Figaro,* they told him.

On Wednesday, March 1, 1922, he published a letter to the directors of *Le Figaro,* which explained his politics:

> You are aware of the violence with which I have been attacked recently in the columns of this newspaper. My response has not been adequately inserted, so certain points seem to remain unresolved. Today, I ask your permission to resolve this dispute over the course of several lines.
>
> It is true that my friends and I possess an important number of stocks or shares at *Le Figaro.* We can thus be called on to have a certain influence over the future and the destiny of this paper. It is toward this eventuality that our group, presided over by Mr. Albert Calmette, asked me to ask you gentlemen, the longtime editors of *Le Figaro,* if you would consent to having total independence to recapture the political and literary direction of the newspaper.
>
> You had replied to me that you were inclined to accept our proposition if a contract could, as I had assured you, guarantee your total independence. Your presence here is therefore a pledge to maintain the integral political traditions of *Le Figaro.*
>
> I was attacked without proper cause. If those who attacked me had only informed themselves before insulting me, I would not owe an explanation. Unfortunately, clear thinking was not part of the argument of my adversaries. They dubbed me a radical-Socialist. I would be hard pressed to find in any of my articles, my conferences, or my speeches any material that would appear radical or radical-Socialist. The execution of the program for the recovery of Corsica, to which I dedicated myself, made it necessary for me to become involved with politics, but I always remained unaffiliated with political parties and kept myself involved for the sake of national interests, therefore on economic terrain. I owe this explanation to the true friends of *Le Figaro.*
>
> Please accept my devoted sentiments.
>
> François Coty

Coty's advisors at the time of his ascendance at *Le Figaro* were Paul Bourget and Maréchal Hubert Lyautey. Lyautey quit in disgust after Coty had the nerve to summon him, along with a number of his editors, to the Château d'Artigny, where they waited for five hours in the parlor for Coty to descend from his boudoir. One of the great ironies in Coty's story is that he and this enemy died on the same day in 1934, and Lyautey, the great general and *maréchal,* took precedence over Coty in the obituaries in France. This would have galled Coty, a news magnate for more than ten years and the richest man in France for twenty years, with all the influence and power such wealth can bring.

When Alfred Capus died, in 1923, his seat on *Le Figaro's* board of directors became vacant. Coty installed himself, thereby increasing his influence. Coty paid his staff well, more than they would have made at other newspapers. As a result, the newspaper was able to retain some good writers and editors, even though many of them disagreed with Coty's political views, and all of them chafed under his managerial style. In retrospect, only the literary writers saved the honor of the journal.

Coty was hardly the only French politician who owned a newspaper. Additionally, in the 1920s many government officials were intellectuals who contributed to newspapers. All shades of the political spectrum and all ethnic groups established or wrote for newspapers, from André Maurois on the left to Charles Maurras on the right.

The period between 1923, when Coty began to influence the newspaper he had bought, and 1933, when he lost total control, was tumultuous: right-wing groups worked to destabilize the government and simultaneously the communist party took root in France. To combat communism, some French businessmen, industrialists, and conservative royalists, inspired by Mussolini's development of fascism in Italy, found themselves contemplating a drastic option: replacing the Third Republic that had disillusioned so many with a Corporatist State. Meanwhile, Coty was not only corresponding with Mussolini but was reprinting his Italian tracts in *Le Figaro.* Coty also reprinted pieces from the Vatican, which was actively battling the communist movement worldwide. None of this sat well with *Le Figaro's* directors. They had set what they considered to be a moderately conservative stance for the newspaper. Coty had become a fierce anti-Bolshevik, having had some of his businesses, factories, and money confiscated in Russia and Eastern Europe. Furthermore, like so many Western European businessmen, he equated Bolshevism with Jews.

Not until 1924 did Coty's name appear on *Le Figaro's* masthead, signifying that he was now in control of day-to-day operations. At that moment, Coty's problems with *Le Figaro* began in earnest. Louis Latzarus, a journalist there since 1917 and also a respected scholar who published on Pierre Beaumarchais, had become director. He was a conservative, but he left *Le Figaro* following terrible scenes with Coty. He was replaced by a historian/writer with an established reputation as a traditionally educated, intellectual conservative, Lucien Romier. Not even a man of Romier's prestige could persuade Coty to moderate his behavior toward the staff. Coty infuriated his formerly autonomous writers by ordering them to create articles about subjects that revolted them and promote opinions they viewed as immoral. Worse, Coty would reverse his strong opinions day by day. He pitched the editorial slant more and more against Raymond Poincaré, alternately president and prime minister of France and at that time very popular with people of moderate views. As a result, *Le Figaro* seemed aggressively hostile toward the head of government. A peace of sorts was reached when Coty agreed to emphasize in the newspaper opposition to increased taxes, international high finance and banking, and communism, all of which were oblique references to anti-Semitism.

At *Le Figaro,* Coty took for himself the roles of publisher, managing editor, and director of politics. However, the ghostwriters he hired supplied most of the text that went out under his name. Most of these men—Maurice Hanot d'Hartoy, Marcel Bucard, and Urbain Gohier— were World War I veterans who despised the Germans. These men, who had established veterans' organizations and lobbied for veterans in their articles, were also rabid anti-communists. Coty's own bêtes noires were taxes and Bolshevism or communism. He declared war on those bureaucrats he termed "budgetivores," accusing them of devising ways to tax the French people.

During the 1920s, outrageous, autocratic behavior was the norm among French press lords. As one historican notes, "Léon Bailby, boss of *L'Intransigeant,* had a flag run up on the front of the building whenever he was in his office. He demanded that two rows of his journalists stand at attention when he walked toward the entrance. As for Maurice Buneau-Varilla, he asserted that his chair as director of *Le Matin* was worth three thrones and 'considered himself to be the savior of mankind because his brother had invented Synthol.'"[1]

As fast as Coty was buying newspapers, he was spending his wealth in ways that made favorable news. Coty was busy, but his mind was constantly working. In July 1930, he hit upon the idea of Radio Branly. When he found out that Edouard Branly, one of the inventors of radio, had been forgotten, he brought him out of retirement with plans to create a radio station to blanket the world with his own ideas. The project never got off the ground, but in his usual generous fashion, Coty provided Branly with an extensive laboratory; that space is now a museum in Paris.

Branly, born in Amiens in 1844, was best known for his research on electric discharge by ultraviolet rays. He invented the Branly radio conductor. In 1903, he and Marie Curie were jointly awarded the coveted French Prix Osiris. By 1911, he had became a member of the Académie des Sciences. Coty appreciated Branly's achievements and lamented the obscurity into which the scientist had fallen.

From science, Coty could easily transfer his interests to agriculture.

He built four farms for deserving agricultural workers whose farms had been destroyed by floods in the Montauban region. The project cost him 80 million francs.

Tensions ran rampant when, in 1925, Coty moved the offices of *Le Figaro* from rue Drouot to one of the buildings he had purchased at the Rond-Point des Champs-Elysées, far away from the traditional boulevards where the intellectuals and dandies of Paris, the boulevardiers, promenaded about and dined, drank, and talked. He moved *Le Figaro* into the Bamberger building while providing offices in the Lautrec building to a series of rightist political leagues.

As if that were not enough to exasperate his staff, he managed to enrage all Paris by changing the name of the newspaper to *Figaro*. Dropping the prefixing article triggered a furor throughout the city. The change was rumored to be the idea of Coty's ghostwriter Urbain Gohier, but Coty defended the move by asking, "You would not say Le Beaumarchais, so why would you say *Le Figaro*?" He would not back down and the newspaper was named *Figaro* until October 4, 1933, when Coty's name left the masthead. Immediately the name reverted to *Le Figaro,* and the intellectuals and the literati and the boulevardiers of Paris celebrated.

With all of Paris in an uproar about Coty's actions at *Figaro,* his support of French Olympic teams was surely one way to redeem his public image. France had participated in every Olympic meet until 1928, when the funds dried up. This was unacceptable to François Coty. The *New York Times* on July 24, 1927, reported, "Upon learning that the French Olympic Committee had decided last Wednesday not to participate in the competition because of failure of the French Government to vote the necessary credits for the training of athletes and other expenses, François Coty, perfume manufacturer and proprietor of *Figaro,* offered a loan of one million francs to defray the expenses of preparation. . . . The offer was accepted by Count Clary, President of the French Olympic Committee. The Senate will reconsider the bill asking for a credit of two million francs. . . . The loan offered by M. Coty will provide the French committee with sufficient funds to go ahead with its training plans."

A well-established competitor to *Le Figaro* that appealed to much the same readership was *Le Gaulois.* Once, it had been a Royalist organ. It had abandoned that cause for the more general conservative and socially elite readers. Under the leadership of Arthur Meyer, the same American Meyer that Coty's ghostwriter Urbain Gohier and his mentor, Emmanuel Arène, had fought in duels, *Le Gaulois* became known as the newspaper that most faithfully reflected the true spirit of the boulevards.

Lucien Romier continued under Coty until 1927. By then he, too, could abide his employer no longer and quit as director. Romier joined Redressement Français (French Rectification), the postwar movement established by electricity magnate Ernest Mercier. Beginning as an economic movement against the policies of Edouard Herriot, France's finance minister, the group promoted constitutional reform.

Emile Buré, another journalist who could no longer take Coty's politics or attitude toward the staff, also left. He reported everywhere that Coty was a megalomaniac. Buré aired his resentment toward his former employer when he wrote Coty's obituary for his new newspaper.

During the twenties and thirties, Paris newspapers, including *Le Figaro,* were features of Parisian social life. Both *Le Gaulois* and *Le Figaro* held receptions from five to seven in the evening on particular dates. Politicians, nobility, ambassadors, members of the Académie Française, and intellectuals, seeking coverage of their ideas, flocked to these events. Coty, often attending with Yvonne, adored these soirées, since he was, after all, interested in nearly everything and everyone. On these occasions, it seemed as though the couple was royalty.

Coty's 1928 purchase of *Le Gaulois* was an event significant enough for comment in the *New York Times,* where a March 31, 1929, article read, "After a notable career of sixty-four years, in which it achieved the reputation of being the most Parisian of all dailies, *Le Gaulois* will disappear from the streets of the capital tomorrow in a merger with *Figaro.* Both of these properties belong to the millionaire perfume manufacturer, François Coty, who, with the aid of a greatly enlarged *Figaro,* is to continue, with renewed vigor, his campaign against the parliamentary form of government."

Coty apparently failed to notice that he had managed to alienate and infuriate the readers of both journals. *Figaro's* readership went into freefall, with daily circulation dropping from 100,000 after World War I to 40,000 (some claimed it was only 12,000) in 1933 when Coty lost control. During his tenure as publisher, Coty spent 85 million francs keeping the newspaper afloat.

Coty Establishes L'Ami du Peuple

When Coty saw that his workmen in Suresnes were reading *L'Humanité,* the communists' newspaper, he decided to establish another newspaper aimed at the working class. The new journal would espouse principles that Coty understood and thought suitable. In 1928, he asked an old friend from his early childhood, Albert du Barry, to head up a newspaper they named *L'Ami du Peuple,* with which they hoped to lure the working class from communist leanings.

ÉDITION DE 5 HEURES

L'AMI DU PEUPLE
DE PARIS

LE JOURNAL LE PLUS LU DU MONDE ENTIER

PARIS, SEINE & S.-&-O. : 15 c.
DÉPARTEMENTS : 20 c.

DIMANCHE 8 JANVIER 1933
6ᵉ ANNÉE N° 1.710

Lisez FIGARO le plus élégant le plus renseigné le plus vivant des journaux du matin

Dans FIGARO on trouve vrai depuis un an et demi les meilleures et les plus politiques les plus utiles renseignements pratiques les plus utiles

L'égalité est un vain mot

La rentrée parlementaire

Les séances de mardi seront consacrées à l'élection des bureaux

A LA CHAMBRE

L'intérêt d'un sénateur franc-maçon contre l'intérêt public

LES JOURS PASSENT

Le musée de la rue

A BORD DE L'«ATLANTIQUE»

Notre envoyé spécial visite le grand paquebot entièrement dévasté par le feu

CINQ CADAVRES ONT ÉTÉ DÉCOUVERTS DANS LES FLANCS DE L'ÉPAVE

EN RADE DE CHERBOURG

(Par téléphone de notre envoyé spécial)

Cherbourg, 7 janvier.

A SAINT-LOUIS-DES-INVALIDES
UNE MESSE A ÉTÉ CÉLÉBRÉE A LA MÉMOIRE DE MAGINOT

Pas un ministre n'assistait à cette pieuse cérémonie

A BORD DU PAQUEBOT

O. K... New-York

Une soirée au Waldorf où l'on danse et où l'on boit beaucoup

(De notre envoyé spécial)

Mgr Ruch est élu membre de l'Académie des Sciences morales et politiques

En creusant une tranchée un homme meurt enseveli sous un éboulement

Lyon, 7 janvier.

La composition du Conseil supérieur de la guerre pour 1933

Un ancien banquier allemand faussaire était aussi un faux nom professeur à l'Université d'Harvard

Berlin, 7 janvier.

Message d'un maître-maçon

Notre fondateur a reçu le 1ᵉʳ janvier la lettre que voici :

À Monsieur François Coty,
LOUVECIENNES.

Montcel,

LÉON MEYER, LE GLAS DE LA MARINE

— Monsieur le ministre, l'incendie est éteint.
— Bon !... Il ne reste plus qu'à éteindre l'enquête.

Dessin de CHANCEL.

Les cours à Paris des monnaies étrangères

Lire en cinquième page :
LES ANCIENS COMBATTANTS ET LES JEUNES GÉNÉRATIONS

Coty established *L'Ami du Peuple,* a conservative, working-class newspaper in Paris, to counteract communist publications. (Library of Congress)

Coty aimed to publish 100,000 copies of the first issue of *L'Ami du Peuple* and to reach a circulation of 1 million within six months. To achieve this larger readership, Coty intended to undersell the other newspapers. They charged twenty-five centimes per copy; *L'Ami du Peuple* would cost ten centimes. The shortfall, Coty felt, could be made up with revenue from advertising. He was prepared to use his fortune to subsidize the new publication.

The first issue was slated for distribution on March 20, 1928. However, the Hachette press-delivery service and the Havas Agency, a powerful newspaper advertising business, joined forces to deny Coty access to the newspaper-delivery infrastructure. When Coty found out what had happened, he raged but switched gears and took effective action. The ensuing battle animated Paris for a season. The issue, as far as Coty was concerned, was freedom of speech and of the press.

Havas had under its control *Le Petit Parisien,* with a million and a half circulation, as well as *Le Journal, Le Matin,* and *Le Petit Journal,* each with a million readers. The agency claimed that Coty had signed an agreement to charge the same price as the consortium papers, twenty-five centimes, but had then reneged after deciding to make *L'Ami du Peuple* available to the poorest worker. The consortium therefore demanded that the printer chosen by Coty break his contract. Havas refused to give advertising space and Hachette refused to deliver Coty's newspaper. The Federation of Newspapers told the newsstands that no papers would use them if they sold *L'Ami du Peuple.* Of course, the printer and the newsstands complied with the federation.

The battle was joined, but Coty thought both astutely and creatively. He set up his own National Publishing and Advertising Company. He found a new printer and established his own French parcel service, Messageries Françaises. He put together a new chain of newsstands, launched a billboard advertising campaign, and hired hundreds of newsboys to sell and deliver 150,000 copies a day. Coty's newspapers spread across Paris on May 28, 1928, and 100,000 of them appeared at new venues: tobacco shops, bars, and cafés.

Coty was winning. Circulation exceeded the publisher's goal of 1 million in six months. American journalist Arthur Train, Jr., reported that the newspaper sold 8 million copies in its first month and 18 million within a year.

Coty's accomplishment was phenomenal. He had applied the Coty system from his perfume business to his newspaper business, owning and managing every aspect of it—paper, presses, delivery trucks, and even some of the kiosks. He said, "I do not want to make a profit on the trade of ideas." However, he was making a profit even while selling the paper for less than half the price of his competitors, because he shrewdly took advantage of the publicity from his distribution dispute to garner advertisers. He applied the same business sense to his journalism venture that he used in marketing his perfumes.

Coty sued Havas, which eventually had frozen out anyone who advertised in Coty's newspapers. The lawsuit lasted from 1928 to 1930. Coty published an impassioned defense of his position in *Figaro*. Titling it "For the Liberty of the Press, *L'Ami du Peuple*: Against the Federation of Newspapers," he wrote:

> Is it necessary to remember this already old affair? Because though several trials are pending, it is truly but one case. It is, moreover, of sufficient importance because it is nothing less than the freedom of the press that lies at stake."
>
> In the name of Freedom of the Press, suppress *L'Ami du Peuple* and award us six million in damages. This is what the Federation, Monsieur Campinchi, the top-notch litigant, upheld last Monday before the court. Why this suppression? Why loyal to forty newspapers of the Federation?

Coty was so enthusiastic about *L'Ami du Peuple* that he decided to publish an evening edition. When it came out on November 18, 1928, a preface delineated the policy for the new journal. Adopting a high moral tone, Coty announced, "*L'Ami du Peuple* represents the sole voice of Truth [in France] and the French people should not have to wait an entire 24 hours between editions. . . . The newspaper represents the rights of ordinary people, freedom of the press and free market rights. Other competing papers are run by people who are disinterested except for the profit they are making."

Premier André Tardieu, then an old-fashioned conservative, arbitrated the suit and ruled in Coty's favor, awarding him 10 million francs in damages on April 9, 1930. Tardieu determined that it was established in commercial court that certain provincial newspapers represented by the consortium were sold below the statutory price that had been set up and applied to Coty's *L'Ami du Peuple*.

Urbain Gohier, Coty's ghostwriter, translated for Coty the anti-Semitic Russian text, *The Protocols of the Elders of Zion*. Coty published it under his own name as *Reform of the State* and serialized it in *L'Ami du Peuple* in 1933. The work made reference to a "collusion" among "international Jewry."

The ugliest expression of anti-Semitism on Coty's part manifested in the early 1930s. He attacked Moldavian Jews, probably because the man Yvonne married in 1929 was one. Some of the language that François published cannot be found in some of today's French dictionaries. For example, he wrote, *"Les youtres aux yeux fardes, les juifs polaks, moldovalaques, rastas, racaille qui se ruent sur notre pays comme sure une proie trop facile . . . "* ("The dark ones with their made-up eyes, the Polish Jews, Moldavian Jews, dark and greasy riff-raff that pounce on our country as if it were easy prey . . . ").

Soon after Coty serialized his inflammatory book, his divorce settlement wrested his beloved newspaper from him. What happened next made an ironic footnote to Coty's court victory against the newspaper consortium. Havas bought *L'Ami du Peuple* from Yvonne for 300 million francs in January of 1934. Coty lost his real love as well as his last hope for fame. The extreme-right political line of the newspaper, however, remained unchanged under Pierre Bermond, the new editor, who was also the new director of Solidarité Française, Coty's right-wing organization. Then, in 1936, the rightist Flandin-Taittinger partnership took over *L'Ami du Peuple,* and that same year it was suppressed by the State.

Another book ghostwritten for Coty, *Tearing Away the Veils: The Financiers Who Control the World,* was available in English translation in 1998 from Sons of Liberty Books in Arabi, Louisiana.

Failure of Coty's Publishing Career

Coty's publishing career can serve as a textbook example of an intelligent person's capacity for self-destruction: brilliant enough to become a billionaire in one field of endeavor, yet so arrogant and given to excess in another activity that he united the world against him. Coty the publisher lacked self-control and the ability to foresee the consequences of his inflammatory or denigrating words. "The Viennese Affair," as reported in the *New York Times* on October 2, 1927, is an example of how François sabotaged himself. Journalist Navarre Atkinson wrote from Vienna:

> M. Coty's Statement That They Want to Join Germany to Avoid Work Angers Them
> M. Coty, the French perfume manufacturer, where most other people in the world have failed, has aroused the ire of the good-natured Viennese. They resent an article recently published under his name in the *Figaro* of Paris in which he speaks of the Austrians; laziness more than anything makes them favorable to an "anschluss" [union] with Germany. . . . The perfumer's story, the Monarchist, Conservative and Socialist newspapers declare with unanimity, reeks of spite as well as of untruths, and there is equal concord in urging the Austrian public to boycott the products of M. Coty.

In fact, the Nationalist papers urge the Government to pass a regulation prohibiting his perfumes from crossing the Austrian frontiers, and it is suggested as unpatriotic to allow any bottle to be shown in windows in Vienna.

M. Coty said in his article that he found the statement that the Austrian people could not exist under the present conditions to be groundless, that the Viennese drink all day and were naturally lazy, and that it is more the idea of getting out of work than anything else that contributes to the desire for an "anschluss." The author [Coty] thinks the Austrians want to shift the burden of keeping up the State to the Germans or any one else, who is more industrious and willing for annexation. Government officials published unofficially data to show Austrians are hard workers and not gourmands.

The *New York Times* reported on September 19, 1928, from Budapest that "Hungary today decided to take vengeance on the French perfumery manufacturer Coty for recent alleged attacks on the Hungarian people in his newspaper, *L'Ami du Peuple.*"

Coty had published an article entitled "Hungary, Land of Counterfeiters and Pickpockets." When this became known in Budapest, indignation reached a high pitch, and all druggists, perfume dealers, and barbershops decided to boycott his products. "Today, the first day of the boycott, it was impossible to purchase any Coty articles or find them in any show window," the *New York Times* reported. The boycott of Coty products in Hungary continued for months.

Coty traveled widely, and if anything set him off, he could vent about it on the front page of one or another of his newspapers. The *New York Times* commented on April 18, 1929, that Coty could take an independent stand on just about any subject that interested him, since he was not a member of the newspaper consortium in Paris.

Coty was alternately autocratic with his writers and editors and then generous with them. Sometimes his ghostwriters inserted their own points of view, often chip-on-the-shoulder opinions that added to Coty's reputation as either a radical or a megalomaniac.

The subject of American films in France infuriated François; on the other hand, he also thought that French films were inferior. By publishing both opinions, Coty garnered enemies on all sides of any question. He defended his views in more than one of his newspapers:

> Very few of the people in France know the inside of the contingent question. The American renting of films is ceasing in France! Bravo! Let us applaud. . . . In the opinion of everyone, and

our own sense of fairness compels us to admit it, the French motion pictures were never so poor or inferior as they are at present.

If the American public does not like most of the French films, it is not because of a spirit of Chauvinism or because of the Monroe Doctrine, but because of their inferiority. As a matter of fact, Americans do appreciate good French films and there never has been an example of a good French film failing to succeed in the United States.

No! American films must not disappear from the French screen. Let us have great French films. Let us have a French motion picture industry and let us suppress this sort of moral tariff wall, which is the contingent question.

In another article, however, Coty railed against the loose morals that infiltrate France via American movies. He comes off as quite a prude, considering his own publicly paraded love life. French society may have snickered about Coty's articles, but they did not shun him, since that may have meant losing his largesse in matters of charity or donations to their own political causes. Ironically, most of his readers agreed with his views. Coty was merely voicing the private opinions of many well-to-do Frenchmen of his day.

In *Figaro* on November 20 and 30 and December 1, 1926, Coty wrote a series of articles, "Settling with America," that was translated in *The Living Age.* In it, Coty exhorted France to pay its World War I debt to the United States in spite of the fact that "the United States is wholly responsible for a disastrous situation wherein France is justified in refusing to consent to the repayment."

Coty had long shared many Frenchmen's resentment of the Americans, who, they felt, had not represented France sufficiently in 1919 at the Treaty of Versailles. He lamented the weakness of France at the subsequent Washington Conference, but he believed that France should honor its debts to America. He wrote, "There are times when we must rise above mere questions of money and think only of the peace of the world and the welfare of humanity . . . we believe that a ratification of our debt accord with the United States under certain conditions is preferable to the present situation . . . because the good will of America is now, and will always be a most valuable asset for France; because America's support is today, and will be for a long time to come, necessary." Coty was anxious, above all, that France not be perceived by any other country as dragging her feet about the debt.

In the articles, Coty recommended repaying the debt to America according to the Dawes Plan, "devised by Americans and administered and directed by American experts." He continued, "This plan is the safeguard, the protection, of all the European nations who are indebted to America, and is running with the cooperation of Germany. We must associate ourselves with it. Either it will succeed and the Allied Powers will pay the United States proportionally to what they respectively collect from Germany, or it will fail and Europe will be relieved of all her obligations abroad."

Coty took this opportunity to criticize the French parliament, which had refused to ratify a payment agreement that the French ambassador signed on France's behalf at the Washington Conference. He tirelessly wrote about the difficulties of having a parliament and an ineffectual and outmoded bureaucracy full of *fonctionnaires,* furthering their personal interests.

Coty's conclusion to the series was strong, revealing his preoccupation, as a nationalist, with France's honor. To shirk on payment of the debt "is an unworthy role for France to play," he wrote. "Harsh and unjust as may be America's demands, we should approve the bill. Germany is responsible for the war. It is for her to ask mercy to solicit reductions, and eventually the general annulment of war debts she no doubt plans in the bottom of her heart. Germany is the only country that can secure a reduction or annulment, for a reason we should constantly keep in mind." Coty's enemies, of course, leapt upon his advice to pay the debt to America. Since Coty made most of his millions in the United States, they said, he was just trying to curry favor at the expense of the French treasury.

Journalists and scholars excoriated Coty for decades for the opinions that he wrote and published. Because of statements like the following, Coty was accused of being a propagandist rather than a journalist: "There are twenty or twenty-five million people of German descent in the United States, many of the more powerful financiers are of German stock, and an influential press is controlled by men of German blood and connections. Let Germany, then, be the first one to default."

Coty accused the "American Jewish cartel," in print, of promoting the redevelopment of Germany's industries after World War I. Indeed, Jewish investors worldwide, in the early 1920s and later, were investing in German steel and providing millions of dollars to redevelop the Ruhr Valley as an industrial powerhouse. The irony was that, by extension, Coty was projecting the idea that German-American Jews were loyal, first, to Germany.

Coty also angered his compatriots with his criticism of the tax laws. After harping against France's then-modest 2 percent income tax in his newspapers, he resolutely refused to pay any taxes and was in constant litigation with the Finance Ministry. Coty wrote in *Figaro* on June 13, 1926:

> Our best, most patriotic and most farsighted citizens have exerted themselves for several generations to drag our stalled bureaucracy out of its ancient rut; but their labor has been of no avail against the invincible inertia of an established system.
>
> [A] system of private patronage has corroded the whole Government service. It has corrupted statesmen and their immediate subordinates.
>
> Last of all is the collection of taxes. We employ for this purpose an army of functionaries who studiously do all in their power to make the Government's fiscal inquisition as complicated and troublesome as possible, in order to justify their own existence. But while they bully honest taxpayers, who neither desire nor know how to conceal their property, they allow the big defrauders of the revenue to go scot-free.

"Sinister Meanings Read into Published Missive to French Fascist Leader," read the *New York Times* headline on January 16, 1932. The article commenced: "The publication of a letter from Premier Mussolini of Italy to François Coty, publisher of *Figaro* and *L'Ami du Peuple,* is the latest incident in a campaign which the Left press of France is directing against the Corsican perfume manufacturer whose troubles have been great since he took over the direction of the Fascist movement in France and ran furiously counter to the Foreign Minister, [Aristide] Briand, in his newspapers."

The alleged letter from Mussolini, published by the liberal Paris newspaper *La République,* began, "Dear Coty." In two sentences it informs the French newspaper director that his report had been received and that within a few days a special envoy from Rome would come to see him and arrange matters.

The New York newspaper reported, "Into this message, which has in some mysterious way reached the Opposition press, there are being read all kinds of sinister things. It is being connected with the charge recently made against M. Coty that he sold, allegedly for strategic purposes, the Forest of Asco in Corsica to Signor Mussolini." When that alleged transaction was first revealed, it was reported that the forest was to be used for secret military purposes.

The article continued, "Mr. Coty so far has not replied to these charges. He has contented himself with denying a report that due to the shrinkage in his fortune and the enormous [divorce] settlement which he had to make upon his former wife, he would be compelled to sell *Figaro.*"

The staff, the shareholders and the readers of *Figaro* were becoming as hysterical about Coty as he was about communists. Finally, the staff and the board devised a scheme to get rid of him, or at least to suspend his articles and influence. In 1933, the Council of Administration of *Figaro* became strong enough to demote Coty. The board of directors met on October 4, 1933, and the council made its decision. The post of director was suppressed and the name of François Coty disappeared from the masthead. The day that Coty first learned of the meeting, he asked, "Who did it?" His source answered, "Saint-Aulaire and Alphaud." Coty replied, "I should have expected it. I saved Saint-Aulaire and was benefactor to all the others."

Coty was chased from *Figaro* under curious circumstances, as one historian notes: "Gabriel Alphaud and le comte de Saint-Aulaire, creatures of Coty on the Figaro Council of Administration, profited from their relationship with him, but they were loath to appear as his representative on the various directorships they enjoyed because of him. In the meeting of the Council of *Figaro* on October 4, 1933, they voted, along with Coty's enemies, to suppress the post of the director of *Figaro*. In spite of his protestation, Coty was not able to annul this decision. Edouard Calmette, son of *Le Figaro's* assassinated editor, became administrator; the banker René Wertheimer took charge of the paper."[2]

Within a year of Coty's ouster as publisher, Yvonne Coty-Cotnareanu used her rights over her first husband's shares to become the largest shareholder of the paper. Alphaud and Saint-Aulaire, despite or because of their betrayal of Coty, were eliminated and replaced by Henri Dubois, a relative of Yvonne. Conservative economist Lucien Romier became director again, with a directors' committee that included André Maurois, Paul Morand, Wladimir d'Ormesson, and Pierre Brisson. Pierre Lafitte was called in as technical consultant. The new team was in place on June 7, 1934, just weeks before Coty's death. Pierre Brisson, literary director, became co-director in October of 1936, and his influence continued to grow. The paper prospered, also profiting by the failure of *L'Echo*.

After achieving her takeover of the newspaper, Yvonne, who was not interested in journalism, delegated the oversight of *Le Figaro* to her husband. Léon Cotnareanu, doubtless as he had long planned, became publisher. Anti-Semitism disappeared from the pages of the newspaper. Cotnareanu worked well with Lucien Romier. In fact, Léon and Yvonne invited Romier and his wife repeatedly to join them on long seagoing voyages on Yvonne's yacht. They were most impressed with Romier's friendship with King Michael of Hungary and his English-born wife, Queen Marie. Romier was knowledgeable about all things Eastern European, which endeared him to the Moldavian, Léon Cotnareanu. When Yvonne and Léon fled to the United States after the fall of Paris in 1940, Romier followed the government south to become a close confidant of Maréchal Philippe Pétain and an active advisor in the Vichy government during World War II.

CHAPTER 11

Prince of Politics, 1910-34

> People of France! The politicians are worthless. As long as they have a stranglehold on the finances of the nation, the collapse of the franc will continue.
>
> François Coty

After World War I, Coty's business in the U.S. boomed. He began transferring the bulk of his great fortune, most of it untaxed, from New York to France and Switzerland. This wealth, gained from sales of perfume and cosmetics throughout the world, would support Coty's venture into French politics. He was determined to transform himself into a leader in France, using the billions acquired from women's purses to do it.

As George Ravon, who once wrote for *Le Figaro,* put it, "Alas! What an unwise commitment of money, effort and time, but his brain, remarkably organized for the flagons and the essences, was badly formed to fight the intoxication of politics. Certain collaborators, interested in the development of intellectual disorder, who worked against all government control and favored pillage, pushed [Coty] adroitly toward megalomania. He became persuaded that he was born to save France."

Throughout the 1920s and early 1930s, two disparate motivations underlay Coty's political activities: virulent anti-Bolshevism was one; antipathy toward and distrust of Germany and Germans was the other. Early on, Coty's anti-Bolshevist fanaticism was stoked by information brought to his attention by Duke Pozzo di Borgo, director of the Anti-Marxist Institute of Paris and vice president of Croix de Feu, an organization for wounded veterans. The aristocrat was a Corsican and a distant relative of François, but the duke differed from François in that he was pro-Nazi, although both supported Mussolini.

Coty also took notice of France's ambassador to Moscow, Maurice Paléologue, a sophisticated knowledgeable diplomat who had been trying to warn his government not to ignore developments in Russia. Coty began to support, not necessarily with wisdom or discrimination, all French organizations that claimed they were fighting French

Bolshevism. His fear turned increasingly to fury when, shortly after World War I ended, French communists organized formally at Tours, near Coty's own Château d'Artigny.

According to Coty, the greatest danger France faced after the First World War was Bolshevism. The Bolshevik Revolution had ripped Russia apart, while Lenin, safely out of harm's way, lived unobtrusively in Paris. The Bolsheviks seized all foreign capital in Russia, including the three former Rallet-Chiris factories that Coty had bought and where his perfumes for Eastern Europe had been produced since 1908. The 4 million francs that Coty had deposited in the Moscow branch of Credit Lyonnais were shifted into Bolshevik coffers. His two retail shops were confiscated. Fortunately, his French employees in Russia were allowed to leave and Coty reestablished his factories near Cannes.

Coty felt that it was folly for France and the West to ignore political developments in Russia. He was sure that the former Allies' failure to support Kerensky's provisional socialist government was a dire mistake. However, he coupled these beliefs with diatribes against Russian Jews, claiming that they had brought about the Revolution. François did not grasp how contradictory his behavior was, since he was at the very same time, along with his wife, Yvonne, acting as patron to Jewish painters and performing artists who had made their way to France from Eastern Europe and Russia. Many of his managers across the world were Jewish, most importantly Benjamin Levy in New York, his closest associate, and Raymond Charles Greilsamer in Suresnes.

Coty's political thinking closely followed that of two conservative factions, the Royalists and Bonapartists. Their anti-Semitism and opposition to the Freemasons fit his belief system, formed in nineteenth-century, tribal, Catholic Ajaccio. Similarly, denigration of the Third Republic became a major theme in his political pronouncements, when he harped on the frequency with which the government fell, to be reincarnated with the same cast of characters, reshuffled into new assignments.

If none of Coty's ideas represented original thinking, he was still ahead of some of his compatriots in realizing that the Allies' victory had been nullified in part by their failure to enforce Germany's total disarmament. According to André Maurois, who had once worked for Coty at *Le Figaro,* François was incensed that the German high command had not been dissolved, that German reparations to France had been paid only at the beginning of peacetime, and then mainly with American money, and that France was having to struggle, hopelessly, to regain its primacy in Europe.

The Spotorno family emigrated from Spotorno, near Savona on Italy's Ligurian coast, to Ajaccio, Corsica, in the early 1500s. This photograph shows the medieval fortress at Spotorno. (Elizabeth Z. Coty Collection)

An advertisement shows a view of Place Vendôme from the
interior of the House of Coty. (Elizabeth Z. Coty Collection)

Coty's house in Marly, France, near Versailles, was used when the family played golf nearby, 1960. (Photograph by Elizabeth Z. Coty)

Muguet perfume label designed for Coty. (Elizabeth Z. Coty Collection)

François Coty had René Lalique design his Fifth Avenue retail shop as the New York headquarters of Coty Inc. Lalique installed an etched-glass facade, a heavy glass stair rail, columns, and other fixtures. For many years, the facade was hidden. It has now been renovated for Henri Bendel. (Elizabeth Z. Coty Collection)

The facade of Château d'Artigny, near Tours, was designed and built by François Coty after Champlâtreux. (Elizabeth Z. Coty Collection)

Coty commissioned this mural for the dome at the Château d'Artigny, incorporating portraits of his friends and family as well as three of his mistresses. (Elizabeth Z. Coty Collection)

Buildings at the Château d'Artigny before Coty's purchase of the property. (Photograph by Elizabeth Z. Coty)

Coty's factory at Suresnes. (Société Historique et Artistique de Suresnes, Archives)

You've only one life to enjoy . . . let it all be fragrant! For your casual hours, Coty has created "Informal Fragrances" . . . crisp, fresh versions in lighter mood of famous Coty Perfumes. "Informal Fragrances" are exceptionally rich, rounded and lasting . . . each breathes the charm of true Coty essence. Prices are keyed to informality. You'll find yourself using your Coty "Informal Fragrances" lavishly, as often as your feminine soul desires!

NOW—ATOMIZER WITH EVERY SIZE . . . Since "Informal Fragrance" is most happily used with an atomizer, Coty now offers you a good one with each of the world-famous odeurs: L'Aimant, Emeraude, "Paris," L'Origan. Three sizes, $1.25, $2, $3.25. Economy Size, a real investment in charm, In matching fragrances . . . silky-soft COTY TALC, 50¢.

Advertisement for Coty's fragrance *Informal.*
(Elizabeth Z. Coty Collection)

Goty advertisement for *Le chemin de la beauté* (The Road to Beauty).
(Elizabeth Z. Coty Collection)

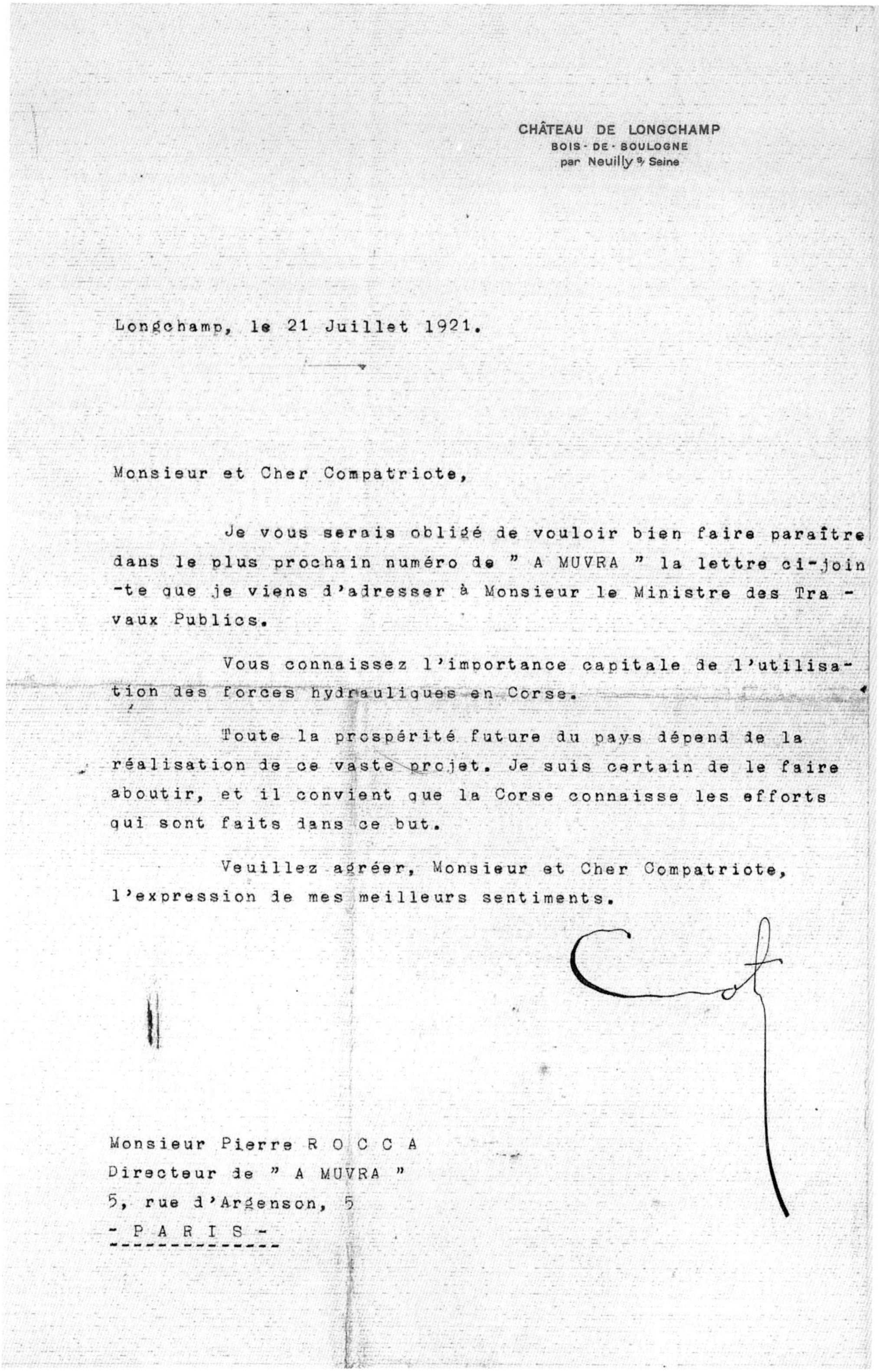

CHÂTEAU DE LONGCHAMP
BOIS - DE - BOULOGNE
par Neuilly ⁹⁄ Seine

Longchamp, le 21 Juillet 1921.

Monsieur et Cher Compatriote,

Je vous serais obligé de vouloir bien faire paraître dans le plus prochain numéro de " A MUVRA " la lettre ci-join -te que je viens d'adresser à Monsieur le Ministre des Tra - vaux Publics.

Vous connaissez l'importance capitale de l'utilisa- tion des forces hydrauliques en Corse.

Toute la prospérité future du pays dépend de la réalisation de ce vaste projet. Je suis certain de le faire aboutir, et il convient que la Corse connaisse les efforts qui sont faits dans ce but.

Veuillez agréer, Monsieur et Cher Compatriote, l'expression de mes meilleurs sentiments.

Monsieur Pierre R O C C A
Directeur de " A MUVRA "
5, rue d'Argenson, 5
- P A R I S -

François Coty sent this letter to Pierre Rocca, editor of Coty's newspaper, *A Muvra,* which was established to preserve the Corsican language, 1921. (Elizabeth Z. Coty Collection)

Villa Rosa in Calvi, Corsica, was one of the homes of Christiane Coty.
(Photograph by Elizabeth Z. Coty)

The sports stadium in Ajaccio was named after François Coty. Corsica has been somewhat unappreciative of the millions of francs that Coty lavished upon the island of his birth. The sports stadium, however, retains his name. (Elizabeth Z. Coty Collection)

Château de Sainte-Hélène, in Nice, was another home of the Cotys. (Photograph by Elizabeth Z. Coty)

Coty rebuilt Louveciennes, the residence of Comtesse Du Barry, mistress of Louis XV. (Photograph by Elizabeth Z. Coty)

Louveciennes's *pavillon* was designed originally by Claude-Nicolas Ledoux and purchased and rebuilt by Coty. He died here in 1934. (Elizabeth Z. Coty Collection)

Filolie, in Périgord, was one of Coty's numerous estates. Yvonne's mother settled here during World War II and died on the estate. (Photograph by Elizabeth Z. Coty)

Top: *Hyphen,* the airplane that Coty financed for a flight from Paris to Tokyo.
Bottom: Pilots Costes and Bellonte are shown with an image of Coty in the
background. (Elizabeth Z. Coty Collection)

Share in Coty, Inc., 1930. (Elizabeth Z. Coty Collection)

"Air-Spun" Make-up

There's beauty in the air, beauty that's yours to command with these four color-related make-up aids. First, "Sub-Tint" to give your complexion that smooth, clear, flawless look . . . Next, "Air-Spun" Face Powder and Rouge—cloud-soft because they're buffed by whirling torrents of air. Then, as a brilliant finale, "Sub-Deb" Lipstick. All four are made fragrant by matchless Coty artistry.

Coty

For Fall Harmony: Dark "Sub-Tint" with Cassis "Air-Spun" Rouge, Café Crème "Air-Spun" Face Powder, and Cassis "Sub-Deb" Lipstick.

Coty Inc. advertisement for Air-Spun powder and makeup with the traditional Coty logo, illustrating the continuing quality of Coty advertisement first established by François Coty. (Elizabeth Z. Coty Collection)

Advertisement for Air-Spun powder. (Elizabeth Z. Coty Collection)

The sides of this Air-Spun powder box show views of Paris. At one time, more than 30,000 boxes of Air-Spun were sold each day, worldwide. (Roulhac Toledano Collection)

Tension and instability in interwar France resulted from the cruel losses in male population sustained during World War I and from dissatisfaction with certain clauses in the Versailles Treaty. Resentment toward America for demanding repayment for the financial help it extended during the war increased. Ever present was the fear of a German resurgence. The French citizens' disappointment in France's parliamentary system rose and spread. The Third Republic was unable to cure the country's worsening postwar economic and social problems.

Both socialist and fascist factions were searching for policies that would heal their country's problems. Indeed, the two groups had much in common during this period. Many organizations were established during the 1920s by intellectuals and journalists who sought the support of France's great capitalists: Renault, Michelin, Taittinger, and Coty. For these people, at this time, the road ahead led toward a Corporatist and paternalistic state.

Over time, many of these leagues took on fascist tendencies and reputations. Some developed into quasi-military groups. Two of Coty's colleagues, George Valois and Marcel Bucard, became league organizers. Each was the son of a provincial butcher who had risen through the ranks during World War I and attained an elite military post. Disappointed by postwar life, the former soldiers sought to translate their right-wing agenda into public policy.

Coty opted to back them. In 1925, he gave Valois 1 million francs to underwrite a weekly newspaper, *La Nouvelle Siècle,* published by the fascist league that Valois had organized. Within a year, Coty had ended his financial support to Valois and his co-worker, Bucard (who later became Coty's personal secretary), switching his commitment instead to Léon Demoge's Association of Wounded Legion of Honor Members.

Sinking Fund

By 1926, Coty was working with Prime Minister Raymond Poincaré to develop a sinking fund that would stabilize France's currency. All that François had learned in developing his global market was applied to the creation of this salvage operation for France. Like so much that Coty did, it was not appreciated. He never collected on the 100 million francs he "lent" the government. That money became a gift to his nation. The sinking fund, and the airplanes that he provided to the nation for round-the-world flights, were probably Coty's outstanding philanthropy for France. However, the way the government and people of the country ignored his largesse became one of his greatest disappointments. His name was often eliminated from the membership lists of the committees and boards that he had envisioned and financed.

In July 1926, Poincaré formed a "national union" cabinet of old Republican leaders, including six former premiers, to deal with the nation's financial crisis. The country's citadel of finance, the Bank of France, announced it would not lend the government one more franc.[1] Poincaré then listened to advice from America, reportedly from the director of the Federal Reserve, who suggested, "Why not turn to those who have more capital than all your banks together— those who have more than 10 billion francs in securities or gold abroad? Why not turn to your own Frenchmen?" He was referring to the well-known "200 families" who possessed most of the wealth of the country.

At the top of this list of 200 was François Coty, who was determined to solve the problem alone, saving the franc and thus his country's economy and honor. Poincaré motored to the Château d'Artigny in the summer of 1926 for a visit with the financial king of France. They spoke about the fall of the franc, France's debt ratification, and payment of the war debt. According to the *New York Times* on August 3, 1926, Coty's influence in French financial affairs was real.

Poincaré, a fierce patriot who respected the businessmen of France, discussed with Coty a plan to stabilize the franc by refunding government loans with a sinking fund run by an independent agency. This became the Caisse d'Amortissement. Poincaré would also manage to impose a tax on part of every Frenchman's capital, for the first time in France's history.

The irony presents itself. The right-wing leagues that Coty supported so lavishly were assembled outside the Palais Bourbon even as Coty was negotiating to save the government. The crowds were so threatening that the prefect of police had to call in mounted Republican Guards for reinforcement.

A *New York Times* article reported, "The idea [for the sinking fund] originated with the great perfume manufacturer, M. Coty, who made an offer of 100,000,000 francs to the fund. It was incorporated in Finance Minister Herriot's Ministerial declaration."

Perhaps Coty envisioned himself being recognized and praised by the nation, but as it turns out, he was not even on the list of notable private persons appointed to oversee the fund. Coty's shock and disappointment is documented. One can only imagine why Poincaré agreed to this terrible slight against the sensitive perfume magnate. Coty claimed that he was not surprised to have been left off the board of administrators of the fund, "but there are . . . individuals at the office of *Figaro* who are eminently qualified." Coty's bombast and his passionate determination to publish all his opinions made him so controversial and unwelcome in so many circles that he was often excluded in a way hurtful to him.

Then, he took his money to New York. The *New York Times,* on February 5, 1929, reported, as did Coty's French newspapers, that he had donated a sizable sum to the French Hospital in New York: "Albert Blum, chairman of the special gifts committee, announced that François Coty had made the largest contribution, with a gift of $100,000, to provide quarters for the nuns connected with the hospital." French newspapers, however, failed to note that Benjamin Levy, Coty's longtime representative in New York, with his wife, "came next, with a gift of $30,000," while Pierre Cartier had presented $25,000 in the name of Madame Cartier.

Maurice Hanot d'Hartoy

Coty sought an organization in which he would have personal influence and not just be a financial backer. He found his opportunity in 1927 when he met Maurice Hanot d'Hartoy, a Norman journalist and author who had been wounded during his army service in World War I. Coty's fellow magnate Pierre Taittinger had formed La Jeunesse Patriote (Patriotic Youth), a group seeking to replace the Third Republic with an authoritarian government. Coty decided that he, in his turn, would provide financial help to the league that d'Hartoy had established, Croix de Feu. D'Hartoy recruited wounded and decorated veterans into its membership. Their manifesto read: "Our association wishes to constitute a great anti-revolutionary and anti-defeatist force of the most moral and military honor. The organization does not care to participate in any electoral combination." The group was growing fast and becoming more and more nationalistic, anti-Bolshevik, and right wing. At the same time, its antipathy toward anything German was expected, since it was a veteran's organization.

Coty gave d'Hartoy a comfortably furnished office at Rond-Point des Champs-Elysées, in the building that housed *Figaro.* When Coty gave him the title of director of his various political undertakings, he initiated a close relationship that lasted until Coty's death, although they were often estranged due to sharing a mistress, Henriette Dieudé.

D'Hartoy, well connected to the government through Croix de Feu, made it possible for Coty to participate far more effectively in political projects to "reform the state." Bernard, d'Hartoy's son, spoke of the commonalities between the two men: "I must tell you that my father was another exceptional man, who had, like François Coty, the will to initiate many things, many ideas, and to pass quickly from project to project." Their similarities also included the "creation of associations, . . . the choice of their residences, [and] their activities as editor or journalist."

Madame d'Hartoy, a well-connected woman, and their four children were ensconced in quarters provided by François Coty, who enjoyed extending his largesse, tastes, and interests to others. When François met Maurice d'Hartoy, the Norman had been married since 1919 to Jacqueline Bruté de Rémur. In 1931, their fifth child, Bernard, was born while Maurice was working for Coty. That fifth child described an amazing event embroiling Coty, his mistress, and the d'Hartoys in difficulties that reverberated for three generations:

> D'Hartoy became involved with Henriette Dieudé, François's premier mistress, there at the offices on the Rond-Point, right in front of Coty's famous "nose." After having seduced her patron, François Coty, [Henriette] undertook to seduce Maurice. His wife, a small saintly and very modest woman, did not have the strength to overcome this elegant and perfumed *dévoreuse*."[2]

Despite the danger to herself and the future of her children, Henriette, François's mistress of twelve years and mother of five of his children, abandoned herself to an affair with Maurice. The seduction played out in the office that François had given his new friend, Maurice. François found out about her affair with Maurice after it had become the gossip of Rond-Point. When François discovered the famous affair, he was "very affected by this misadventure and furious with both of them," according to Bernard d'Hartoy, who was just an infant then. "Monsieur Coty wrote a letter to [Maurice] demanding that he leave France for a year, giving him a project, an investigation of the subject of 'The United States of Europe,' which proves that M. Coty had a gift of prophecy."[3] It also proves that Coty was dependent upon Maurice, because he did not fire him. He kept him on the payroll and continued to support his family.

The imbroglio among François, Maurice, and Henriette became more melodramatic when the woman who had introduced Maurice to his wife heard about the situation. Janine Dumas d'Hauterive was the daughter of Alexandre Dumas fils. She was also married to a general and had been head nurse in the hospital where Maurice had recuperated from his wounds in 1916. Having organized Maurice's engagement and marriage to Jacqueline, Janine arrived in Paris to lecture Maurice, warning him never, ever, to leave his petite, quiet, refined, and lovely wife. Janine was wasting her time.

Coty Flirts with Mussolini

Sensing that Frenchmen's preference for a strong and authoritarian government would be the answer to the country's problems, Coty looked for leaders who had proven to be financial successes or who had descended from ancient, recognized families—like himself. Was he not the scion of the Spoturnos, among Corsica's first families for centuries? So, when he learned about Mussolini's activities in Italy, he became another member of the sizable group around the world, including many in the United States, who admired Il Duce.

The Frenchman and the Italian had much in common. Both owned and wrote for newspapers—Mussolini's was socialist, out of Milan, where Coty had a large factory and retail stores. Coty had visited Milan numerous times and knew that Mussolini had been publishing his *Popolo d'Italia* since 1914. Both men were self-educated and shared a fascination with the role of newspapers in public life. Coty saw Mussolini as a man who had used his own paper to launch, first, reform in Italy, then his own movement, then ultimately a government. As Mussolini wrote in his autobiography: "Without that modern weapon, capable of all possibilities, ready to arm and to help, good for offense and defense, the newspaper," there was no way to inform the public. He continued, "On November 15, 1914, the first number of the *Popolo d'Italia* appeared. It was my platform up to 1922 [when elected a deputy]. It was an instrument for the making of me." It was certainly enough for Coty to decide to finance Mussolini's March on Rome, which launched Mussolini into power in Italy. Coty sent money to Il Duce every year through 1926, sometimes enthusiastically, but sometimes with regret that there was no greater man, especially after Mussolini established his rigorous policy in Abyssinia and moved strongly towards dictatorship.

Coty was satisfied with the platform of Mussolini's party that favored worker participation in industrial management, an eight-hour day, and a national militia. Apparently, Coty failed to read the section advocating a heavy tax on capital and confiscation of Church property—both anathemas to Coty. He agreed with the Italian's anti-Bolshevik sentiments and manifested his endorsement of Mussolini's political philosophy by reprinting one of Mussolini's expressions of it in *Le Figaro:*

> Fascism . . . does not march against the police, but against a political class both cowardly and imbecile, which in four long years has not been able to give a government to the nation. Those who form the productive class must know that Fascism wants to impose nothing more than order and discipline upon the

nation and to help raise the strength that will renew progress and prosperity. The people who work in the fields and in the factories, those who work in the railroads or in offices, have nothing to fear from the fascist government. Their just rights will be protected. We will even be generous with unarmed adversaries.

Heritage and ethnicity as components of a national gestalt interested both Coty and Mussolini. Coty fervidly promoted Mussolini's idea of Latinity, or cooperation among Mediterranean nations. Coty followed the lead of a coterie of French intellectuals who sought the return of France and Italy to the world of the Caesars. Pan-Mediterranean Caesarism became a catchphrase of those seeking meaning for, and a path to, their country's civil and political redevelopment. Coty found solace in the idea of France's return to the days of the Roman conquest.

A contemporary viewpoint about the Coty-Mussolini amity appeared in the January 1935 issue of the magazine *Class Struggle*. In "Fascist Trends in France," S. Herman wrote: "In France alone lies the hope of the world proletariat of administering a defeat to fascism before the large industrialists substitute it for the bourgeois democracy which has become too burdensome for them. Ever since Mussolini was put in command by the Italian bankers and industrialists, many of the greater French bourgeoisie have considered his example an excellent one to follow. . . . It should be mentioned that in 1923 François Coty, whom we know as the perfume magnate, acquired *Le Figaro*, for anti-communist propaganda. When it appeared unsuccessful, Coty, in 1928, issued *L'Ami du Peuple* and sold it below cost. This was his way of trying to obtain a mass base . . . he advocated Italo-French amity and the use of the idea of Latinity as a rallying cry for fascism."

Such policies intrigued Coty. Family lore has it that François "lent" money to the pope during the 1920s. The verb "donate" was not used. The sum must have been large, and the objective, anti-communist propaganda. Yet even the Church's actions could cause Coty inner conflict. When Germany halted reparations payments to France, as its currency went into freefall, the Vatican sided with Germany against France. Coty felt challenged.

Anti-Semitism in France

In 1886, Edouard Drumont, who coined the term "national socialism," authored *France Juivre,* an inflammatory exposition of the belief system that underlay French anti-Semitism at the end of the nineteenth century. Vigorously denouncing the so-called Jewish financial oligarchies, Drumont's book incited anti-Semitic activity among the lower echelons of the clergy and also among many socialists. Five years later, a member of Parliament proposed that Jews be expelled from France. Thirty-two deputies supported him, but the proposal was not placed on the agenda. Many Frenchmen considered Jews strangers no matter how long they and their ancestors had lived in France.

Jews who became active in the mainstream of French life inevitably became the targets of prejudice—the longstanding Dreyfus case had become the most notorious example. Even a man as internationally recognized as Gustave Eiffel, creator of the Eiffel Tower, was the object of anti-Semitism. Like millions of his compatriots of his generation, Coty grew up harboring anti-Semitic beliefs. Publication of Emile Zola's *J'accuse* in Clemenceau's newspaper, *L'Aurore,* jolted some literary figures into reconsidering what the continuing furor about Dreyfus was doing to poison relationships among the various groups in France's population. Others were not rehabilitated. Most of the men who became Coty's associates in his journalistic endeavors were in the latter group.

François's ghostwriter Urbain Gohier had written as early as 1909, in *Les hommes du jour,* "From the age where I knew that actual society reposed in hypocrisy, cruel injustice and lies, I have not ceased to repeat that it is necessary to destroy the present society, and I have worked by all means to destroy it. I have proclaimed without rest the necessity of a violent commotion, a total renovation, of a revolution." Unfortunately, Coty had not read this when he hired Gohier, who proceeded with an anti-Semitic, anti-communist agenda as well as a program to bring down the government in Coty's name.

On the other hand, Coty, the businessman, had Jewish colleagues who represented his interests in Europe and Central and South America. The bankers and brokers who served his corporations included such eminent Jews as Lehman Brothers; Heidelbach, Ickleheimer and Company; and Kuhn, Loeb and Company. François relied completely on his partner Benjamin Levy, who ran Coty Inc. Mr. and Mrs. Levy attended charity balls, dinners, and parties, both in Europe and the United States, with François and Yvonne. In Paris, François specifically exempted the Rothschilds as well as his own Jewish employees and managers from his vicious denunciations; he sometimes used specious terms that indicated he was referring to Romanian and Bulgarian Jews. He pointed out that the Rothschilds, his neighbors on avenue Raphael, were hardly to be considered Jews.

Nevertheless, he introduced *The Protocols of the Elders of Zion* into France. The *London Times* revealed in 1921 that the *Protocols* were a plagiarized adaptation of a pamphlet that French attorney Maurice Joly had written in 1860 to criticize Napoleon III. Whether this was correct or not, exiled Russians living in Paris, imbued with the anti-Semitism rampant in their home country, brought the text as a screed against Jews as early as 1903. However, it took someone like Coty to publicize it in French. He paid Urbain Gohier to translate the Russian-language text into French, then published the work under his own name and serialized it in *L'Ami du Peuple.* This occurred before Hitler issued his version in German.

Coty accused bankers not associated with his firms, particularly German-Jewish international bankers such as the Jacob Schiff group and Warburg Brothers, of harming European civilization throughout Europe, Russia, and Japan. The irony appears once again, since Coty needed international bankers for his business.

Coty conveniently overlooked that it was his idol, Napoleon, who had granted full citizenship to Jews and Protestants in France. With his associate, Maurice d'Hartoy, Coty ignored the fact that during World War I, Jewish soldiers fighting in the French army were awarded 174 Croix de Guerre, 150 Distinguished Service Crosses, and 1,100 citations for valor. Nor did they acknowledge the 10,000 Jewish commissioned officers who served in the military. After Coty had litigated for years against accusations that he had defamed Jewish veterans of World War I, a French court fined him for his criticism in 1922. The scandal left Coty unfazed.

Coty played critic as he kept abreast of developments in the United States. In his newspapers, he harped on the "Hoover Moratorium," blaming that president for the cancellation of Germany's war debt, although it was decided during an earlier administration. Even worse, from Coty's point of view, Hoover had appointed the Sephardic-Jewish jurist Benjamin Cardozo to the Supreme Court. He excoriated Franklin Roosevelt in print for raising Jews to influential positions. Coty alleged that President Roosevelt's advisor, Bernard Baruch, was "the absolute overlord of about ten million Jews in the Western Hemisphere."

In *Reform of the State,* Coty's translation of *The Protocols of the Elders of Zion,* one finds both totalitarian and liberal ideas in the same text. It stated that the "reform of the state is a necessary precursor to the reconstruction of order, authority, hierarchy and social and democratic discipline without which no civilized nation can survive." Yet it also broached the then-radical idea that women should have the right to vote: "The full exercise of political rights by women as is proclaimed by our reformed constitution does not even require justification. . . . The question is not what women will do with their voting rights, but to ensure their defense in a society which has not been able to preserve it. . . . Women have the right to vote because they are human beings, because they are wives and mothers, because they contribute to public expenditures." French women finally gained their suffrage in 1945, eleven years after Coty's death.

When Coty serialized *Reform of the State* in *L'Ami du Peuple,* he made recommendations about the environment that seem prescient: "[There should be] periodic competitions for the best wines and other natural produce of France; methodical cleaning up of the atmosphere in the cities, in the countryside and on the roads [ruined] by the absorption of smoke, dust and odors; elimination or substantial attenuation of street noise which, in large cities, attacks the nervous system, causes irritation and insomnia which soon lead to stress, mental unbalance and neurasthenia."

At the same time that François was damaging his country through his fanatic journalistic agenda, his personal efforts demonstrated that the honor of France was his mantra. The way he ran his business was a model for the entire nation. He brought tens of thousands of people into the middle class by the wages and pensions that he paid. He exported French goods throughout the world. Through his individual effort and practices, France became the global leader in cosmetics. Even the forty newspapers that he underwrote supported many notable journalists and authors, artists, and cartoonists, paying them the best wages available in their professions.

Coty managed to get published in *Figaro* on August 23, 1931, an article with a map of France that Coty claimed proved Hitler's evil aims toward France. Coty alleged that the map of a partitioned France was circulating among Hitlerites in Germany. The Germans repudiated the map, calling it trumped up. The map showed Germany in possession of a double row of French departments in the east, running from north to south; the northwestern departments, and those that border on the Bay of Biscay, belonged to England. The departments of the south were in the possession of Catalonia, which cut off France from the Mediterranean. The United States, Coty claimed, would get a naval base on Finistère to keep the nation neutral. "Thus dismembered," Coty wrote, "ruined by loss of her richest regions, deprived of both maritime and mountainous frontiers, her fleet and colonies suppressed, France henceforth could only be compared to Austria or Switzerland, capable of maintaining a gendarmerie, not an army." Coty's article was newsworthy enough to be covered in the *New York Times* on September 2, 1931, in an article entitled "Map Shows France Partitioned in 1935."

At the beginning of the 1930s, Coty's desire to undermine the
Third Republic took center stage in his life, and his efforts to sway
public opinion took a more ominous form. While he was not alone
among the rich capitalists in this, he was a strong exemplar of the
trend. In an article dated February 7, 1933, in *L'Ami du Peuple,*
Coty announced that he was going to create "a great party of French
solidarity which will do in France what has been done on the other
side of the Rhine." He then referred to his new rightist league,
Solidarité Française.

The Coty family is convinced that if it had not been for Maurice
d'Hartoy, Solidarité Française would never have existed. This former
president of Croix de Feu, representing François, both advocated
for and organized the new league, paramilitary in character and
more fascist than any of the organizations that Coty had previously
backed. Coty persuaded le comte de Gueydon, dit Vinceguide, son
of a governor-general of Algeria, to train the recruits of his private
army. He launched a new journal, *Solidarité Française,* to serve as
the voice of the new group, whose participants wore identifiable blue
shirts, with gold braid giving a nod to Mussolini's marchers on Rome.
Coty paid his recruits, attracting former colonial soldiers. Those who
signed on learned the Solidarité anthem: "Arise, the time has come,
your voice is sovereign/The lone man raised the Torch of Truth/
Defying the cries of hatred."

*The anthem's metaphor of the "lone man" was all too true. By
this time, Coty was ruined. His poorly managed newspapers sang
his praises, to the distress of the responsible men on his payroll.
Irresponsible in the use of his personal fortune, he now threw away
the money from the Coty fortune in Europe and in America in a last,
frantic bid for glory and power—and to keep what was left of his
money and property out of the hands of Léon Cotnareanu, Yvonne's
second husband.*

By this time, Coty was no longer thinking about reforming the state;
he had moved close to calling for replacement of the parliamentary
system with a strong central government authority. His numerous
newspapers abounded with his diatribes: "People of France! The
politicians are worthless. As long as they have a stranglehold on
the finances of the nation, the collapse of the franc will continue."
His criticisms of particular officials appeared daily, and his general
opprobrium appeared in his own words or those of his employees
at his newspapers. "We have in France an abundance of able men,
but they are either driven from public employ or withdraw disgusted
and go into private business. Meanwhile the government inherits all

the castaways of private enterprise whose indolence, incapacity and natural servility lead them instinctively to the public crib."

In 1933, *L'Ami du Peuple*, an instrument for Coty's personal views as well as those of his ghostwriters and managing editors, had a circulation of 400,000, with 80,000 subscribers, Coty's newspaper had gained, in the words of Léon Blum, "a kind of emotional hold over its readers and consequently over a considerable portion of public opinion." The moderate right of the suburbs read it, as did the workers who had waged a long campaign against what Blum called "the fat, the plump, the well-endowed."

In February 1934, Coty joined with other right-wing leagues, most of which he had supported financially, to coordinate a march against Parliament. The marchers converged at the Place de la Concorde on February 6. Though hard to believe, it was reported in various newspapers that Coty had a 125,000-man contingent, outfitted with shiny black boots and uniforms trimmed with designer gold braid.

The march was a display of anger against parliamentary corruption and inefficiency, not a fascist putsch. Rivalry among the power seekers—financial backers like Coty and men of action like Taittinger—made it impossible to succeed with any specific plan, program, or goal. No cooperative, single insurrectionary party was to be found.

Although *Le Figaro* had been wrested from Coty's hands by February 1934, the newspaper's reporting about the march suggested that the communists were the sole culprits in the march and the riots that followed. The right-wing and paramilitary marchers were referred to as patriots, implying they were trying to defend the government against the communists. In reality, the right-wing league marchers and the ensuing riots forced Premier Edouard Daladier to resign, causing the first collapse of a French government due to pressure from the streets since the French Revolution.

Shortly after the march on Parliament and not long before his death, Coty signed a National Front pact that allied his Solidarité Française with the Patriotic Youth of Pierre Taittinger as well as the National Volunteers and the Camelots of the King. This move was probably engineered by Maurice d'Hartoy. It made possible his exit from an active political life in France before he endangered himself.

Coty never gave up. Until the eve of his death, he was frantically working on the political front, primarily through *L'Ami du Peuple*. At the same time that he was designing new scents at d'Artigny, he was calling his journalists to both d'Artigny and Louveciennes.

Less than a month before his death, on June 29, 1934, Coty planned to give a speech to Solidarité Française. He was not able to do more than present himself to the public at the Salle Wiegand. He was too weak and too emotional to proceed with his prepared speech. D'Hartoy read it on Coty's behalf. Later printed in *L'Ami du Peuple*, it can be considered his farewell to what he hoped to make of his life.

Today I want to limit myself to state that by the miracle of an intrepid will, all the people that surround us have been reconstituted into solid nations: an Italian nation, while France only formerly made a territorial and political unity; the German nation, in spite of its defeat in the formidable conflict that set in motion its dream of universal hegemony, and the English nation, have all skirted many times the abyss which seized the day to avoid collapse.

The Swiss themselves have taken efficient measures so that their regime of liberty and neutrality will not be overturned.

Belgium, this model of countries, small in territory and grand in heart; Belgium to whom we owe so much, whom Europe and the Christian civilization ought to really salute because she has given in an historic hour the example of the most sublime heroism, Belgium now has given us the most splendid example of energy for the resistance of evil.

Only our people of France have not begun to break the chains of servitude, because they have been forged by generations of incompetent and avid politicians, greedier still than incompetent: and this does not say little.

These politicians by stupidity and complete absence of moral sense have allowed to be formed around us, around the country, the frightful web of internationalism.

They do not themselves see that France has almost ceased to count among the great forces—one does not dare say that she is going to die as part of the Pact of Four, that we have called *le Pacte à Quatre Pattes* [the Pact on All Fours]—by the sole fact of universal deficiency of her leaders.

We don't want to docilely stand by to be led by foreigners! These wretched persons who always speak in the name of the people and pretend to serve them plunge them each day further in an abyss of gloom where they are left to envelop themselves to the point that they are no longer capable of finding an issue to seem honest. There is less and less a French nation because the Foreigner wants it thus, the Foreigner whether it be German, English, or Italian, the Foreigner en masse.

It is up to you Frenchmen to react. Your fathers have been the great emancipators of humanity. Now Frenchmen, the moment has come to free yourselves—to become again the masters of your country and of your destinies!

CHAPTER 12

Fortune Fades

N'était-ce donc que cela? [Is that all it amounted to, then?]

André Malraux

When François said one day that he would not trade places with Napoleon, he astounded his family, friends, and colleagues. They all knew he not only resembled Napoleon and behaved like him but also was obsessed with him. To their queries as to his meaning, he answered, "Napoleon never had any money." Little did François know that after 1929 he would, for the first time in his adult life, begin to lose almost all of his money.

In financial matters, Coty was his own man, though often inconsistent. Taxes were an anathema to him, as they are to most men of great wealth. "They keep business from expanding," he said. The most successful businessman in France, he opposed the income tax, which was barely 2 percent. Successive ministers of finance failed to extract even this amount from him. Not until Coty achieved international dominance in the manufacture and sales of his perfumes and cosmetics did he develop a phobia against excise taxes. The wealthiest man in France refused to pay them, writing, "France can become rich and powerful, providing an indiscriminate tax system does not take away from men of experience the means of developing and organizing business abroad."

In the 1920s, Coty's apoplectic anger was directed against Russia's post-revolutionary government, headed by Vladimir Lenin, who had returned from exile. Earlier, during World War I, he had vented equal fury at Charles de Lasteyrie, finance minister of France, who demanded from the Coty company 4 million francs in taxes on wartime profits. After all, during the war, the firm had continued to operate, built up its Suresnes factories, and sold an enormous amount of cosmetics to the American soldiers in France. Additionally, Coty Inc., established in 1912 and incorporated in Delaware in 1913, flourished during World War I. Lasteyrie also imposed a tax-evasion fine of 4 million francs on Coty as a private citizen.

Historically, tax evasion was a sport in France during the late Third Republic. Coty's staff included a bevy of lawyers, headed up by Justinius, on whom he depended more and more since he exhibited knowledge of all the strategies to use in court. Coty himself knew what to do with the government investigators—shower their relatives with gifts or provide jobs in distant subsidiaries for their friends or in-laws. The precedent had been set in Corsica; Coty had seen payoffs all his life on the island of his birth. It seemed to him the accepted, traditional way to conduct business. François Coty felt that bestowing his largesse on both enemies and friends would make things run smoothly, and, for a while, it did.

The first time the French government investigated Coty's account books and corporate finances, in the early 1920s, the civil servants who conducted the probe announced that nothing was improper in Coty's affairs. The second investigation, by anonymous investigators whose names were not released to François, found fraud that led to a fine of 8 million francs. When, in 1928, the left-wing newspaper *La Rumeur* revealed that Coty had paid nothing, the general public began to express disapproval. By that time, reports had been widely published that Coty had wasted millions of francs in illegal, though traditional, payoffs during his abortive political campaigns in Corsica. Liberal newspapers then lampooned the public life of this private man. The sardonic weeklies of France published cartoons and articles about his wealth and personality in the most disparaging terms. His mistresses' diamond bracelets and pearls were targets for the press, along with his tirades on every topic to which he had subjected his newspapers' readers.

Articles about his international factories and their profits hit the front pages of his own newspapers, usually followed by his personal rebuttal. His overpayment for the purchase of *Le Figaro* in 1922 for an outrageous 10 million francs was public information, as was his spending in 1925 of another 10 million francs to move *Le Figaro* to its new headquarters at the Rond-Point des Champs-Elysées, so detested by its staff. The public knew of his use of the expensive Rond-Point properties for headquarters of Croix de Feu and Marcel Bucard's Fascisme Français. Such profligate spending incensed the French public. Criticism of his wealth and the way he spent it erupted all over Paris and in Corsica and fed his enemies' ire over his rampant denunciations of the Third Republic.

In the counterattack against Coty's increasingly right-wing presence in Paris, opposing newspapers investigated his financial games with the French treasury and the small investors of France. *La Rumeur* reported that the tax collector sent to force Coty to pay back taxes and fines had

two sons employed by Coty Inc. The tax imbroglio provided fodder for
the press for years, but after Coty established his own rightist league,
Solidarité Française, in 1931, the attacks multiplied. Camille Aymard
wrote vitriolic pieces about Coty in *La Liberté*.

Aymard's series of articles about Coty's finances damaged the Coty
SA corporate image so much that the price of Coty shares traded on
European stock exchanges was cut in half. The existence of Coty's
Geneva Financial Holding Company, in which he placed profits from
Coty Inc. in order to avoid paying taxes in France, had already been
revealed but was now publicized throughout France. Coty agreed
with many other wealthy taxpayers that it was enough to pay taxes
in one country. To pay them simultaneously to several different
jurisdictions was beyond reasonable expectation. It was reported that
either Monsieur Marais, Monsieur Dubois, or François Pittet, three
straw men, held Coty's Swiss accounts in their names. Even Coty
could never have imagined the trouble his heirs would experience
once it became clear that these people would never be produced.
Some of Coty's secret Swiss accounts would never be opened by his
heirs, either the legitimate children or the illegitimate offspring.

The French public read that shares in Coty Inc. earned a dividend
of over three dollars on stock certificates whose average selling price
was twenty-seven dollars. To hear of Coty's wealth stemming from
these American operations, and his subsequent legal avoidance of
paying taxes on it, infuriated the French.

François pulled a clever arbitrage maneuver to profit from the
decline in value of the Coty Inc. stocks traded on the New York Stock
Exchange. When Lehman Brothers, in conjunction with Heidelbach,
Ickleheimer and Company, had brought the Coty Inc. initial public
offering to the stock exchange, the firm's capitalization came to $11.5
million. Only one-sixth of the company had been sold to the public.
The 50,000 shares that had been made available were offered at $78
apiece. (The bank had paid $45.) Wall Street's 1929 crash occurred just
when business was beginning to justify the confidence of Coty's small
shareholders. At the time of the crash, the stocks' equity value had
risen to $130 million (more than 4 billion francs). Five-sixths of the
company were still owned by Coty, Benjamin Levy, and the company's
bankers and associates. The family told the story that François, who
was in touch with his bankers, learned the news about the debacle in
New York six hours before Americans did. Aided by this information,
Coty invested $10 million in France, where the crash had not yet
occurred. He netted a profit of $10 million from this short selling and
regained ownership of the shares he had sold to Lehman Brothers.

When the depression deepened in Europe in 1931, Coty did the same thing in France that he had done in America. This maneuver increased his fortune, but it destroyed his reputation with small investors. Of the billion francs in profits of Coty SA in 1929, all that remained was a package of worthless shares. The shareholders denounced Coty's maneuvers and demanded a refund, which, of course, they did not receive. Shares, both in America and in France, plunged to a new low. Coty lost huge amounts of money for the first time in his life. His financial ruin had begun with his divorce in 1929 and Léon Cotnareanu's subsequent diligent maneuvers to secure more than one-half the Coty fortune for Yvonne. By 1933, it was accelerating.

Both sides of the political spectrum used investigative reporting to expose Coty's extensive financial manipulations to avoid taxes. They brought him to court. Léon Blum, from the left, and Louis Latzarus, from the right, became his most effective political enemies, gathering evidence about the *parfumeur's* blatant disregard of tax laws and his outrageous methods of dealing with bureaucratic investigations. They published condemnations of his blasé treatment of small shareholders. Blum, in his newspaper, *Le Populaire,* and Latzarus, in his book about Coty, presented the results of their research to expose Coty's methods of appearing not to make a profit and thus not owing any taxes on Coty Inc.'s revenues.

Coty used his newspapers to defend his financial actions. At the same time, he garnered more cash and kept the French government from collecting taxes from him. Accompanied by Robert de Flers, one of his early editors at *Figaro* and author of *Comédies Boulevardiers,* he called upon Charles de Lasteyrie, minister of finance, to seek relief from the longstanding past-due tax debt related to Coty SA. When Coty denounced the injustices of the "fiscal inquisition," Lasteyrie retorted that the controllers of contributions had unanimously pronounced in favor of Coty's payment and that he, Lasteyrie, had stayed out of it. Coty responded that there was nothing else to do but to condemn "your proceedings or process" in *Figaro.* Unlike some of the politicians Coty confronted, Lasteyrie showed Coty the door. Coty promptly published his opinion that "Lasteyrie is a dangerous man."

Louis Loucheur, a well-respected French minister, was one of the signers of the Treaty of Versailles, a treaty that Coty, not alone among the French, increasingly blamed for France's fiscal problems, the depression, and the country's loss of its onetime position as cultural and political leader of the European powers. Coty reproached Loucheur for being signatory to the treaty, which he said "Loucheur signed for the American stocks." In this case, Loucheur was one of those men who accommodated Coty and offered reconciliation.

François was forthright in criticizing what he called America's unfair treatment of France at the Treaty of Versailles conference. He fomented in his newspapers France's outrage that England was awarded so many German colonies and territories following World War I: "England is copiously served. She has taken the German colonies, the German fleet in order to sink it, the German commercial fleet to exploit it, Mesopotamia and its oil, and Palestine in order to command the Suez Canal and the near East. What has England not taken? France doesn't even have the distant hope of gathering the crumbs."[1]

Since France had more newspapers per capita than any other nation at that time, critics abounded to ridicule François's defense of himself in his own newspapers. English, American, and other European newspapers reported all his financial activities. Articles abounded about Coty's wealth and continual successes in business as well as his lawsuits, politics, mistresses, and scandals. Journalists wrote that François Coty demonstrated the talent, vision, daring—and weaknesses—of his contemporary, William Randolph Hearst. François was labeled the "Hearst of Europe" as early as 1910,[2] while his endeavors to improve the lives of his factory workers caused him to be compared to Henry Ford.

Yvonne, who loved François even as she was divorcing him and bringing him to financial ruin, always said that his passion caused ideas to tumble out and that he would print them in the newspaper before giving them careful consideration. Each new day and each experience in his travels round the world brought new observations, so that he published opinions that often clashed with previously published ones.

Then too, François was never a good public speaker. His voice was weak, and he could not effectively marshal his thoughts for the political arena, something that always upset him. François or his ghostwriters wrote articles on subjects that he should have just spoken in conversation and let go afterward.

Coty's critics found it hard to comprehend that he spent such a disproportionate amount of his money to disseminate his ideas. Emile Buré, in *L'Ordre,* was particularly vitriolic but always tried to be fair. He wondered why Coty endured and even relished the loss of up to 90 million francs on *L'Ami du Peuple*—and more staggering losses on his other papers. Here was a man making millions in America, Europe, and Australia, yet he drained these fortunes on right-wing journalism. He wondered why Coty did not fund universities, hospitals, and laboratories, which could be named after him.

Of course, François did not use all his fortune on his newspapers. Nor was his Corsican initiative carried out solely for political gain. His charities were legion. He funded four hospitals at least, farms, and Edouard Branly's laboratory. His generosity was widely known, and it was recognition he was after—recognition and affection, appreciation and fame.

Coty was intensely sensitive to criticism. He countered it by proceeding full steam ahead, holding grudges, carrying his reactions to perceived insults to surprising heights. He agreed with Friedrich Nietzsche, whom he quoted in one of his books, partly to prove that he was not a fascist: "Man does not aspire to happiness—only Englishmen do that. I do not want happiness. I want to do my work." A man of extremes, and more so as he grew older, Coty had no tact or discretion or patience.

In 1923, when Raymond Poincaré was minister of foreign affairs, Coty entreated him to alleviate his tax problems. Poincaré failed to respond. In 1924, Coty looked to Poincaré, to no avail, to validate his election to the French Senate after the Chamber of Deputies had annulled it. After this episode, Coty published two articles called *"L'Expiation."* He recognized in Poincaré certain positive qualities, "but they were negated by a major defect." He continued, "He lacks courage before certain demands; the flagging of his will before the obstacle." As Latzarus concluded, "So Coty both attacks and defends Poincaré."

Coty "admired Aristide Briand, the French premier," according to Latzarus. "He offered him an automobile, which Briand politely refused." But not even Briand would validate Coty's election in Corsica. He did, however, invite Coty for lunch at the Quai d'Orsay. On another occasion, Coty attacked Briand in his newspapers for being a milquetoast and a compromiser, his usual complaint about politicians.

André Tardieu was among the first politicians to denounce Coty's harangues in print. Tardieu, then minister of the interior, brought attention to Coty's activities in Switzerland, where he hid his American profits from France, the French people, and the French tax system. On the other hand, Tardieu, as arbitrator, had ruled in Coty's favor in the flurry of lawsuits regarding the distribution of *L'Ami du Peuple* in 1930. Political inconsistencies abounded.

Coty mixed personal affairs and business in his position as editor of *Figaro*. After all, he had two of the most powerful positions in France, or in any capitalist country, for that matter. He was France's richest citizen in the 1920s, the Frenchman with more international business and connections than anyone else. He was also on the masthead of Paris's most influential newspaper. Despite his penchant for bombast and his insistence on pushing his own political ideas and agenda on France, he gave copious financial support to philanthropic and political projects. It is no wonder that he was received at the Quai d'Orsay, Le Matignon, L'Elysée, and Le Palais Bourbon—all the corridors of power in France—and was also acknowledged in Italy and England. In March of 1927, Coty was invited by the government of London to an official banquet given in honor of British industries, visiting with Sir Austen Chamberlain, brother of the future prime minister, Neville Chamberlain.

Corporatism and Fascism—Coty Style

Coty personalized French politics and published his own grievances against the government as a rich citizen, businessman, and philanthropist. The brisk sales of *L'Ami du Peuple* attest to working-class interest in what he had to say. France was full of fierce and patriotic nationalists who resented their country's loss of power and prestige after World War I; Coty was one of millions of disillusioned Frenchmen. Whether royalist, bourgeois, socialist, or centrist, a Frenchman could open a Coty newspaper every week and read something that he agreed with. Coty's vituperative criticisms found their niche among Frenchmen of all persuasions who were tired of the depression, constantly changing governments, and rising taxes, which for some people went from less than 2 percent to 20 percent between the wars. Confusion reigned for many French citizens as they searched for meaning in their lives and in their state. Many followers of rightist thinkers, such as members of Ernest Mercier's Redressement Français, read François Coty's opinions.

Coty supported corporatism vehemently. An integral part of French fascism, it aimed to erect a barrier against international capitalism, as represented, for example, by Standard Oil or Shell Oil. To resist the "interference of the great trusts" was ever on the minds of the corporatists, both the intellectuals and the big-business men like Mercier. He and Coty, and many other industrial giants of France, believed that "ordered liberty" would replace "the present anarchic liberty" when employers would direct the economic corporation, emphasizing the supreme importance of discipline and the collective interest.

Logic was not one of François's strong points, but thought and action were integral to his character. Here was François, an international capitalist himself, who developed one of the first global businesses, aligning himself with men of the right, believing that businessmen could best serve the workers of France and replace the methods of the Third Republic. He produced results for his own employees, and his own record would give credence to such a view, but he knew that his fellow industrialists failed the test. One relative said, "François wrote what came to his mind. He changed like the winds, but never consider that he was not interested in everything and everyone."

Coty presented the French with his ideas and programs that he believed were good for the country. He paid high salaries to scores of intellectuals and thinkers of the period to expose their thoughts to the public in dozens of his newspapers, both in the capital and the provinces. *L'Ami du Peuple* added to the ideas fermenting in France between the wars, providing what could be called a civics education to the masses through newspapers that were blatantly political, with neither the left nor the right consolidated into one driving force.

Jean Prouvost, the wealthy textile industrialist whose family owned the woolworks of Roubaix, and later owner of *Le Figaro,* published *Paris-Soir* from 1931 on.[3] He reinvigorated French journalism by using many photographs and drawings and an entirely new format that intrigued and attracted the French public. Coty's *L'Ami du Peuple*, by contrast, had few photographs and page after page of long articles day after day. Coty lectured and taught, while Prouvost intrigued and made his presentations visually interesting.

Nonetheless, Coty's newspapers became laboratories of ideology. His various newspapers serialized a number of books of right-wing authors who would never otherwise have reached a large readership. For example, Thierry Maulnier's journal, *Combat,* sold only about three thousand copies, and Maurice Barr's works sold even fewer. When these authors were serialized in Coty's papers, many more thousands of Frenchmen received their messages.

Some of Coty's small projects may also have had long-lasting impact. For example, his establishment and support of the journal *A Muvra* preserved the Corsican language in its written form. By extension, this may have encouraged another cycle of independence movements and revolutionary ideas that swept Corsica from time to time. Here again appears the dichotomy that was François Coty—a French nationalist, supporting the independence movement in his native island of Corsica, which had been integrated into France before Napoleon's time.

William Shirer, in *The Collapse of the Third Republic,* opines that the free press, supported by industrial and financial tycoons who also supported the rightist leagues, manipulated the public, both the left and the right. The public came to be "so scornful of the Republic and so cynical about its policies" that survival of the republic came into question. Coty and his associates from the rightist intellectual pool, and the upper echelons of French industry and finance, of course, must bear some of the responsibility for the ensuing prejudice against the government. As the moderate historian René Rémond understood, "it is the press of the Right that formed public opinion," since "the average Frenchman, even if he voted Left, read most often a newspaper of the Right."

The rightist leagues' march on Parliament on February 6, 1934, Solidarité Française among them, suggests that the intellectual right-wing journalists used Coty and the rich tycoons to finance their newspapers and propaganda, with the journalists themselves tending to disappear when the action or the march became dangerous. Action Française suffered the heaviest casualties on February 6—four killed and twenty-six wounded by gunfire alone—yet their leaders did not participate in the mêlée. Writer and activist Charles Maurras, the chief of Action Française, stayed inside to write his daily editorial that day. He remained home until dawn, composing some verse in his provincial dialect in honor of rightist Léon Daudet's wife, Pampille. Tired and put out by his literary efforts, he slept until late the next afternoon. Coty, on the other hand, is said to have been present with his six trusted bodyguards surrounding him.

Premier Edouard Daladier (1884-1970), having seen bloodshed in the Great War, was appalled at the sight of Frenchmen killing one another in the streets during the rightist leagues' march. Deserted by his cabinet aides, harassed by a frightened president, and reviled by a reactionary press, he would not risk any show of force. He stepped down, and the French president was able to coax Gaston Domerge out of retirement. Monsieur Domerge, a conservative republican, but a Protestant and Freemason, was the very thing Coty and the marchers, Catholics and strongly anti-Masonic, had professed to hate.

François remained militant, argumentative, and engaged in his political projects. The intellectuals might hide at the moment of crisis, but François, basically shy, always joined the fray with his protective guards, right or wrong, left or right. His best friend and colleague, Maurice d'Hartoy, always prudent, lingered in the background and protected his own reputation. Maurice wrote in Le Courier Français *to explain his rightist activities and painted them all as appropriate.*

Politics seized center stage in Coty's life in 1929, and until his death he poured all the millions he could get his hands on into *L'Ami du Peuple* and Solidarité Française. At the same time, the non-political yet socially aware Yvonne Coty, prompted by her new husband,

Léon Cotnareanu, the Romanian consul in Paris, was continuing her lawsuits to capture as much of Coty's remaining fortune as possible. As a result, Coty became even busier and more frenetic than he had been in the first decade of the century when he was building his perfume empire.

His divorce was the defining moment of the last five years of François Coty's life. Once Yvonne was gone from his life, he had no center. What little order and consistency there were in his habits were due to her presence in his life. After 1929, Coty had no restraints whatsoever. Yvonne's absence made it easier for Maurice d'Hartoy to insinuate himself ever closer to François, to influence him to ludicrous undertakings and to ruin. No matter how many châteaux he worked on, how many perfumes he created, how many times he traveled the world over, he was staggered and weakened when Yvonne divorced him.

The continuing relationship and friendship between François and Maurice, even after François had been cuckolded by the latter, meant that Maurice in some ways replaced Yvonne. Yvonne had tried to rein François in while Maurice spurred him into even more outrageous activities. Maurice was the facilitator of François's overt anti-Semitism. He encouraged François to promote the fall of the Third Republic. Over time, Maurice encouraged François in his fascist leanings and instigated his ultimate ruin. On the other hand, Maurice was, at the end, François's only intimate.

CHAPTER 13

1929 Catastrophe:
Divorce and Yvonne Remarries

Praised by some, blamed by others, mocking fools, braving the wicked,
I hasten to laugh at everything—for fear of having to cry.
              Pierre Beaumarchais (printed on the masthead of *Figaro*,
                                                      May 18, 1928)

Yvonne Coty, handsome, beautifully dressed, and sophisticated, had grown gracefully into wealth. With her natal family, she had contributed to the development of François's perfume business. Her background had been a great asset to him. She developed a keen interest in sailing, and after 1911, they had often sailed to the United States. After the Great War, she, François, and the children had sailed to Corsica, Italy, and England, as well as across the Adriatic, for business and pleasure. She led his cultural philanthropy, especially in the restoration of the Opera in Paris.

Watercolor of Yvonne Coty. (Elizabeth Z. Coty Collection)

She loved the social life of the city, and as the wife of France's richest and most publicized personality, she had the opportunity to meet some of the most powerful people in the world. *Figaro*, under François's ownership, hosted elegant parties, held in a beautiful room on the Champs-Elysées at the newspaper's headquarters. Attending these events with François, she met the literati of Paris, who swarmed there, along with the elegant nobility who wanted to influence the press. Artists, actors, and performers arrived in their finery to impress the art and theater critics of *Figaro*.

200

François's protégés in the visual arts, ballet, and opera thronged to the events. Editors and contributors of other dailies and weeklies attended for the conversation, stories, wine, and cuisine.

Yvonne and François seemed to be king and queen of Paris in their public life. Not only did they attend the Ballets Russes and the opera together, but the audience responded in a furor of clapping when they entered, in recognition of their sponsorship of the Opera. Artists, stage performers, and screen stars—some of them Coty's mistresses—dined with them at Avenue Raphael and attended soirées at the Chateau d'Artigny. Princes, premiers, sheiks, the Aga Khan, and other notables sat down to dinner with them in Touraine. They entertained royalty from across Eastern and Western Europe as well as potentates of the Middle and Far East.

A regal quality was evident in Yvonne's beautiful poise, exquisite skin, and sharp olive-green eyes. She had opinions about everything and was quick to give them. At the same time, her look indicated that her privacy would not be invaded. On many occasions, her sense of humor was evident, though her anger could be well defined. She was her own worst enemy because she wanted people to like her, although she made it difficult for them to do so. Her friends were loyal, however, and Yvonne returned that loyalty. When she loved, she loved deeply, sometimes sacrificing her family to the demands of these loves. Money, because she had it in such vast quantities, came last in her concerns.

Wherever they went, François had projects, whether related to his perfume industry, philanthropy, politics, architectural interests, or newspapers. As time went on, his manic activity took him farther away from Yvonne. Their residences grew in numbers so fast that going from château to villa to *hôtel particulier* became burdensome.

Yvonne did not enjoy prolonged visits in the countryside. The mansion at Avenue Raphael, where she was ensconced with the assistance of thirty-four servants, suited her best. With François absent most of the time, she assumed the responsibilities of collecting decorative arts and positioning the eclectic art that François acquired, as well as running the large complex. Her social life was frenetic, but the pressure of being one of the richest women in France did not faze her.

In 1929, tragedy struck François Coty when Yvonne divorced him, a move instigated by her lover, Léon Cotnareanu. This sophisticated and attractive woman had gone her own way for years, though she still loved her brilliant, wayward husband even as she cringed to see what was written under his byline in his various newspapers. She was increasingly saddened in the twenties to see him become unbalanced in his passion for French nationalism, but she continued to assume social duties in their private and public lives. She represented Coty SA and Coty Inc. at charitable and business functions around the world, with or without him. Her mother, Virginie Dubois Le Baron, continued to be active in the Paris- and New York-based companies.

By 1928, Yvonne had had enough. Stories of the twelve mistresses on the special floor of the Hotel Astoria, and later in the Hotel Georges Cinq, appalled her. François's love life was described in all the liberal weeklies, especially the sarcastic *Dépêche de Toulouse*, along with images of Coty's five children by Henriette Dieudé, the former shop girl at Place Vendôme. How galling it was for Yvonne to realize that anyone could read about this extramarital situation. The ever-present staff at d'Artigny and the Coty residences in Corsica received Henriette and her brood openly whenever Yvonne was elsewhere. It was all too much to bear.

Coty's growing intensity in all things—his multiple architectural projects, his quest for influence through his dozens of newspapers, and his determination to form the Cotyiste party of the right—embarrassed Yvonne. Support of the increasingly aggressive rightist leagues discomfited the entire family. Certainly, his importance on the national political arena was evident, yet Yvonne realized that her husband would drive their great international business into the ground by supporting his newspapers and the ever-growing fascist leagues.

Yvonne was confronted with François's insupportable activities at every turn. During one of the periods when François was housing Henriette and the children in Corsica, Yvonne came face to face with Corsican culture and the vendetta tradition, as well as the enormity of his brazen unfaithfulness.

One rainy day in Paris, as her car was moving through the wide gates of her Avenue Raphael residence, she noticed a man who had been sitting outside the gate for several days. In fact, she had seen the same small, swarthy man at least three times on the same bench. She asked Jean, her chauffeur, if he knew who the person was. "The guard told me that he was from Corsica, and he wants to see you, madame." Yvonne directed, "Send him in." That he was Corsican must have intrigued her. She received him in her library.

The man took out a small white box, wrapped in sheepskin, and handed it to her, saying, "This is for you, madame, and it is from le Roi des Bandits." *When she opened the sheepskin, she saw a white leather knife holder, from which she cautiously removed a small, beautifully carved pearl-handled dagger. It was slightly curved and about six inches long, with hammered-gold inlay on the blade and the dagger tip bearing an etched cover. The Corsican explained that this was a poisoned dagger and that she ought to establish her position by stabbing her husband at some propitious moment to punish him for his irreverent, adulterous behavior.*

Horrified, she exclaimed that she could never do such a thing and asked why she should. He spoke of the presence of the "other lady" in Corsica and the children who were also a part of François's household. Yvonne knew that the vendetta was a strong and longstanding Corsican tradition. Her husband's open life with a mistress and a bevy of illegitimate children on their island was offensive to the Corsican people. They were as insulted as she was. Thanking the man, she offered him coffee and cakes, much to the distress of the servants. She also kept the dagger.

Later, she told the story to her daughter, Christiane, who claimed the dagger. Many of us in the family saw it. Sometimes Yvonne stated that she wished that she hadn't been so surprised and so weak. Perhaps the Corsican himself would have been delighted to use the dagger on her behalf, she would say, half-laughing. We could see, though, that despite everything, she still felt love for François Coty.

As growing outrage consumed Yvonne, Léon Cotnareanu came into her life. She had met him in the early 1920s in Nice at the casino, where she had gone with one of her many escorts while staying at the Château de Sainte-Hélène. Her dismay at François's antics had climaxed, and here was a younger man to take her mind off all these unpleasant, troubling things. Léon sat at a table with another gentleman, discussing business. The small, elegantly attired, energetic man intrigued her. She developed strong feelings for him, and they became lovers.

Léon had come from Bucharest, Romania, where his father owned one of the finest of Eastern Europe's Belle Epoque hotels. His family name derived from a town called Cotnari in the eastern Romanian wine region of Moldavia. Anti-Jewish incitement became one of the important factors in the evolution of the Romanian state and Moldavia's history, and the Cotnareanu family, though of a professional background, were not exempt. One by one, the five Cotnareanu sons had made the long train voyage to Paris for their education. Léon's eldest brother, Albert J. Cotnareanu, had gone to New York after earning a degree at the University of Paris. He became a U.S. citizen, changing his last name to Leo. He was the only one of the five brothers to have children, one son and three daughters. In the 1920s, he established a steel business in New York, the sole American company at that time to import steel into the U.S. as well as into France. The company, Petro-Metal, imported the steel from Belgium. The Paris-based Cotnareanu men ran the French end of the business.

Philippe, the youngest Cotnareanu brother, changed his name to Cortney and became the attorney for the Coty-Cotnareanu interests, representing Léon in matters relating to *Le Figaro.* He and his wife, Marcelle, an aspiring opera singer, came to the United States just before the German invasion of France in 1940. Lucien Romier, an editor of *Le Figaro* for Cotnareanu, described Philippe as extremely bright and alert in any negotiation at the newspaper office. In New York, he became president of Coty Inc., while Léon was chairman of the board.

Léon himself had attended the military college at Saumur, the prestigious cavalry school that developed from a regiment of cavalry or carabiniers stationed there in 1763. A young cavalry officer in World War I, Cotnareanu was an intellectual who maintained an interest in Eastern Europe, especially Romania. When he and Yvonne met, he held the post of Romanian consul in Paris.

Yvonne's filing for divorce was Léon's idea. A genius and mastermind of her lawsuits, he quickly acquired for Yvonne much of François's remaining fortune in Europe. What he didn't get there, he obtained for Yvonne in the courts in Brooklyn, New York. Besides her own complaints against François was the moral indignation Americans have toward a married man who has five illegitimate children while he conducts affairs with other mistresses.

When they decided to marry, Léon knew what he was doing. His first efforts would be to secure as much of the remainder of the Coty fortune as possible before François squandered it in his political maneuvers. François's massive expenditures on architecture and art were no problem for Yvonne, because she knew that their value would increase. The fortune had been so vast that losing it was unimaginable to her, but Léon recognized the risks.

As a Jew from Romania, where anti-Semitism was rampant, Léon was interested in a takeover of *Figaro,* since he and his colleagues saw that it had become openly anti-Semitic under Coty's leadership. Suppression of *L'Ami du Peuple,* with its equally anti-Semitic rants, was another one of their goals.

In 1943, a German supporter of Hitler, Bernhard Payr, wrote *Phönix Oder Asche,* his defense of the "Aryan" ideology. Payr attacked what he saw as the corruption of the French press by the Jews, and he propagandized "against four Jews who have the Panama Canal scandal on their conscience, Gustave Eiffel, Baron Jacques de Reinach, Doctor Cornelius Herz, and the cosmopolitan financier [Aaron] Arton." Payr pointed to Coty's ruin, his ouster from *Figaro,* and his loss of *L'Ami du Peuple* "as proof of the brutal suppression and the absence of scruples that these Jewish press potentates utilize to suppress the creations of the Aryan journals like Coty's." Payr recalled the "scandalous asphyxiation of *L'Ami du Peuple*," which had attempted to face down the Jewish press in France. The fascist Payr excoriated the methods employed to injure the industrialist, Coty. Defending Coty, Payr mentions "attacks carried on in the domain of his private life, by disclosures in divorce proceedings."

This fascist, anti-Semitic material was not translated into French until 1984, and it suggests that Léon Cotnareanu had been a representative of Jewish activists, concerned about the rising anti-Semitism in France. At the same time that anti-Semites were filling the French press with propaganda, they were accusing Jews of taking over the French press.

Before Léon had come into her life, Yvonne consistently refused to divorce François, even though her relationship with her husband was in steady decline and she was experiencing mounting emotional deprivation. Whatever Léon's motives for courting and then marrying Yvonne, we can do no more than infer them from his subsequent behavior as a husband. To the end, Yvonne understood François and adored him, in her way. However, she was happier after becoming Madame Cotnareanu. As François's attempts to lead France away from constitutional government became more frantic and bizarre, giving the impression that François was veering away from reality, Léon's timing was psychologically brilliant when he proposed to Yvonne that she divorce François in order to take himself as her second husband.

Wife and Mistress Problems

Léon and Yvonne were just one part of Coty's problems with his colleagues and relationships. By the end of the 1920s, Henriette's and Maurice Hanot d'Hartoy's lives had become intermingled with his. The intrigues and machinations of this group of lovers, friends, enemies, and colleagues, interchangeable in their roles vis-à-vis Coty, began to wear him down. These four men and women—Henriette and Maurice, Yvonne and Léon—wielded power, either real or psychological, and caused trouble for François and for each other in their respective and varying families, in Coty's enterprises, and in French politics.

Yvonne's marriage to Léon dismayed François. He had never expected her to leave him. Early in his involvement with Henriette, he had asked for a divorce from Yvonne, in view of his fast-increasing illegitimate family, but Yvonne had realized the disastrous implications of such a move for herself at that time. They had adjusted their relationship. He depended on her socially and emotionally. In addition, her mother for years had guarded their interests in the United States.

François was as surprised as anyone when Yvonne divorced him. For years, she had put up with his mistresses and the lack of privacy in her life. Even after the divorce, François assumed that things would go on with Yvonne as before. He even expected to arrange voyages on the Alphée, *the oceangoing yacht that Léon and Yvonne purchased. According to François, the idea to purchase it had been his. One of the many things he demanded, and to which Yvonne acquiesced, was to retain large offices at the Avenue Raphael residence in the Bois de Boulogne.*

Greater than his dismay, however, was Coty's developing fury toward Yvonne's new husband. His wife not only had pursued an open affair with a Romanian Jew, but she had married him. Coty, a xenophobe, fined by the French government for publishing libelous criticism about the Jewish veterans of the Great War, was rabid over losing his wife to a representative of what he called the international Jewish cartel. He went so far as to write a harangue about his former wife and her new husband in *L'Ami du Peuple*. He always included the term *Moldovaïques* in his vituperative pieces about foreign Jews stealing France from the French, because Cotnareanu's family sprang from Moldavia.

Henriette Dieudé, who had waited ten years for her moment, producing a child every two years in the interim, was delighted by the divorce. François married her just a few days later. They planned to move into the pavilion at Louveciennes. This proved impossible because François, in his usual zest for rebuilding, had reduced the place to piles of bricks and was passionately involved in a clever reconstruction. It was based on the exact proportions of the original, using the same materials, but larger, with room after room dedicated for laboratories, storage, kitchens, and bathrooms.

It seems that Henriette, after five children, was no longer suited for the married state. She found a new lover right before François's eyes. The man she chose was his best friend, Maurice Hanot d'Hartoy. Coty's cuckolding by Henriette with his best friend and employee went undetected only by François. When he discovered his new wife's continual propensity for sexual intrigue outside of marriage, he seemed not to blame d'Hartoy. Maurice continued to handle many of François's responsibilities with the leagues and with Figaro and L'Ami du Peuple, *even as everyone close to François was subjected to the blatant affair between Henriette and Maurice, who had a lovely wife as well as five children, like Henriette.*

Coty even paid d'Hartoy to travel around Europe to investigate the possibility of a United States of Europe. Coty suspected a renewal of their love affair upon Maurice's return to France. Consequently, he initiated divorce proceedings against Henriette within the first year of their marriage. However, he made sure that his five children by her were taken care of, with a hefty bequest in a Swiss bank to be overseen by his straw men. He placed 10 million gold Swiss francs in a separate account for Henriette.

While Coty writhed in anger at Yvonne's marriage and Henriette's indiscretions with Maurice, not once did he suspect the "good lawyering" on Yvonne's behalf by Léon and his brother Philippe. Philippe's astute work would, in the end, deprive Coty not only of the rest of his personal fortune but of his beloved newspapers, along with most of his American assets. Three years later, by 1932, François found himself without enough money to pay his huge staff from month to month.

As the lawsuits were under way between Yvonne and François, life had to go on. Coty refused to leave his office in the mansion on Avenue Raphael, where Yvonne lived with her new husband. When Coty and his bodyguards drove up, a runner made sure that none of Yvonne's guests encountered Coty. Two footmen opened the gates and four butlers helped guests avoid Coty when they entered the house.

Yvonne embraced the entire Cotnareanu clan when she married Léon. Geraldine Leo, daughter of Léon's eldest brother, Albert, raised in New York, arrived in Paris in the early 1930s to study music. Yvonne welcomed her at the Avenue Raphael mansion. Geraldine said:

> My father in New York feared that I would come to love the exciting life in this atmosphere of untold wealth, but, in reality, it cured me. To see my aunt dealing with so many people, in order to live in accordance with her financial standing, made me realize that wealth is not everything. Monsieur Coty's problems showed me that great wealth could be a misfortune. When I lived at Avenue Raphael, everything fell apart for him. We all knew he was trying to hide his fortune—from the government and from Yvonne.
>
> Life with Aunt Yvonne and Uncle Léon was fascinating. If we were in Paris, we were at the Opera or a concert every night. Yvonne had a heart as big as she was. A born charmer, she was full of warmth. I always thought of her as my loving aunt.
>
> I was always protected from Monsieur Coty, who insisted on retaining his office at Avenue Raphael, even after Aunt Yvonne's marriage to Uncle Léon. At the end of his life, Monsieur Coty was known as a kook,

and since I was a young girl, the kind toward which he had a proclivity, I was always surrounded by Aunt Yvonne's entourage as I entered the house.

Throughout his marriage to Yvonne, Léon retained an interest in his Romanian background, as did his family wherever they settled. Geraldine Leo was presented into Romanian circles in Paris in the early 1930s, before Coty died. She was visiting with Léon and Yvonne when she fell in love.

> I met my husband, Edgard Feder, a Frenchman of Romanian background, in Paris while I was staying with Uncle Léon and Aunt Yvonne. Monsieur Célèbaire, the important music publisher in Paris, gave a cocktail party. Edgard was there because his father, who lived in Romania, was the largest impresario for musical talent in central Europe. He placed talent everywhere. He insisted, however, that his son become a lawyer, although Edgard played the cello and wanted to become a musician.
>
> When I became engaged to Edgard, my father insisted that I retain my U.S. citizenship. Little did I know how right he was. I was married from the Avenue Raphael house, and the affair was absolutely perfect, as Yvonne directed everything.

During this time, Léon initiated a series of court appearances and lawsuits that lasted for years to secure the Coty fortune and business. Yvonne's divorce from Coty had become an international affair, with lawsuits in Switzerland, France, and the United States. However, not wanting to leave anything to chance, at the rate François was spending what money was still available to him, her lawyers, led by Philippe, refused any delays in payments or seizures of property. The courts in France and the United States received Yvonne and her briefs well. She prevailed, garnering most of his fortune that he was not frantically giving away to friends, political organizations, and charities.

Yvonne Enjoys New Marriage

After their marriage, Yvonne introduced Léon to the powerful men who ran all the Coty enterprises and looked after her private wealth. At the Morgan Bank at Place Vendôme, they met with her personal banker, André Cheveneau. Yvonne tried to give Léon her power of attorney. In an unprecedented move, Cheveneau refused to let Yvonne relinquish control over her money. To the family's horror, however, Yvonne did this later. She was no longer interested in participating in the international business affairs that her first husband and his wealth had spawned. By 1931, she had turned everything over to Léon, including Le Figaro, *the Cité des Parfums at Suresnes, Coty Inc., and her share of the real estate worldwide.*

Yvonne did, however, run Avenue Raphael. She planned the daily menus with Pierre, the maître d'hôtel, and Anna, the housekeeper, after she had finished her breakfast on a tray in her bedroom. Each day she telephoned her "chums" from a little ten-inch-high stool, chatting with Helena Rubenstein, Antoinette Pietre, Gabrielle (Coco) Chanel, and Jeanne Lanvin. Still agile in her eighties, she exercised daily.

Once possessed of one of the world's great fortunes, and certainly France's greatest fortune, Yvonne did not continue her course as the outstanding philanthropist she had been when she represented François. As Madame Cotnareanu, she made the appropriate donations but spent most of her time enjoying being rich, sailing around Europe and Asia in her yacht and playing golf at Marly, outside Paris.

Yvonne was saddled with a charming, much-loved, but spoiled son, Roland. Eventually she decided that she had to have him declared incompetent to control his finances, and she did so with a heavy heart. Meanwhile, she and Roland funded sailboats that won awards

for France in international races, with Roland at the helm. Their largest sailboat, *Le Gaulois,* fifty feet long, won many competitions. Another sailboat was named *Coupe-File,* built for her by Archachon in 1936. This one sailed numerous times out of Le Havre, representing France in international races. The emblem of the Cotnareanu prize in sailing can still be seen today at the yacht club in Marseille. Yvonne received the Legion of Honor for her sailing vessels that had raced to victory for France. Her citation read in part, "Yvonne Alexandrine Le Baron, born . . . in Paris, the sixth arrondissement,

Yvonne Coty Cotnareanu's sailboat *Le Gaulois* won prizes for France in the 1930s. (Elizabeth Z. Coty Collection)

has been named *Chevalier de la Légion d'Honneur* by decree of July 30, 1935."

Yvonne's greatest interest, however, was her yacht, the *Alphée*. The *Alphée* logbooks from 1933 to 1936 describe her voyages with Léon. The list of guests provides evidence of Léon's literary and political interests. These logs also give testimony about the vast wealth that went into the Cotnareanus' travels and entertainment for their guests.

After her divorce, Yvonne had completed the purchase and renovation of the yacht that she and François had arranged to purchase from the Caliph of Turkey. It was 297 meters long, traveled at thirteen knots, and was the second-largest private yacht in the world at that time. She called in François's old friend René Lalique to have it appointed with spectacular glass columns and doors. A teakwood railing set in bronze hinges and joints was an eye-catching component of the decoration.

Yvonne named the yacht the Alphée, *after her mother's father. Dignitaries loved the mink bedspreads. In the master suite, Yvonne's was ermine. On board, she entertained at various times Queen Marie and King Carol of Romania, Winston Churchill, singer Maurice Chevalier, who later worked for Coty Inc., artists Raoul Dufy and Henri Martin,* Le Figaro *editor Pierre Brisson, André Maurois, and American authors Ernest Hemingway and F. Scott Fitzgerald, among others.*

Inside the yacht *Alphée*, with Lalique glass details. (Elizabeth Z. Coty Collection)

The *Alphée,* belonging to Yvonne Coty Cotnareanu, was the second-largest private yacht in the world. (Elizabeth Z. Coty Collection)

In 1933, Yvonne and Léon sailed from Deauville to Portugal and Spain, then on to Corsica, Capri, and Naples. From Civitavecchia, where they docked, Roland drove the party to Rome. There, Yvonne wrote in the log, "I found with much emotion and pride the portrait of

Yvonne aboard her oceangoing yacht, the *Alphée,* with her pug dog.
(Elizabeth Z. Coty Collection)

my grandfather, Alphée Dubois, winner of the *grand prix* of Rome,"
for the medals he designed. On their return, they anchored in Nice,
then proceeded to the Château de Sainte-Hélène.

Paul Morand, the French author and a contributor to *Le Figaro,*
joined the Cotnareanus on a trip they took from March 4 to April 12,
1934. Hélène Vacaresco; Admiral Joubert; his wife, Princess d'Ancone;
and Monsieur Cutzarida, minister of Romania, were among the other
guests. They sailed from "Nice for Genoa, Naples, Messina, Sicily to
Alexandria, Haifa, Athens, Katakola, Naples and back to Cannes." On
that trip, Yvonne received an award for another sailboat she owned,
the *Qu'importe,* from the Marquis Pallavicini, president of the Reggio
Yacht Club in Italy. Roland Coty drove the groups to Mount Thabor.

Madame and Monsieur Stefan Osusky joined Léon and Yvonne on the
Alphée in April 1935 for a voyage to the "Oriental Mediterranean," as the
logbook called it. Stefan Osusky (1889-1973) was the Czech representative
to the Reparations Commission of the League of Nations between 1919
and 1932. Lucien Romier, editor of *Le Figaro* under Cotnareanu, and
his wife, Yvonne Palmer, came along on the voyage. His Majesty King
Carol II of Romania attended a reception that the Cotnareanus hosted on
May 7, 1935. The voyage took them back to Turkey, then on to Greece,
Yugoslavia, and Italy until they docked again at Nice.

CHAPTER 14

Miracle Man Meets His Maker: 1934

Twenty-five thousand francs to place a grille over the grotto [in Ajaccio] where Napoleon came to dream.

> François Coty, in his last will and testament

The attorney who called himself Justinius became one of Coty's principal advisors in the late 1920s. He installed himself in La Namouna, Coty's villa in the south of France. Justinius found himself involved in numerous lawsuits related to Coty's divorce from Yvonne, then his second marriage and almost instantaneous divorce from his longtime mistress, Henriette Dieudé. Justinius and a veritable retinue of François's attorneys were bested repeatedly by Léon and his brother Philippe.

By 1933, Yvonne and Léon, plaintiffs in lawsuits on both sides of the Atlantic, had divested François of most of his unimaginable fortune. The courts in the United States were far friendlier to Yvonne than to François. American courts decided on the basis of lawyers' briefs, but tax evasion and François's attempts at bribery did not help him, and blatant adultery and five illegitimate children were, perhaps, au courant in Paris, but they were not, then, in the United States.

Léon was a short man with a mop of heavy silver hair and a good physique, wearing his perfectly tailored uniforms or suits well. A vain man, he wore highly polished riding boots and always expected compliments. He had a quick, financially oriented mind that probably aided his success during nine years of court proceedings.

In his 1929 French divorce settlement, Coty was expected to pay Yvonne 425 million francs in three installments. In exchange, the ex-Madame Coty waived all her interest in his property. Coty made the first payment of 38,812,318 francs on the day the agreement was signed. The second payment of 100 million francs was made a year later. Then he defaulted on August 5, 1931, on the third and final payment. Léon understood well that most of Coty's money was in the United States. To cover the default and other expenses, Yvonne demanded all of Coty's American assets in Delaware in May of 1934, just two months before his death. Finally, Madame Coty-Cotnareanu filed a request through her New York attorney, Francis L. Kohlman, for a default judgment for $5,760,622 in the Court in Brooklyn. An attachment for $1,091,351 was granted in New York by Justice Callahan. Furthermore, she did not have to waive her interest in Coty's property.[1]

Coty had outlined in *Figaro* his difficulties with his former wife and tried to explain why he had not and could not make the final payment. He had not been able to finance the sale of his stock in Coty Inc., from which he expected at least $8 million, in time to make the payment of $5.2 million. His wife, he explained, had taken advantage of his difficulties and, on Léon's advice, had attached his properties throughout France and Switzerland, including furniture and artworks. He continued these articles in *L'Ami du Peuple,* in which his raving against Léon crossed over into overt ant-Semitism.

In October of 1933, Yvonne Coty had become the principal shareholder of *Figaro* through court action against François. She ceded to Léon the management of the newspaper, and Lucien Romier was named director once more, having served in that capacity for François Coty between 1924 and 1927. Pierre Brisson, also Coty's director and later once more director under Yvonne's ownership, took over the literary editorship, as well as the dramatic page. A brilliant team was built and overseen, according to Lucien Romier, by Léon Cotnareanu, since Yvonne allowed Léon to run the paper without her interference. The staff included André Maurois, Paul Morand, Georges Duhamel, François Mauriac, and Tristan Bernard.

French intellectuals and boulevardiers have a long memory and often hold a grudge, calling it wit. The first thing the staff did under the new directorship was return the name of the newspaper to *Le Figaro.* In a move that excited all of literary and journalistic France, the newspaper published a facsimile of its first issue of January 1826 with the article *Le* in its original place. Furthermore, Romier and Brisson, with the financial encouragement of Léon Cotnareanu, who was vitally invested in the rehabilitation of the newspaper, transformed and modernized *Le Figaro* for the first time since 1919. Photography made an appearance and rapidly took an important place in the paper's layout.

Enraged at the changes at *Le Figaro* and sincerely hurt at his removal from the masthead, Coty had numerous other newspapers where he could publicly vent his rage at his ex-wife and her new husband. He wrote in *L'Ami du Peuple* on July 31, 1933:

Are not the games of fate to be admired when one discovers that the poor orphan of yesterday is an authentic descendant of Isabelle Bonaparte, first cousin of Napoleon I? The struggle is continuing, bitter, fierce, and implacable with the same adversaries that were to defeat the Emperor. Will they defeat me? I have already found Moscow, in spite of the wiles, betrayals and pitfalls. I do not see Waterloo.

He was wrong; his Waterloo was racing toward him. Having lost *Figaro* in October 1933, he lost *L'Ami du Peuple* in December of the same year to Yvonne, who sold it the next month to a group controlled by his old enemy, the Havas Agency. The *London Daily Observer* of May 3, 1934, noted:

> On Monday will be sold at auction *L'Ami du Peuple,* the third of the three daily papers of which François Coty, the perfume manufacturer, had been proprietor. He had begun by buying *Le Figaro* and the *Gaulois,* and merged the latter in the former. His ambitions then turned to something of a more popular appeal and he founded *L'Ami du Peuple,* to be sold at the revolutionary low price of ten centimes— the near equivalent of ten cents.
>
> Even now, though he is beaten, he has established a paper which has one of the biggest circulations in France; but he could not hold out long enough to put it on a firm footing, for his industrial enterprises were no longer giving him a surplus to spend on journalism. There is a cynical French proverb, "Money has no smell," or cannot smell bad. "Smell has no money" is the pitiless Parisian quip, referring to the perfume manufacturer [and his nose] now that he is losing his fortune.

Richest Man in France Dies

François's perpetual anxieties became more and more pronounced after his divorce. Believing these to be cardiac troubles, he checked himself into a number of hospitals for the rich and famous in the south of France. He demanded absolute privacy in these places, but he found that he had more privacy at La Namouna, his villa in Beaulieu-sur-mer. Rumors ran rampant that he had a persecution complex and delusions of grandeur that he would take over all France because the country needed order and a good businessman.

In 1934, François's spirit remained unbroken in the midst of his legal, financial, and journalistic disasters. At the lowest point of his political downfall, he called one of his perfume-department staff, Pierre Camin, to d'Artigny and supervised the creation of a new scent, *A'Suma*. Something was terribly wrong during this period, however. He seemed to be adrift. Week after week, he had himself chauffeured from d'Artigny to Louveciennes and back, over and over, for no apparent reason. He transferred residences, causing great confusion to his enormous staff of drivers, dressers, bodyguards, and secretaries. From *coiffeurs* to physicians, everyone remained in a state of fear, because François displayed terrible fits of temper. Without Yvonne, he had no anchor. At least he had quit appearing at all times of the day and night at Avenue Raphael, scaring Yvonne's guests and staff and Léon's niece, Geraldine Leo.

In the late spring of 1934, François suddenly became reclusive. He abandoned his staff and closeted himself in the penthouse apartment he had installed in the *pavillon* at Louveciennes. The stairwell was unfinished, and François pulled up a ladder after he had climbed to the space. Then he locked himself in. About the only friend he had left was Maurice d'Hartoy, who kept close to Coty and even proclaimed that he had cut off his own affair with Henriette. And what a friend he was, running the ultra-right-wing Solidarité Française and what remained of the newspaper empire. Coty's fascist and corporatist colleagues descended on the *pavillon* in droves to request money for any number of projects. Only d'Hartoy and his old friend Paul Reboux could coax him out of his retreat. Reboux just shook his head at the situation.

Coty's last illness was reported in the *New York Times* on June 18, 1934. The story stated that François Coty, a billionaire six years earlier, was wiped out financially and physically. Less than a month later, the newspaper announced on July 16, just days before Coty's death, that Benjamin E. Levy had been elected chairman of the board of Coty Inc.: "[Levy] has been associated with the Coty interests [in the U.S.] and in France for the last twenty-four years and will henceforth direct the organization both in this country and abroad. François Coty remains as president of the company." The business in the United States remained in good hands for the time being.

When François lay dying at Louveciennes, reportedly of pneumonia and complications after an aneurysm, the archbishop of Versailles arrived to perform last rites. Alfred Dubarry, a longtime conservative associate of Coty and a beneficiary, published in *Le Matin* July 26, 1934, that, "at death, Coty was attended by Doctors Bourgeois, de Macary, Courcoux, Linaret and Coudert as well as by Monsignor Chaptal."

Maurice d'Hartoy sent for Christiane and for Roland Coty's family at nearby Château de Vaux. *Le Matin* stated that family members surrounded François, but they exaggerated. François's eldest grandson, Henri, a twelve-year-old, came to the *pavillon,* but little François was deemed too young and Michel, the youngest, was in his crib in the nursery with one of the nannies.

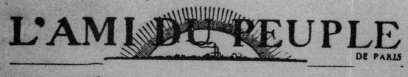

L'AMI DU PEUPLE
DE PARIS

LA RÉFORME DE L'ÉTAT
PAR
FRANÇOIS COTY

FRANÇOIS COTY
ARTISTE, INDUSTRIEL-TECHNICIEN, ÉCONOMISTE, FINANCIER
SOCIOLOGUE
PROMOTEUR DE LA *CROISADE DES PATRIES*
AUTEUR DE LA *REFORME DE L'ÉTAT*
PRÉLUDE NÉCESSAIRE A LA RECONSTRUCTION DE L'ORDRE
DE L'AUTORITÉ, DE LA HIÉRARCHIE
DE LA DISCIPLINE DÉMOCRATIQUE ET SOCIALE
SANS QUOI NE PEUT SUBSISTER
AUCUNE GRANDE NATION DU MONDE CIVILISÉ
MAIRE D'AJACCIO, DEUX FOIS ÉLU SÉNATEUR DE LA CORSE

Coty and his ghostwriters devised a plan to transform the Third Republic into a corporatist state. He was campaigning for this until his death. (Elizabeth Z. Coty Collection)

Surely, François understood toward the end how he had been deceived about Henriette and his Solidarité Française by the very man who now stood beside him, Maurice d'Hartoy. Well, he had heard it all, and seen more, since he had traveled the world over and had financial interests in five continents. Since his Corsican childhood, he had heard about continuing insurrection and the many vendettas in the mountains around Corte. He had seen how the Great War with Germany had brought his country to its knees, leaving France bereft of young men and world influence. Had he not seen the Bolsheviks rise just when he had invested in three factories in Russia and nine more in the Red zone? His factory and fashionable retail establishments in Milan had thrived while Mussolini published his socialist paper there. He had seen fascism grow, bringing Mussolini to power in 1922 as the youngest premier Europe had seen. He was glad to have helped Benito then. But soon Benito censored the press and destroyed hundreds of Italian newspapers. Why had Mussolini disappointed him? Everyone did.

François could have recalled with pride that he had been asked to counsel three presidents and two premiers of France. England, too, had called on him for advice, and he had lunched with Sir Austen Chamberlain himself, so well known for his work on the 1925 Locarno Pact. François was proud to have personally saved the French franc. Had he not passed through all the corridors of power in France? Was he not an intimate of heads of state, Winston Churchill, the Aga Khan, the richest maharajas, the most powerful financiers of the post-World War I period? His fragrances created an aura around all the crowned heads and nobility of the world. He had spent millions purchasing and restoring beautiful châteaux, ensuring that his name would live on in the architecture world. Twenty-five thousand francs would go to putting a grille over the grotto in Ajaccio at a place where Napoleon and he had both dreamed.

Why, though, had he been ridiculed for what he wrote in his newspapers? Is it not a good thing that someone should champion law, order, and discipline in France? What was wrong with going to corporate leaders for governance? They had already proven themselves by their successes and should be encouraged to lead. Was not everything he said coming to pass? Why had the Senate negated his seat from Corsica in the French Senate? Why had Yvonne schemed against him after all their years together? Henriette had seduced Maurice, his friend and advisor.

Had Solidarité Française gone too far in its efforts to defeat the communists and socialists? He was only searching for a way to organize the government so that it could operate effectively.

Had he forgotten any of the people loyal to him? Of course not. Servants, bodyguards, his attending physicians, and, oh yes, even his personal tailor and hairdresser were taken care of. Yes, he had remembered the families of Emmanuel Arène and Raymond Goëry— those friends of long ago—even the family of Henri de Villemessant, director of the department store that had sold his first perfume. His children were taken care of, and he had settled a title on his illegitimate son and established a trust in Geneva for Henriette's five children's education and livelihood. Henriette had a huge stipend, though Maurice would be there to help her spend it.

Nor had he forgotten bequests to the places he remembered best: Ajaccio, first and foremost; Calvi; Coti-Chiavari, the seat of his mother's family; Marseille, where his grandmother, Anna Maria Spoturno, had raised him; Grasse, where he had learned his trade; Suresnes, where he made his fortune; Tours, near his beloved Château d'Artigny; and even Spotorno, Italy, the land of his ancestors.

François Coty died at 8:30 in the evening of July 24, 1934, with Maurice d'Hartoy at his side. D'Hartoy arranged the funeral, where his body, shrouded with the French flag, was surrounded by 200 members of Solidarité Française in blue-shirted uniforms, carrying pennants designed with roosters before a rising sun. Two thousand more activists from Solidarité Française marched by the coffin, saluting it. A Corsican pilot named Reginensi from Bastia circled a plane above the *pavillon* in honor of the Corsican patriot.[2]

Maurice d'Hartoy arranged this tribute from the organization that had proved to be Coty's undoing. Perhaps d'Hartoy failed to see the irony, taken in as he had been with the development of fascism a decade after he had been wounded at Verdun in World War I. He had convinced Coty to finance the future merger of Solidarité Française and Taittinger's Patriotic Youth into the National Front, to oppose the newly formed Communist Front of the left. D'Hartoy could easily energize the league to support his anti-communist goals; he had created Coty's projects for him and set them into motion. Now he had Henriette back, too.

Jean-Louis Arène, son of the senator, presented the eulogy. Young Arène had been in Coty's employ since entering adulthood. François always remembered the families of those who had supported him and his ideas. Also present at the funeral was the minister of air, Colonel La Montagne, to recognize François's role in the development of French aviation. François's former mother-in-law, Virginie Dubois Le Baron, stood close to the coffin, although Yvonne did not attend. Since the family crypt Coty had designed for d'Artigny was unfinished, the funeral cortege proceeded to the little cemetery at Montbazon, with contingents from Solidarité Française, Patriotic Youth, and Croix de Feu.[3]

Le Figaro published an obituary on July 25, the day after Coty's death. The editor summarized Coty's failures and successes as they were assessed at that time:

> The name and the work of Monsieur François Coty will remain inseparable from postwar history. In this paper, which Monsieur Coty directed for ten years, we remember, now that he has died, the qualities of vigor that he placed at the service of what appeared to him to be the good of the public.
>
> The journalistic methods of M. Coty offered a new character, especially marked with passion, which could not fail to raise strong reactions. This is neither the time nor the place to mention the excesses and errors that inevitably resulted from the concepts of such a man and the reflexes of his temperament. It suffices to recognize that M. Coty, observed serenely, outside his successive and disparate surroundings, sincerely desired to be useful to his country and to protect it. He may have been mistaken as to the means, been unfair to certain people, or not have taken circumstances sufficiently into account, but no one can deny the spontaneous eagerness of most of his campaigns.
>
> It must not be forgotten that M. Coty had succeeded, through hard work and determined perseverance, to impose his firm and his name on all the markets of the world.
>
> Like others, M. Coty could have placed his wealth at the disposal of unworthy causes or used it selfishly. Attracted by a kind of national mystique, he preferred to expose himself to blows.
>
> At a time when poverty of character and mediocrity of ambition deprived many [public] individuals, we must salute the rare spirit of enterprise demonstrated in the complex boldness of the man.

Paul Reboux commented, "This realistic industrialist was romantic about government. He was driven to madness by toadies and ruined by petitioners. He was, however, gifted and capable of making his mark on history."

Le Matin published a dry, though not negative, obituary two days after Coty's death. "He was in a coma from the afternoon. Monsignor Chaptal was called and administered the last rites, and at 8:32 pm surrounded by family members, François Coty succumbed to death. He was sixty years old."[4]

The life of this complex, brilliant, but contradictory man illustrates that brilliance can be flawed when accompanied by passion, if not a final mental derangement. Here was a man supremely talented at perfumery, art, industrial development, marketing, and assembling a staff and colleagues to achieve a successful global business. Coty's goal for the use of his vast fortune was well intentioned; he sought to return his country to its pre-World War I eminence. His means to achieve this, however, were flawed. He toyed with fascism, which he saw as Charles Maurras defined it—socialism emancipated from democracy—but Coty added that it was a logical move from capitalism, from which it was derived. To him it was a system that united action and thought under the leadership of proven businessmen. His efforts were not understood, nor were they appreciated. His was an unlucky fate.

Like so many Frenchmen between the wars, Coty was searching for significance for France. During these turbulent times, ideologies abounded. His program to address France's problems emphasized order and discipline, but neither François Coty, Ernest Mercier's Redressement Français, nor France itself had found the optimal formula at the time of his death.

François Coty's life was a theatrical performance of a play he developed for his own stage. He was driven from scene to scene, from act to act, by determination, indefatigable energy, and talent. Intensity guided him.

Newspapers all over the world covered Coty's demise. At the time of his death, Coty's politics, as expressed in his printed works and articles, were controversial. Even the most complimentary of obituaries, such as the one in the *New York Times,* offered stories that gave offense. Maréchal Hubert Lyautey's death, on the same day as Coty's, was front-page material throughout France, trumping coverage about the country's first billionaire. News of the assassination of the diminutive premier of Austria, Engelbert Dollfuss, under the aegis of Mussolini, also took precedence over the death of France's most interesting genius.

A former Coty employee, Emile Buré, director of politics for *L'Ordre,* capped the reports of François's death with an insulting assessment of the man and his reputation. The Friday, July 27, 1934, edition of his newspaper published a scathing front-page announcement of Coty's death. It was a eulogy, but one of celebration that the industrialist-turned-journalist-politician had died. It was titled "François Coty, When Money Is King."

François Coty is no more. His life is such a lesson; it denounces with such an explosion the hideous misery of his époque where money, acquired through good or bad works, is king, where money serves all as a law, often imbecilic, not to say odious. . . . Death has a right to the truth. Never, assuredly, a better occasion will ever be offered for the criticism of the misdeeds of the plutocrat in our democracy, said to be free, which carries the cruel irons of its frightful materialism.

[Coty] fabricated good products, and he presented them well. His flasks signed *Lalique* obtained the greatest success; he made *fureur* as one says, and he found with ease the indispensable capital for development of his business. His wife, who also had sure taste, helped him extensively in his enterprises, on her own admission. Becoming a millionaire in selling perfumes and rice powder—that is nothing extraordinary. But billionaire—that is another affair! The war and, above all, the postwar period, which unleashed speculation, [contributed] much to the incredible richness of François Coty, and it is not at all astonishing that his head was turned.

François Coty, in the course of each day's chats, invoked the image of Bonaparte. If I had not worked for him, I would have had no idea of the extent of his dictatorial dreams. His megalomania appalled me to the point that, called to take the directorship of one of his papers, I had to resign instead. I could not support the atmosphere of a satrap, raving among his courtesans, who flattered him basely when he was in their presence, but who were villainously treasonous when he had his shoulders turned.

Each time I left the Rond-Point des Champs-Elysées I was reproached, "What are you doing there? You know well that a crazy man directs that place!" If I showed myself to be satisfied with a conversation that I had at the Avenue Raphael residence and that I showed the desire of signing my contract, he would always find something to stop me.

Buré explained that his problem was that Coty could be so charming, so penitent, that Buré would feel guilty—that he had been led astray and he had no one to blame but himself.

When I entered into relations with him he was not then compared to the heroes of Kipling, to Goethe. He had not then published in his newspaper frightening articles that should never be reproduced. He changed over time.

[Coty's] clairvoyance, his true unique intelligence makes him see quickly the objective that he distinguishes immediately. His ability and perseverance were never conquered and he never gave up, never. Anyone who knew him understands the determination he had to succeed.

Christiane Coty Dubonnet, who used the name Spoturno, insisted that she knew her late father's real wishes. She waited until 1968 before having François's remains exhumed and carried to Corsica. "The last wishes of my father have been granted. He wanted to sleep his last sleep at the cemetery of Ajaccio," Christiane declared. François was laid to rest in the chapel of the Château of Pinto d'Antigues, the last property he bought, on the route des Sanguinaires along the coast just outside Ajaccio. He does not rest alone there since, on December 12, 1971, the same day the stadium bearing Coty's name was dedicated in Ajaccio, Christiane moved his grandmother Anna Maria Belone Spoturno's remains next to François's gravesite. At that time, Christiane moved into Canicciu, a new home that she had built in the Ajaccio area. She died, over one hundred years old, in a nursing home in Nice in 2005 and now lies beside her father and great-grandmother.

This second burial of François Coty was covered in the Ajaccio newspapers and attended by throngs, just as he would have wished. After his burial there, the property became part of the old cemetery. Even François Coty's burial is controversial!

CHAPTER 15

Cotnareanu at the Helm

Man is neither angel nor beast, and the one who wants to be the angel, becomes the beast.

Pascal

Léon Cotnareanu, like François Coty, was interested and active in world affairs, but on a more intellectual plane in his early years. He initiated correspondence with Henri Bergson, France's most eminent twentieth-century philosopher. His interests naturally concerned Romania and all of Central and Eastern Europe. He arranged luxurious voyages on the *Alphée* with guests who were influential diplomats, Middle Eastern potentates, princes, and even kings in exile.

His prime interest, however, was restoration of *Le Figaro*'s pre-1922 reputation. Yvonne still owned and theoretically controlled the newspaper but chose to take no role in its operation. Léon worked with conservative intellectual Lucien Romier, who ran the newspaper for Yvonne, but he also saw to it that anti-Semitic elements in its news reporting and commentary were eliminated, working closely with his brother Philippe in this regard.

As for Coty SA in Europe, Léon left it largely in the hands of the managers Coty had appointed at Suresnes. Coty Inc. was another matter. Taking the advice of his brother Leo in New York, he learned the Coty business there and applied himself to its further expansion, even though by 1934 it was by far the largest moneymaker in the worldwide Coty enterprise.

Between 1934 and World War II, Léon immersed himself in managing Yvonne's inheritance and all that she had won from François in court battles in France and the United States. Acting on Yvonne's behalf, he began to sell her properties and art collections, taking fees as her business agent and paying his brother for the attendant legal services.

On Monday, November 30, and Tuesday, December 1, 1936, the Coty Collection was sold at auction at the Jean Charpentier Gallery,

76, rue du Faubourg-Saint-Honoré. It consisted of art from the Château d'Artigny that Yvonne had decided to sell, on Cotnareanu's advice. She was no longer interested in François Coty's vast project of establishing the perfect eighteenth-century French estate, since her life now was centered in Paris. It must have been clear to her by then that neither Christiane nor Roland would ever be suited to the proprietorship of a great estate. However, the land and buildings, as well as many of the interior accoutrements at d'Artigny, were not sold in her lifetime. In the end, Roland's sons and Christiane inherited them.

The sale at Charpentier included sculpture, furniture, tapestries, paintings, drawings, and gouaches. Among the paintings where oils by Watteau and de Largillière; pastels by J-B Greuze and J-B. Perroneau; and watercolors and gouaches by Baudouin, Demachy, and others. The cloisonné pieces were advertised as dating from the Ming Dynasty. The furniture of marquetry, lacquer, and scalloped wood included that made and signed by master cabinetmakers Carel, M. Criaerd, J-P Dusautoy, M. B. Evald, L. Moreau, and P. Roussel. A suite of four Beauvais tapestries, called *Les Divinités Marines,* carried the signature of Béhagle. Other tapestries were from Gobelins, d'Aubusson, and Des Flandres, dating from the late sixteenth to the eighteenth centuries.

The *New York Times* of December 2, 1936, published an article about the Coty Collection headlined "Charges of Fraud Halt Sale of Art." Lawsuits over the authenticity of some of these pieces dragged on for years after Coty's death, when he was no longer able to refute the allegations. Even after his bombastic newspapers were sold, his name removed from the mastheads, and many of his personally selected employees dismissed, Coty still made headlines, whether about art, architecture, fragrance, or politics.

Christiane's relative by marriage, Geraldine Leo Feder, described Christiane's activities toward the end of her father's life and beyond. "She did not stay with Paul long, and then she and the baby returned to Avenue Raphael by 1929. Christiane did not get along with her mother, and she was already a bitter woman, and, we thought, unattractive. In 1933, Christiane married another magnate, William Saurin. His family had long been associated with the development of French cuisine and methods to keep French specialties from spoiling." Christiane soon divorced Monsieur Saurin and moved to Corsica, where she continued the generous charitable contributions to the island begun by her father. She bought a house on Cours Grandval in Ajaccio and presented collections of military letters of Napoleon and other rare Napoleonic artifacts to the city. She became honorary president of the Sporting Club of Bastia and a major donor to the Church in Corsica.

In the Paris of 1935, warnings of impending war did not penetrate life at Avenue Raphael, nor did any growing threat for Jews in Europe infiltrate the gold-colored walls of Yvonne's boudoir. Léon kept his activities relating to Jewish affairs to himself. The viability of the Third Republic continued to consume public interest. However, without the passionate François Coty at Avenue Raphael or in the lives of his family, there seemed to be little concern about the future of France's republic. Art, golf, sailboats, and voyages on the *Alphée* reigned supreme, at least in Yvonne's life.

Geraldine Leo's father in the United States kept her and her husband, Romanian Edgard Feder, informed of the growing problems for Jews in Europe. Mr. Leo sent letters to them at Avenue Raphael, where they often visited, and their apartment. Geraldine recalled:

> My father, living in New York, was the one to warn us in the late thirties that Edgard and I must reestablish ourselves in the United States. We could not imagine what he was talking about. We were living so well in the Paris of the thirties, Edgard and I, as a young married couple, with a flat at 164, avenue de Neuilly, in Paris. Uncle Léon and Aunt Yvonne never seemed concerned, and life went along as usual in their exalted set. In the end, however, we left our car in the garage to flee to New York to escape the Germans. Léon and Yvonne did not leave for the United States until after Paris fell. How fortunate, though, that they had taken my father's advice and concentrated on the perfume business in the United States, since Europe was to be embroiled in war for years.

Roland's wife, Marguerite, died in an auto crash on February 4, 1938, when she was thirty-seven years old. Having just finished dinner at the home of her mother-in-law, Yvonne, Marguerite telephoned Roland. He was on his yacht near Cannes. She heard women's voices in the background. She reacted by picking up her best friend, and the two women took off for the south of France. While they were driving on the A6, near Vierzon, a hay wagon pulled out in front of their speeding car. In the resulting crash, the two women were killed.

Yvonne found herself in charge of Roland's three sons, with the aid of several nannies. The youngest, Michel, was just six and would not be informed of his mother's death for some time. As for Roland, it seemed he was not going to take an active role in his boys' upbringing. He had his own house on the coast near Cannes, where he moored

Roland (far right) and Marguerite (far left). (Elizabeth Z. Coty Collection)

his yacht. He was frequently elsewhere, managing either the Alphée *or François's massive racehorse operation in Normandy. At any rate, his three children had been in the hands of nurses and tutors at the Château de Vaux, near François's Château d'Artigny, for most of their lives, so not much changed with their mother's sudden death.*

The family decided to send all the children to boarding school, even six-year-old Michel. When Michel returned from the Saint-Gervais boarding school in Villars to Avenue Raphael, little Michie, as Yvonne called him, had to ask Madame Clarisse, Yvonne's secretary, if he could speak with his grandmother. Michel wished to ask her the whereabouts of his beloved mother. The excuses, going on now for two school terms, were getting so thin that the boy knew he was not being told the truth.

Barricading himself in a corner of the library, he refused to eat for two days. A series of platters brought by sympathetic servants accumulated in front of his chair while he waited for an explanation of his mother's absence. Granné had made a mistake and knew that she could ask no more of her small, beloved grandson.

Yvonne had not set eyes on Michel since his arrival from school, and she was weeping when she walked into the library. "Michie, your mama died in a motor accident a year ago. That is why you were sent off to school when you were barely six years old." Finally, after hearing the full story, little Michie prayed by his grandmother's side, hoping his mother had had a second to repeat the prayer that she had taught him in his infancy.

Michel never forgave any of his family for deceiving him. Boarding school for little Michel had been Léon's idea, Michel always said. The two older boys were of an age at which children of their social stratum would have been at boarding school anyway. Only Michel had been shipped off at an unusually early age before he could have expected it. The abrupt change in the life to which he was accustomed had to be explained.

CHAPTER 16

Henriette's Havoc

Reader, have you at times inhaled/With rapture and slow greediness/
That grain of incense which pervades a church,/Or the inveterate
musk of a sachet?

Charles Baudelaire, *Les Fleurs du Mal*

Henriette Dieudé's affair with Maurice d'Hartoy ruined her for marriage to François. Forbidden sensuality apparently appealed to her more than the comfort and security of married life, notwithstanding her five children by Coty. Antoinette Mouchet, Roland Coty's second wife, summed up the situation with her comment, "François was quite a stud, but Henriette liked Maurice because he was younger and more powerful in politics." After François's death, the divorcée resumed her relationship with d'Hartoy. In 1935, within a year of Coty's death, he divorced his longsuffering wife, Jacqueline, left their five children and married Henriette as soon as the two could legally arrange it.

D'Hartoy lived with Henriette, her children by Coty, and their own three children in Geneva throughout World War II. He secured a post as consul of Rafael Trujillo's Dominican Republic. The Coty family suspected, however, that the money Coty had settled on Henriette, as well as funds from another Geneva account that Coty left solely for his children by Henriette, supported them. D'Hartoy certainly needed extra money, what with obligations to his first wife and their five children, as well as his three children with Henriette—Catherine, Elisabeth, and Frederic. By 1948, d'Hartoy had divorced Henriette. Perhaps Henriette, now mother of eight, no longer had the allure of a paramour.

Antoinette Mouchet said that "Henriette spent everything" during her marriage to d'Hartoy. She was referring to the sum that Coty had set aside for her in a Swiss bank in 1932, reportedly 10 million gold Swiss francs. She has also been accused of raiding a similar amount from the trust François set up for their five children.

The Geneva bank in question claimed that before anyone could

François's longtime mistress, Henriette Dieudé (left), sits with her daughter France, her longsuffering mother, her son, Christian, and her sister in the 1920s in France. When Coty squired his mistress around Paris, she was considered one of the great beauties of the day, according to numerous sources, including her own grandsons. (Elizabeth Z. Coty Collection)

gain access to the children's money, signatures were needed of the two trustees Coty had appointed, one Marais and one Dubois. These men were never found, and it was sworn in one court that they were just "straw names" used by Coty. Ironically, Dubois is Yvonne's mother's maiden name. Perhaps one of Yvonne's brothers or her deceased uncle was one of the trustees.

Coty had arranged for his only son by Henriette, Christian, to be adopted by Theodore Spreng, the childless, aging, penniless duke de la Châtre. Coty hoped that his natural son might inherit the title. The arrangement came to fruition when the duke died in 1940, after acknowledging Christian as his heir in 1936, two years after Coty's death. At the same time, Henriette's four daughters—Françoise, always known as France; Anne-Marie; Josette; and Marie-Louise—were authorized to use the name Spreng instead of Dieudé. Titled, but without access to the money that Coty had set aside for him, Christian became bitter, but not incapable of action.

In Antoinette's view, Christian "was not loyal and turned out to be bad." She disapproved of his behavior when he sued his own mother in 1953 for the money that François had set aside for him. He aimed to recapture any money that Henriette and d'Hartoy had not spent.

The *London Evening Standard* of April 12, 1953, reported, "Under French law, which protects legitimate children against the claims of those born out of wedlock, [Henriette] had the power to revoke the bequest bestowed on the five children she had with Coty before her marriage to him." The article concluded, "The courts are trying to discover what has happened to the Coty perfume millions." Besides the courts, the French government, the Spoturno dit Coti descendants, and the Dieudé-Coty descendants have all tried to find the millions that Coty hid in Geneva and elsewhere. Even now, one or another periodically seeks access to sealed bank accounts in Geneva that purportedly contain various Coty monies, including some of the 10 million gold Swiss francs that Coty had set aside for his illegitimate children. Léon's niece, Geraldine Leo Feder, said quietly at age ninety-five in her lovely apartment overlooking Central Park in New York City, "Some people have even dared to suggest that the Cotnareanu family somehow made off with the money." While this idea was shocking to her, Coty's descendants on both sides accuse one another as well as Cotnareanu of taking François's money.

The *London Evening Standard,* in a long article published on December 12, 1953, described the lawsuit against Henriette by Christian and three of his sisters to recover their Coty inheritance. Henriette and her children were not, in effect, in agreement over Coty's intentions for this money. Henriette claimed that it was destined for her. But four of the five children disagreed: they insisted that their father, not wanting to bequeath the money to them directly, had taken this action in order to secure their educations and their futures.

The children's suit turned out to be fruitless. No money was retrieved. Christian had better luck in 1955 when he sued Yvonne Coty-Cotnareanu in Brooklyn for the 10 million gold Swiss francs that François Coty placed in a Geneva bank for his five natural offspring.

The *London Daily Herald* of April 22, 1955, described Christian's financial situation at the time: "Christian de la Châtre, the only illegitimate son [of Coty], . . . works as a clerk for a building firm and lives with his wife and three children in one room in a Paris hotel." The hotel was the Astoria, where his mother had conceived him and where he previously worked as a waiter."

Sam White, writing for the *Evening Standard* from Paris, quoted

Christian as saying in court, "I earn 35 pounds a month as a clerk, and with it I have to support a wife and three children." White added, "The perfume millionaire [Coty] placed 10 million gold francs, now worth 700,000 pounds [in 1955] in a Swiss bank in Madame Hanot-Dieudé's name. But he laid down that the money was to be handed to his illegitimate children."

With Judge Kohlman presiding, the court granted Christian 700,000 English pounds. This precedent-setting lawsuit inflamed Yvonne, since Christian was no relation to her, and indeed, his and his sisters' very existence had caused her a great deal of heartache. The courts, which had once favored her over François, now turned in favor of François's children. This ruling surprised everyone, especially the French, who were accustomed to the civil law that stipulates exactly where money from a marriage goes—and it is not from the hands of the former, legal, wife into the hands of her husband's natural children by another woman. Apparently, such maneuvers and judicial decisions could happen in Brooklyn.

This woman, Henriette, wrought havoc. She broke up the first marriages of two men. She bore eight children, five with Coty and three with d'Hartoy, much to the distress of each husband's first wife and family.

The entire Coty family referred to Henriette as Mamou Chat because she constantly smoked cigarettes from a package with a picture of a cat on the label. In spite of some opinions, however, "she was considered one of the loveliest women of Paris," one descendant said.

D'Hartoy, "despite the differences between the two men, . . . always had a great esteem for Coty," said Bernard d'Hartoy, youngest son of Maurice from his first marriage. "I have known for a long time [Coty's] qualities as a leader of men, his political will to fight against communism and his concern for the common good, in particular that of the less rich. Who speaks now of his achievement in the social sciences for society or of his creation of a popular and successful journal, *L'Ami du Peuple?* No one does because Coty's name has been all but obliterated from the lexicon of French history due to his political stand and the perception that he was unstable."

Bernard d'Hartoy described how Henriette, then the head of a relatively considerable fortune, made contact with Maurice after Coty died. He "succumbed again to her charms, divorced his wife, left his children and married her." Janine Dumas d'Hauterive, who had introduced d'Hartoy to his first wife, "was furious and my father returned to [Janine] all the furniture, silver and art that she had given to him" upon his marriage to Jacqueline. "As for my mother, she contented herself by saying, *S'il est heureux, je le suis*" (If he is happy, I am).

"To complete the portrait of my father [Maurice d'Hartoy] for whom you have divined that I have a great admiration, in spite of the bad that he did to us, I will tell you another thing: he was a man of great culture, author of more than twenty works, doctor of political science from Washington University, doctor of letters from Columbia, member of the academies of Rouen, of Lisbon and of Rome, eight times laureate of *l'Académie Française,* consul, then consul general, then [permanent consul] for the Dominican Republic."

PART II

World War II to 1965

CHAPTER 17

Flight from France

You've only one life to enjoy—let it all be fragrant!
Coty Inc. advertisement, 1944

Yvonne had assumed that if war ever came again to France, she would simply board the Alphée with everything she wanted and sail across the Atlantic. Yvonne had such faith in the Maginot line that it never occurred to her that she would not be able to flee on her floating palace when the warnings came. However, no warnings arrived: the Germans did. Yvonne and her family were trapped in their home. Neither she nor Léon had heeded his eldest brother, who had been suggesting for years that they relocate in New York.

The German military governor of Paris, Gen. Hans von Boineburg, after taking over the Hôtel Meurice on Place Vendôme, knew just where to go for his residence in the most beautiful city in the Western world. François Coty's Avenue Raphael residence was renowned for the magnificence of the estate, the splendor of the interior decoration, and all the modern conveniences installed by the late owner. The general's emissary broke the news to Yvonne and Léon. They were given four days to evacuate the property, with orders to leave it perfectly appointed and staffed.

The two youngest grandchildren, François and Michel, were home from their Saint-Gervais boarding school in Villars. Both Roland and his eldest son, Henri, were away in the navy. Yvonne and her most trusted staff managed to get to the Morgan Bank on Place Vendôme with cases of jewelry and small objets d'art. The little troop carrying boxes was not stopped as it went first to the House of Coty boutique, also on Place Vendôme, then to the bank. André Cheveneau, director of the bank, received millions of dollars worth of Yvonne's jewelry, which remained safe with him during the war.

Yvonne also hid place settings of vermeil, Lalique glasses, and Sèvres china made especially for her, along with seven statues by Rodin. Original drawings and paintings by Fragonard and her paintings by Gauguin, Manet, Monet, Dufy, and Renoir were removed from the salons for safekeeping. They were carried to the sublevel cellar, which housed her vintage champagne, to be hidden behind a new wall along with thousands of bottles of wine in old wine racks and then covered with dirt.

While the German army was scouring the city and country for objects worth much less than these pieces, the German high command in Paris unknowingly guarded and preserved the Coty collection at Avenue Raphael throughout the war. The Germans never investigated to find the treasures resting below the floors.

Pierre, Yvonne's faithful Yugoslavian butler, and his wife, Anna, remained to serve the Germans and guard their mistress's estate. Yvonne knew they would be there whenever she returned, supposing it to be quite soon. She never dreamed that World War II would be such a long and disastrous war for France and the Western world. Indeed, before she returned for good, she had lived in America for twenty years. She raised two of her grandchildren in North America, and they became United States citizens, something almost beyond her comprehension.

During the German occupation of Paris, Annabella Waldner became the official hostess for General von Boineburg at this elegant estate, the Coty home on Avenue Raphael. As one historian described, "Each night for four years, she lit the massive silver and crystal candelabra in the residence of the French perfume king, François Coty. Through its salons, she watched the flower of the Third Reich, of fascist Italy and Vichy France drift by. The wine cellars and pantries over which she presided had housed the rarest wines of France, caviar from Russia, the rich foie gras of Périgord—every delicacy that occupied Europe had been able to furnish its conquerors." For this young girl, these four years would be a Cinderella existence. She had her own car and driver, a dressmaker, and, as the final accolade, a box at the Opera, in the building that François Coty had restored just a few years before through a large donation.[1]

Escape from the Germans

As the Germans were consolidating their grip on Paris in 1940, Léon, who had Madame's chauffeur, Jean, ready and waiting, insisted that the entourage of refugees leave. He finally managed to get Yvonne and her two grandchildren Michel and François into the Bugatti with him. Author-editor André Maurois, Jewish and one of Léon's employees at Le Figaro, climbed into the large Délage, driving it with a mountain of Yvonne's luggage. Yvonne's Citroën, piloted by the assistant chauffeur, followed with more luggage and with Yvonne's maid, Annabel, without whom Yvonne could not manage a trip. Just as they were about to drive away, Yvonne dashed back into the mansion to retrieve the Mirabel figs she could not live without. She stuffed masses of figs into the pockets of the enormous sable coat she was wearing for her getaway. "How could I forget the figs!" she exclaimed, trying to keep a sense of humor for the boys.

The file of automobiles proceeded toward the Spanish border and their destination, the Lisbon airport in Portugal. The family group waited for Roland and his son Henri to join them at a prearranged rendezvous. After several hours had passed, Léon insisted that they could not endanger the entire family by waiting longer and they drove on. The trek through the center of France included a stop at Yvonne's tobacco farm and its ancient stone château, Filolie, in the Dordogne. Yvonne and François had renovated the quaint medieval complex for Virginie, Yvonne's mother.

They insisted that the Widow Dubois-Le Baron escape with them, but she refused to leave. "I have been to America many times, before and after the Great War. Now, I cannot leave my country." So Yvonne said to Léon, "I must respect her feelings."

Even with all the tension and hurry, Yvonne, who loved her country, felt it was impossible to pass the beautiful border area of the Pyrenees in early summer and not find joy in the surroundings. The range of mountains dividing France and Spain was exquisite. She enjoyed them despite the difficult conditions and despite two little boys, ages nine and fourteen, crowded into the car with her. She had never experienced such conditions during her life of leisure with her staff of thirty-odd people.

To avoid the main roads, the motorcade proceeded south from the Dordogne through Pau and on to St.-Jean-de-Luz, where the chauffeur, Jean, bid them a tearful farewell and headed back to Paris with Annabel.

When the family and Maurois arrived at the Spanish border town of Irun, Léon convinced the guard to find someone to drive them to Portugal because they had to leave their own cars behind. For a hefty fee, the guard's brother, whom the family forever remembered as Pedro, provided an old car that resembled a large English taxi. Juan, Pedro's cousin, drove a rickety pickup truck behind them with Maurois and the mountain of luggage, as they headed to the Portuguese border.

When Yvonne reached the Lisbon airport, travel worn and with the figs crushed in her pockets, another crisis awaited them. "There *are no seats on the plane," shouted the airline attendant in broken English. When it was revealed, pointedly, that the editor of* Le Figaro *and its publisher and owner were present, a Pan American Airlines official appeared. Money prevailed: vast sums of it. Five bags of English mail destined for the United States were removed from the Pan Am clipper. The authorities allowed the five passengers to board the last plane headed for New York City, and the apprehensive pilot prepared to take off, late.*

They made a sad picture: a fifty-seven-year-old woman, overheated but clutching her fur coat, with two frightened boys and two spoiled Parisian men, Léon and André, grumpy about the inconvenience of their situation. These two men, who were well-known Jewish intellectuals and businessmen, did not realize how fortunate they were to have escaped France at that time.

Landing in New York in June of 1940 was almost as dramatic as the trip across France, Spain, and Portugal. Léon expected the entourage to be met by notable officials and guided into a luxurious life in the United States. Instead, customs officials blocked their entry. Back in Paris, there had been no time to obtain U.S. visas for their passports before their hasty exit. Yvonne, in her accustomed manner, telephoned the highest official of the city from the airport. Grover Whalen, the official greeter of New York City and a longtime friend of François and Yvonne, rushed to the airport, sure he could begin arranging everything for her stay in the United States. He was the right-hand man of the popular mayor of the city, Fiorello La Guardia.

Whalen ensconced the group in the Hotel Pierre, the finest hotel available. Yvonne, Léon, the two boys, and André Maurois were advised to remain quietly inside the hotel, with assurances that available services were sufficient to take care of them. Fortunately for the journalist-intellectual Maurois, his papers were in order. With Grover Whalen helping her family, Yvonne felt sure they would be able to remain in the United States. The group came with three passports, the two boys on Yvonne's passport. The officials needed for her passport to claim the children as her own. The passport did say that the children were adopted, but there were no papers. Her role as grandmother would not suffice in the U.S. "Luckily, no one asked to see the adoption papers," Michel remembered, even though the U.S. immigration service had been tightening regulations because so many immigrants were flooding in from Europe.

Although Mayor La Guardia was to sponsor them, they still needed to come in on a quota. That meant a two-year delay. The troop left for Quebec on Air Canada, a new airline with sparse accommodations. They soon checked into the Seigneurie Club, a chic place near Montreal that the wealthy used as a secluded vacation resort. Maurois was at home in French Canada and soon found his own way.

La Seigneurie du Triton in Quebec remains today a private club that since 1923 has been the rendezvous for multimillionaire Americans who go there to hunt and fish and to enjoy nature and each other's company. The club has had as members Pres. Harry Truman, the Rockefeller family, and Winston Churchill. Accessible only by boat or hydroplane, La Seigneurie was a well-guarded secret, but also a lonely place for Michel and François. Ironically, on those premises they could play boule, their grandfather's favorite game. He had played it as a youngster in Corsica.

One of Granné's priorities was to have her two grandsons learn English in preparation for their return to the United States. Miss Rose, a trained governess, was hired by Grover Whalen's secretary and sent to Canada to assist the family. When the boys had trouble with English, Miss Rose used a unique method to aid their memories. She accompanied them into the dining room of the resort, requiring them to read the menu and order for themselves whatever they wanted. François said, "Sometimes we got ice cream and sauerkraut, but she made us eat it so we would never forget those words and their meaning." The boys' vocabularies grew very quickly, but Yvonne herself never considered learning much English, either in Canada or during the years she remained in the United States.

Life in Canada at a secluded club was very different from the gay life in the grand city of New York they had envisioned. Léon had expected to burst upon the American scene with gusto.

Yvonne sent the boys to a camp at Loon Lake in Maine for two summers, a definite relief to both Léon and the boys, who always resented their grandmother's husband. The boys did not encounter passport problems since they were rowed over quietly at night. Michel ("Mike") never forgot those summers. He told me of being awakened by the loons after long days of excursions and exercise. The "loony" call fascinated the boys, who had fun imitating the "oahaoo" calls in deep-throated voices. Mike said that when the loons awakened him, he had lots of time to dream of his coming life in the United States.

New York at Last

After two years in Canada, they were allowed to enter the United States. Mike made only one mistake on his exam. When asked,

*"What is the Fourth of July?" he promptly replied, "Bastille Day."
Mike ultimately became a more devoted American than most of
his friends at Yale. Nevertheless, he always said he didn't like it
when someone called him a French Canadian. "After all, we are
very Parisian." Gratefully and diplomatically, he did not criticize or
ridicule the way French was spoken in Quebec.*

*On arriving in New York City, the family moved into suites at
the Pierre, since Yvonne had such fond remembrances of her times
there with François. This venue was not so much to the liking of the
two boys because they constantly had to be on their best behavior.
At nights in New York, Mike couldn't help wondering what was
happening to his brother and father in France. He began to hear
of the French Resistance, and he had an idea that his father was
surely a hero in it. He hoped so, because by thirteen years of age he
already knew that some of the family was privately disappointed in
his father, Roland. How could they be? He was fun loving—taking
them for fast rides in the "Coty Special," his racing car, or to the
horse races at Longchamp and Deauville. He had even taken Mike
flying in his Lysander once. He was still a polo champion. Yes, his
father was bound to be a hero.*

*The Coty-Cotnareanu retinue settled in New York City to put the
boys in good schools. Yvonne knew that education meant a lot in the
United States. Mike, with his quick François-type brain, was sent to St.
Ignatius Loyola, a Jesuit school on Park Avenue, Léon's idea, so that
some of Mike's vigor and love of life would be subdued. Mike told me he
immediately began to complain that the priests watched his every move.
Naturally, they caught the mischievous boy in many misdemeanors. His
favorite story was when he became a corporal. He was very proud of his
new stripe, and he could blow a bugle. He was asked to blow reveille
the first day. He recalled, "I got halfway through the piece when I began
to laugh into the bugle, which spoiled the musical tone and sounded too
much like a large raspberry." The boys teased him gustily. He lost his
day-old corporal stripe, never to regain it.*

Léon Cotnareanu returned to a flourishing Coty Inc., in New York.
Perhaps he had been traveling back and forth between Montreal and
New York to oversee extraordinary changes for retail sales. He had
authorized the installation of a spectacular new salon in the "sunken
plaza of Rockefeller City." "The Coty Inc. première . . . had, to begin
with, an incomparable background as well as foreground," according
to the *New York Times* on July 10, 1941. "It had the [Paul] Manship
masterpiece, Prometheus and the splashing spillway, as a backdrop
and a tiered stage opposite him against the grand stairway." Wafting

across the floors was "a galaxy of beauty, in a corps of the city's prettiest, most willowy manikins." There was also a quartet from the Music Hall ballet and "Rockettes, ten in full costume." Rollo Hudson's orchestra and Rose Bampton were featured. The reporter was impressed with "a suggestion of de Mille," and Grover Whalen was, as always, a part of the drama and presentation. Whalen had obtained the services of Dorothy Draper for the Coty interior and it was up to the minute, with John Powers models displaying collections from Altman, Wanamaker, Mary Lewis, and Stern Brothers. The president of the New York Board of Aldermen officiated over the two-hour-long extravaganza, which concluded with "The Star-Spangled Banner" and the requisite ribbon cutting.

During the time that Parisians were wondering when to leave, Cotnareanu was appointing substitutes for the Jewish officers and employees of Coty SA whom he had sent to Coty Inc. Meanwhile, the company was thriving in New York. Grover Whalen's help was everywhere evident, and soon he was an officer in Coty Inc.

In 1942, Léon attended Columbia University, where he received an honorary Ph.D. and put together an anthology of *Le Figaro* articles that had appeared between 1934 and 1940, during his tenure as publisher. The two volumes, *Chroniques du Figaro: Suites Françaises,* were published by Brentano's in 1945 with an introduction by Cotnareanu and a note from the editor, Robert Tenger.

Cotnareanu collected 220 pieces for publication, organized under eleven subject headings. The contributing authors included many who had written under Coty's stewardship, although Cotnareanu's objective was to show how the newspaper had returned to its exalted state after Coty's departure and his own arrival. Most of the writers remain internationally recognized. The books, classics of French journalism, have been reprinted a number of times.

Yvonne chose a Renaissance-style stone apartment building on the corner of Seventy-fourth Street and Fifth Avenue, next door to the Guggenheim townhouse, in which to house the family. It was near one of the entrances to Central Park, and she could see across the park and the lake from her windows. She said she could "keep an eye on the boys too." As always, Yvonne wanted to be in the middle of urban activity. She rented an entire floor of the building, which she then had magnificently furnished in the art-deco style, very different from her formal Parisian interior decoration. A coincidence: I myself would be a neighbor to my future family in 1959, in my apartment in the marble Guggenheim townhouse. Without even knowing it, I was moving closer to their world.

The first year in New York, mischievous Mike, whose personality and lust for fun resembled his grandfather's, found a kindred soul in Laurent, son of the French ambassador. One Saturday afternoon, they were allowed to go see the movie Sergeant York, *starring Gary Cooper as the World War I hero from the mountains of Tennessee. They became so fascinated with the hero's "mountain" speech that they sat through the movie three times. These sons of wealthy, prominent French families emerged from the theater after dark to see dozens of police cars cruising up and down Lexington Avenue. Everyone believed they had been kidnapped. François Coty had been afraid of this and had always surrounded himself with many bodyguards. Yvonne had grown accustomed to the idea that it could occur in the family and now she was frightened for the boys.*

Not satisfied with the excitement they had caused, the two boys upped the ante the following week by dropping bombs, made of water-filled paper bags, out of the upstairs windows of the French Embassy, hitting dignitaries walking to the Russian Embassy next door. This time the boys' families were notified by an enraged group of Russian diplomats. The two "warriors" explained that they realized the Russians were not really friends of either France or America. The subsequent punishment meted out to the boys, courtesy of Léon, just about convinced them they would have been better off living through the war in France. All Mike's grandmother could think to say was, "Is it true that boys will be boys? But for how long?"

Yvonne's newly formed family enjoyed New York immensely. They were well received due to their wealth, their connections with Mayor La Guardia, and their Coty name, so familiar to Americans at that time. Yvonne entertained beautifully: her sense of humor and vast knowledge about wine and food made her a wonderful hostess. She developed her own style of dress and décor for her new life, so different from Paris in all ways except for the plentiful wealth.

In the summer, Yvonne grew restless after having been accustomed to at least thirteen residences prepared for her arrival on a day's notice in France. As Mike said, when asked, "we always needed all thirteen so we could spend one month in each place and have the thirteenth for vacations." She found a beautiful seaside home in Madison, Connecticut, a socially prominent but secluded village, where she immediately joined the beach club. The population included several of America's industrial giants, including Grover Whalen.

Learning English and acclimating to America were more difficult for François, now called "Frank," Mike's senior by five years. The older brother was never able to assume his role of guiding his

Frank and Mike Coty pose in their American military-school uniforms. (Elizabeth Z. Coty Collection)

younger brother. Frank's long bouts with tuberculosis as a child in France had put him in and out of hospitals. His schooling was interrupted, and he remained slow most of his life. In 1942, Yvonne sent him to the progressive Clark School in New England, where his learning skills improved. Later, he was able to join the U.S. Army, where he became a military policeman.

Frank Coty's story is brief and tragic. While in the military police, he fell for the daughter of a Japanese bartender at the canteen. Her name was Akiko, which she said meant "September," but Frank called her "June" because he liked this name better. Frank and Akiko married, and he took her to Alaska to finish out his duty. They came home to Yvonne's houses on the east coast of Virginia and Connecticut. This became difficult for them because of the prejudice against the Japanese people after the war. Ultimately, they lived in an apartment building that Frank bought in San Francisco. After suffering repeated insults in the elevator there, Akiko begged to go to Hawaii to live. After all, they could afford it. Frank bought a fabulous house on a cliff in Honolulu. Doris Duke's house was next door. It thrilled Frank to be recognized as a Coty and to live in such a neighborhood. The couple then adopted two Eurasian children, a boy and a girl. Despite all that, Akiko remained insecure and Frank began to drink heavily. Akiko filed for divorce and won a good deal of Frank's resources. Then she and the children moved to Kyoto, where Akiko's family lived. Frank died soon after, at age fifty-six of a heart attack. Mike and I had visited the family in Hawaii in 1963 and were deeply saddened by the later turn of events.

Romier in Vichy France

Lucien Romier had continued to lead *Le Figaro* during Yvonne's ownership and Cotnareanu's involvement. After their departure for America as the war got under way, he, like many intellectuals and conservative Frenchmen, supported Pierre Laval and Maréchal Philippe Pétain at Vichy, bent on saving what was left of France. Romier remained loyal to Pétain and was, in effect, his first councilor, his intimate friend, the only man whom Pétain could trust. "Throughout this period Romier was independent in his thoughts and work," Cotnareanu said. Although Romier was an intimate of Pétain and worked on behalf of the French at Vichy, the Gestapo put him on a list of Frenchmen to be arrested in January of 1944, because of constant marked hostility to the Germans. He died of a heart attack on the night of January 5, 1944, at age fifty-nine, under questioning by the Gestapo. It has been reported that Pétain could have saved him, but, apparently, Pétain did not see the list or know of the arrest until after Romier was dead.

Had Romier survived the Gestapo interrogation, his decisions probably would have motivated the French of the postwar era to accuse him of being a collaborator. The posthumous collection of his papers available for study enlightens scholarship today on the difficult problems that well-educated and honorable men of a conservative bent wrestled with in Vichy France.

Cotnareanu Seeks American Entry into the War

Across the Atlantic, in America, Yvonne and Léon Cotnareanu knew little of what was happening in either occupied or "free" France between 1940 and 1945. Nevertheless, from the moment they set foot in North America, Léon embarked on his literary efforts to convince the United States to enter the war against Germany. In New York, he began a book that he probably finished in Canada. *The Alternative* was published by Dodd, Mead and Company in 1941. It commences with the family's 1940 arrival in the United States. "As I landed from the clipper at La Guardia Field, New York, after having lived through the nightmare that accompanied and followed the French military disaster, it astonished me when I realized that only twenty-four hours' flight distance away a great nation lived 'at peace' in a political climate so different from its Atlantic neighbors and apparently unmarred by a foreboding sense of what is to come—a quiet comparable to the ominous calm of nature preceding a hurricane. On the way from [the airport] to New York, one scene struck me: next to our car there rolled along an open sport coupe in which two young men, twenty-two or twenty-four years old, seemed to 'enjoy life' while their radio was playing beautiful jazz. Only then did I realize that in over a year this was the first time that I had seen men—young men—not in a uniform. . . . At that moment, I could not help thinking of the youth in Europe, everywhere under the colors, far from their homes and families and friends, constantly exposed to the dangers of violent death, of illness, of hunger. And all these people here, men and women and children, walking about without that anguishing and terrorized look of the men and women and children over there, fleeing the murderous bombardments from the air. Are we really only twenty-four hours from a Europe harrowed by a hideous war let loose by the incredible ambition and mad visions of an unscrupulous man?"

Cotnareanu made an effort to explain why the U.S. should intervene in World War II to save the world from German domination. He also explained how it was that the French waited too long to act against Hitler. The French press, for one, had failed the people: "The French press, like its readers, was very much less news-minded than the English or the American press. For the French press, comment was the main business; I would say that most of the editorial expenses of the French newspapers went for commentators and columnists. No newspaper in France, or even in Great Britain, however, can offer any comparison with the important American newspapers, the *New York Times,* the *Herald Tribune* or the *Christian Science Monitor.*"

Like François Coty before him, Cotnareanu objected to France's treatment in the Treaty of Versailles and the gratuitous opportunity that Germany had to rearm.

CHAPTER 18

Coty Inc.: Winnie Awards

This year the needles of Paris have been suspended, temporarily we hope, by the fortunes of war. . . . What will America do without Paris fashion?

Edna Woolman Chase, *Vogue,* 1940

When Grover Whalen became CEO of Coty in the 1940s, he joined Benjamin Levy, who had served the company since its American inception, about 1910. The two men ran Coty worldwide out of New York. As onetime general manager of Wanamakers, Whalen was suited for the job at Coty. He had chaired the World's Fair in New York in 1939 and received accolades for his success. When the handsome pavilion reserved for American fashion design at the fair remained vacant, Whalen filled the empty space with Coty products. As a result, the art-deco structure with a two-tiered octagonal dome was known as the Coty Building. Marketing was Whalen's strong suit. Purportedly, it was he who introduced the ticker-tape parade to New York City.

As soon as Yvonne and Léon and the two boys were able to return to New York from Canada, Léon settled in as chairman of the board of Coty Inc. The factory and executive offices occupied a block of leased buildings in the heart of midtown Manhattan, on Twelfth Avenue between Fifty-fifth and Fifty-sixth streets. Philippe Cotnareanu, now Cortney, was made president of Coty Inc.

During World War II, Eleanor Seymour Lambert, active in *Women's Wear Daily* from its inception, worked with Whalen. The two of them conceived the idea of the Coty American Fashion Critics' Awards, with Whalen utilizing his penchant for lavish spectacle to promote their novel idea. This concept would have appealed to François Coty, who had created perfumes as signatures of the great fashion houses.

During the war years, the prestigious annual Coty Awards promoted the ascendancy of an independent American fashion world. At the same time, the awards were a marketing mechanism to associate Coty perfume and products with the fashion industry, suggesting those Coty products were as essential to great style as fashionable clothing. This, too, would seem to have been inspired by François himself.

The Coty Award-winning fashions were displayed in the Metropolitan Museum of Art, placing fashion in the wider context of art and design. This continued François's tradition of combining art with fashion and beauty products. The awards also employed radio advertising in New York; François had been in the forefront of this movement in France. The Coty Awards also encouraged window displays as a "vehicle for stimulating consumption and to familiarize the captivated consumer with the latest wares." Elaborate window displays and exhibit cases had always been a priority for François Coty. In his day, exquisite presentation and attention to detail were bestowed on everything from the product itself to its packaging and display. Lambert and Whalen were able to build on this achievement with longtime Coty colleague Jean Despres, who had moved to the United States from Paris.[1]

Coty Inc.'s American Fashion Critics' Awards sought out and promoted original American talent in fashion during a time when French fashion leadership was unavailable because of the war. Ironically, Coty, the French perfume company, caused American designers and manufacturers to stop depending on French ideas and leadership in the fashion world. For example, Stanley Marcus, cofounder of Neiman Marcus, in the 1930s had stated, "The *Normandie* shuttled so many American buyers back and forth between France and New York that the ship was familiarly known as the Seventh Avenue Express." Coty's awards gave credit to America's own designers and advertised their original work. According to Bernadine Taub in *Women's Wear Daily* on March 4, 1968, the Coty Awards "empowered American fashion designers by granting them public recognition that resulted in greater authority and creative control vis à vis the manufacturers who produced the clothes and the retailers that sold them."[2]

The Coty Awards carried generous prizes: $1,000 and a trophy by sculptor Malvina Hoffman for first place; $500 and a plaque by Cartier for Special Awards. The Eleanor Lambert Archive notes, "What began in February of 1943 as a small private function, with a dinner and fashion show of the winners' designs, grew to a major yearly event and gala fashion show of past and present winners with a guest roster of dignitaries from the worlds of art and politics."[3] The first presentation in 1943, held at the Metropolitan Museum of Art, was followed in subsequent years with galas at Gracie Mansion, New

York City Hall, and the Waldorf Astoria. National coverage of the Coty Awards ran the full range of radio and print media to an extent not previously experienced in this country.

Following the criteria for innovation set by François Coty, the awards were a mark of distinction. Hall of Fame winner Pauline Trigère said, "The Coty Awards were the beginning of recognition for anyone who designed in America."[4]

The Coty Awards became so influential in the New York fashion and design world that they were referred to as the Winnies, an allusion to the better half of the Oscar of movie fame. A Winnie was the fashion equivalent of a Hollywood Oscar. The Coty Awards were still one of the major yearly events in the New York fashion world in the 1960s. Although they lasted until 1984, they waned in importance after the sale of Coty Inc. to Pfizer in 1963.

In 1963, I was excited about going to my first Winnie Award ceremony with Mike. We arrived from France just in time. I knew that the occasion had the fashion world agog and that the press was poised to interview anyone who was beautifully dressed. My long-awaited pregnancy was just beginning, but I could still squeeze into the heavenly original Patou gown in a delicious shade of fuchsia, made to fit like a glove, that I had chosen in Paris with Yvonne's approval.

Jean Despres, our company's executive vice president, walked down the aisle with me to our reserved seats. Suddenly, I realized that I couldn't possibly sit down. The fabulous dress that I adored was of such heavy satin that the swirl, at least six inches deep, that started at the waist and curled like a snail around the back of the dress, was like a bodysuit. I could hardly consider sitting on this batch of satin and creating a huge rosette on my derrière. What would I look like? I was horrified; but as I was contemplating this, Jean made everything much worse. At six feet two, he was tall for a Frenchman and had a voice like a foghorn. "What is that awful odor? What perfume are you wearing?" he blared. I had purposely chosen Coty's Emeraude, since it was very heady and I thought it quite suitable for this dress and the stunning stole of the same fabric. Jean said, "Oh, lord, you smell like a Chinese whore. Your body oil does not bring out the best in this fragrance. Don't ever wear it again."

I could have fallen through the floor. What had happened to my beautiful night in New York as Madame Coty? Life had entered into the unreal, but so be it. I loved the show and Mike loved my shimmering Marilyn Monroe look.

Coty Inc. Expands Its Cosmetics Business

By 1955, Jean Despres, backed by Benjamin Levy and Léon Cotnareanu, saw mass marketing as the future of Coty Inc. This was logical, because François Coty himself was the first to perceive that all classes of women worldwide wanted to use cosmetics. Of course, the company expected to continue its sales of prestige products at the same time.

For some reason, the Coty organization in New York declined to embrace the medium of television. François Coty had always been on the cusp of innovation and would have turned over in his grave at this decision. Coty himself had used creative marketing techniques to attract buyers for his fragrances—spilling a bottle at Les Grands Magasins du Louvre and dragging sausages through small rural villages in southern France in the first years of the twentieth century.

Still, fifty years later in the United States, Coty Inc. was transforming cosmetics sales into a giant business, one of the biggest on the planet. The volume of sales was staggering.

As Coty publicist Bernard Lee wrote, Jean Despres also developed the import order, a special opportunity for large stores. He arranged irrevocable import orders of goods shipped directly from Paris at a substantial discount for big department stores that signed orders for $5,000 or more worth of product. "Many of the best stores signed and benefited, such as Neiman Marcus, Bullocks, Filenes, J. L. Hudson, Joseph Horne, Marshall Field and others. This encouraged store advertising and promotions, resulting in increased sales. Nothing like the modern boutiques existed, where one area of the store featured one brand, but volume prompted a fresh approach and [Coty] boutiques were opened at Marshall Field and John Wanamaker to be followed soon by ones in Burdines, Maas Bros., Cohen Bros., Macy's and other leading stores." This started a trend in the United States: cosmetics counters, as we know them today, in the country's top department stores. At the same time, the technique of having demonstrators offer customers a sampling of the product—Coty's original idea in Paris in the 1920s—became widespread in U.S. department stores. "Over 100 girls 'on the line' worked in stores for Coty by 1926, and salaries were generous, $16 a week," Lee wrote. Imagine, almost $3 a day.

In the U.S. during the 1930s, Coty used special events such as Valentine's Day and May Day to arrange elaborate display windows and festive trimmings throughout the various department stores, particularly in the bridal salons. The inspiration was May Day in

A Coty Inc. advertisement in the November 1953 *Women's Home Companion* for Coty's "Cream Powder" compact featured a hat designed by Lilly Daché. (Elizabeth Z. Coty Collection)

France, where everyone presented a sprig of lily of the valley, or *muguet,* to their loved one and received a kiss. Sales for *Muguet des Bois* climbed to over $1 million in the early 1930s.

Another beautiful promotion featured the famous "Coty Girl" in the Lilly Daché hat. It was another in-house project, because Daché was Jean Despres's wife. The Coty Girl appeared in the ads with a dramatic sweep of her black hat, wearing elegant French designer clothes and Coty makeup.

CHAPTER 19

Return to Liberated Paris: 1945

People of France who have lost all, safeguard the dignity that these terrible times have conferred upon a fallen nation.

François Mauriac, *Le Figaro*

Yvonne was desperate to return to Paris when the war was over. She did not know whether her son Roland or her oldest grandson Henri were alive. Nor did she know the fate of Christiane, her daughter, or her granddaughter, Rolande, thought to be in Italy. For five long years, she had lived as an American, raising two grandsons and developing the trappings of life as a rich socialite in the United States, but her heart was in France.

Roland and his son Henri had stayed behind in France to support their country. Roland joined the army as an aviator the minute the war broke out, arriving with his own airplane, which was accepted with alacrity since it was much needed. He served under the youngest commandant in the French military, Emile Villomé. War was a good career for Roland, a sportsman whose bravery in international polo, as well as horse and car racing, was recognized but not much appreciated by his family. Roland was captured by the Germans but managed to escape en route to a prison camp in Germany.

After the war, Yvonne, with the paid help of a number of emissaries, located Roland in an army hospital with pneumonia and other complications from his war ordeal. Exactly where he had served remains a mystery, although he did not leave the army until 1947. Both he and Henri were faithful to the ideals of Charles de Gaulle, whom they revered. Family stories circulated about the maquis, or French underground resistance to the German occupation of northern France. However, I never heard anything solid about Roland's role in the maquis. Everyone spoke of him as a fervent Gaullist, but he was a quiet man and never discussed anything political that I know of. This added to his aura of mystery.

Henri Coty did not have his father's luck. Because he was an open supporter of Charles de Gaulle, Henri was judged by the maritime tribunal of Casablanca in 1941 for inciting youth to desertion and for outrageous statements against the chief of state, Pétain. He was sent to maritime prison for three months by the Vichy government. Afterward, he rejoined the underground; there was a resistance unit bearing his name, the Coty Network. Henri worked closely with Jean Moulin until they were both captured. Moulin was caught by Gestapo chief Klaus Barbé and tortured terribly at Caluire near Lyon, after which he died on a train taking him to Germany. Henri was captured in 1943 at Toulouse, where he was repeatedly beaten and humiliated by torture under Klaus Barbé. He spent jail time there and at Lyon, Bordeaux, and Biarritz before his deportation to Germany, but the Coty Network, eventually based out of Cannes, remained active throughout the war while Henri was in prison.

Henri Coty wrote of his long ordeal: "Men, women, and children of twenty-two nationalities, of all tendencies, of all confessions—from Jews, resistance fighters, and others opposed to the Nazi regime— have been deported, martyred, starved, and are dead of exhaustion, gassed, burned. Arrested at the end of 1943, I passed through different French prisons. I arrived at Compiègne, from which I was sent to Buchenwald in January of 1944. On March 10, 1944, we proceeded to [Harzungen, then] Dora." He became head nurse there among 3,000 detainees. His fellow prisoners included the German communists who were, with their leader, Ernst Thaelmann, killed by the SS. Henri, like some other French detainees at Harzungen, Dora-Ellrich, and Buchenwald, became part of a Committee of French Interests. Henri said that he was inspired by Col. Frédéric-Henri Manhès and Marcel Paul, who gave to the desperate prison community "a surge of energy, courage, and solidarity."

He noted, "At Harzungen, for a young resistant like myself, men like André Clavé, André Schock, Dr. [Jan] Cespiva [a Czech democrat], and the Hungarian rabbi gave us examples of courage, human dignity, and dedication that inspired in us the desire and the will to equal them and to stand together."

Henri described the evacuation of Harzungen and Dora-Ellrich in March and April of 1945, when 8,000 detainees left on foot and 1,800 sick men were loaded onto a train. About 1,000 of these detainees were dead before their arrival at Bergen-Belsen. Henri survived and described the new camp as "absolute horror"—this from a man who had been in a number of death camps.

On April 15, 1945, the English arrived to liberate Bergen-Belsen. Henri, who spoke English, was called, along with Roger Latry, to explain the conditions of the camp and plan a way to save the survivors of what once had been 60,000 detainees. "[I remain] indebted to Major Chapman and Capt. John Turner, who forced the SS officers and the soldiers of the Wehrmacht to bury the dead (19,000 cadavers were blocking the streets of the camp before the English arrived)," Henri later wrote. "Within a few days, after arresting Joseph Kramer, the SS commandant of Bergen-Belsen, and Irma Greese, head of the SS for the women's camp, the ninety Englishmen departed to continue fighting the war, which was not yet over. They left food for the starving occupants remaining in the camp charged with the difficult task of taking care of those too weak to leave." Henri managed to survive there until the war was over. He returned to Paris, where he discovered that his grandmother and younger brothers were in New York. He sailed for New York as soon as he could make arrangements through Yvonne's banker, André Cheveneau, at the Morgan Bank in Paris.

Immediately after Paris was liberated, there were whispers about Christiane Coty having had her head shaved in public for associating with German officers. Whether this occurred or was a rumor, I do not know. Christiane had worked all her life to be worthy of her father, making a good first marriage to Paul Dubonnet, whom she had divorced after their daughter, Rolande, was born.

Divorced again, now from William Saurin, after World War II, Christiane moved to Calvi, where she bought La Casarella—the Maison Rose—and oversaw construction of a major tourist hotel for Calvi, the Grand Hotel. It opened in 1948, featuring a state-of-the-art kitchen and restaurant. Christiane's presence in Calvi brought many international jet-set members to Corsica and her hotel. She also restored her great-grandmother's flat in the Vieux Port of Marseille.

Yvonne learned that Avenue Raphael had been the site of major events and decisions during the occupation. On the granite steps of the elegant townhouse that he had taken over, German general Hans von Boineburg had often greeted emissaries from Hitler. Boineburg was commander of Gross Paris, thirty square miles, for a critical eighteen months. While he lived at Avenue Raphael, the first German commander in Paris pondered the plan he had been ordered to prepare "for the widest destruction possible of Paris in case of an enemy assault." After the July 20, 1944, plot to get rid of Hitler, Boineburg, drinking Coty wine at Avenue Raphael, agonized over what to do. He ordered his German troops to arrest the 1,200 men of the SS and the Gestapo stationed in Paris.

Hitler's harsh voice often rasped through the radio loudspeakers at Avenue Raphael. There, Boineburg waited glumly for his own dismissal and punishment. On August 3, 1944, it arrived. He was suspended from his functions as military governor of Paris. August 9 heralded the arrival at Avenue Raphael of his replacement, Gen. Dietrich von Choltitz, a Prussian from a long line of military leaders in Silesia.

Von Choltitz sat on the green velvet Louis XV chairs in Yvonne's salon with six anxious fellow senior officers. There, the new military commander politely rejected the Avenue Raphael quarters. Von Choltitz's first order in Paris was to the corporal beside him. "Prepare for me a bedroom at the Meurice." Turning to Boineburg, he said, "For the days ahead, Herr General, I shall need a headquarters, not a residence." Boineburg watched von Choltitz's Horch automobile disappear past the full-leafed chestnut trees of the gardens, down toward the Bois de Boulogne. He said to his aide, "The good days of Paris are finished." The previous German command had enjoyed their luxurious quarters at Coty's mansion too much.

Yvonne and Léon returned to Avenue Raphael in 1945. Surprise turned to gratitude when they realized that the German staff left it in good condition. Surely to Boineburg's relief, Gen. Dietrich von Choltitz had not only saved Paris from a Hitler-ordered burning after meeting with Mayor Pierre-Charles Taittinger, probably in Yvonne's house, but he had preserved the Coty estate in Paris. Taittinger, one of François Coty's old conservative cohorts, had admonished von Choltitz, "Often it is given a general to destroy, rarely to preserve. If you do not burn Paris, you will be able to say, 'One day I could have destroyed all this, and I preserved it as a gift to humanity.'" This the German did, though at great cost to his future in Germany.[1]

When Léon Cotnareanu returned to the Coty offices, he found that tragedies had taken place near the Cité des Parfums during the occupation. Mont Valérien, on the heights above Suresnes, was a prison where the Germans incarcerated Frenchmen. Between the summer of 1940 and August of 1944, 4,500 Frenchmen had been executed in the courtyard, perhaps within the hearing of the employees at the Cité des Parfums. On Assumption Sunday in 1944, deportations to Buchenwald took place from the Pantin freight station, where Coty SA shipped crated cosmetics every day. French Jews were brought to Pantin from Drancy, and other French Resistance prisoners were herded from prisons at Fresnes, near Mont Valérien, and Romainville.

Faithful Pierre and his wife, Anna, had remained at Avenue Raphael throughout the war and the occupation of Paris. Delighted to have their kind mistress return, they continued to work for her until her death. Their work would be simple for a number of years because they remained in Paris while Léon and Yvonne retained houses, hotel rooms, farms, and apartments in the United States. Just after the war, Yvonne's primary residence became Geneva. This move was made for tax reasons. Léon devised the plan. To become a legal resident of Switzerland, she could not leave that country for two years unless she wanted to pay taxes in three countries— France, the United States, and Switzerland. Her absence allowed Léon free rein in Paris and the United States to plunder François Coty's properties and acquire mistresses as had his predecessor.

After Roland left the military in 1947, he resumed his playboy habits. He had gambled throughout his adulthood, and Yvonne always said the green tables that attracted Roland so strongly contributed to his ruin. Before World War II, within a radius of a quarter-mile of the Madeleine, over twenty gambling clubs lured the well-heeled men of Paris. One gambling-industry publication stated that "the son of one of the wealthiest businessmen of Paris tried to dissipate his father's fortune" in those clubs. After the war, Yvonne said he gambled incessantly, in Deauville at the winter casino and in Nice in the summers. The family was well acquainted with Monsieur Blanc, who owned the casino at Monte Carlo, since François had bought the Château de Sainte-Hélène from him. Blanc had popularized the historic game of roulette in the twentieth century. During his last winter of gambling, Roland lost the equivalent of $600,000 in two weeks in Deauville.

Between nights of gambling, Roland found time to meet a divorcée, Antoinette Mouchet, who had a young son, Claude Mouchet. Antoinette and Roland were married. Their only son, Yvon Coty, was born in 1950 but they were soon separated. Roland continued gambling. Over time, it became his undoing.

Yvonne had little patience with Roland. "None of his condition was necessary. He could have come with us to New York and worked in Coty USA. Instead he stayed in France." She was brokenhearted by Roland's downward spiral. To assuage her pain, she began to help raise his eleven-year-old son Yvon, just as she had done for two of his three sons by Marguerite Charlot. Finally, Roland's eighty-year-old mother had him legally declared "incompetent" not long before his death in 1963. She was very brave to go to court against her only son. She must have known it was too late for Roland, but she could save her grandchildren's inheritance.

In the early 1960s, when Roland became my father-in-law, he was living back in Tours with Renée, his former nurse in the army hospital where he had found himself at war's end. Renée was so tranquil and so successful at restoring his health that he wanted never to leave her, though he made exceptions for an occasional stroll to the neighborhood bar where "the boys" met.

After the house at Avenue Raphael was sold, Léon and Yvonne moved to Hotel Plaza Athenée. From her strategic headquarters there, Yvonne oversaw the creation of her apartment on the Rond-Point des Champs Elysées. Yvonne proceeded to design an exquisite five-story residence, hiring dozens of decorators, assistants, buyers, and consultants including, as usual, Jansy.

Yvonne Coty-Cotnareanu, photographed by Studio Harcourt, Paris. (Elizabeth Z. Coty Collection)

Newspaper Developments

After the fall of Paris, *Le Figaro* had been set up in Lyon. It continued to be published there until the Germans took control of Free France in 1942 and suppressed it. The newspaper did not publish again until World War II was over. Working with Pierre Brisson in postwar Paris, Léon restored *Le Figaro*'s offices, and the newspaper resumed publication in its old quarters as quickly as possible.

The *London Evening Standard* of February 17, 1950, clarified the newsworthy affair of the future of *Le Figaro*. It reported that Jean Prouvost, of the Lille woolen manufacturing family and onetime minister of information, had bought half the shares of *Le Figaro* from Yvonne, who owned 97 percent of its shares. Brisson would continue as editor. Prouvost intended to run his weekly *Paris Match,* with its circulation of 200,000, along with *Le Figaro*. Wresting *Le Figaro* shares from the longtime Coty interests was a big coup for Prouvost, who before the war had been one of the most powerful newspaper figures in France with *Paris-Soir*.

Pierre Brisson died in 1964 at age sixty-eight. After that, the Cotnareanus seemed to lose heart for the battle to save *Le Figaro* for

A homage to Pierre Brisson was held at the Paris city hall. Brisson was a notable conservative intellectual and editor of *Le Figaro* at various times during François Coty's ownership and afterward. (Elizabeth Z. Coty Collection)

Léon's own purposes. Léon's retinue of lawyers toiled on Yvonne's behalf, but in 1965, she lost her long legal fight and Prouvost became *Le Figaro's* majority stockholder. Thus ended François Coty's venture into French journalism that tracked along with his quest for political power.

In 1945, a man named Robert Hersant was jailed for collaborating with the Germans. In 1975, *Le Figaro* would be sold to Hersant, for 75 million francs. The paper became one of the properties controlled by his holding company, Socpresse. In 1980, the conglomerate merged *Le Figaro* with *L'Aurore.* A year later, Socpresse sold a 20 percent stake in the newspaper to the Carlyle group, a private equity firm that usually invested in defense contractors and that counted American president George H. W. Bush among its directors. The following year, Carlyle sold its shares, and in 2004, the Dassault Group, the major French defense contractor, bought *Le Figaro.* This small history would indicate that although fewer people read newspapers, they are considered powerful tools in world affairs, just as Coty thought.

CHAPTER 20

The Next Generations

Perfume is a love affair with one's self.

François Coty

Back in the United States, Michel Coty settled into Yvonne's house in Madison, Connecticut and commuted to and from Yale University in nearby New Haven. He was a C student, which he assured his grandmother was "a gentleman's average, and only proper." At the Madison Beach Club, Mike met a sophisticated blonde named Elise Kullman whose mother was a Swedish beauty and whose father, Charles Kullman, was the leading Wagnerian tenor at the Metropolitan Opera. As soon as Mike graduated from Yale in 1953, they married. This alliance provided the Coty family with further American connections, and Elise's father was gracious enough to sing occasionally at Yvonne's grand soirées when she was in residence at Madison.

Mike registered for the army when he finished Yale, not wanting to accept the commission as a navy officer that his family had arranged. That meant three years in the military. Mike said, "After discipline in several Catholic schools and my New England boarding school, Taft, I had had quite enough regimentation to last a lifetime. I was not military material." He was advised to choose Thule, Greenland, the most remote military post of the United States and the bleakest place for duty. Mike said, "I'm no fool. If I signed up for Thule, I would only have to stay in the service for nine months. I quickly learned the Morse code and was eligible to become the radio operator. This kept me busy, and I knew that if I could keep the guys in touch with the outside world, they would be my buddies." He added, "Never mind the fact that I was almost swept off the safety walkway by an ice storm. That goes with the territory."

Nine months later Mike returned to the United States to meet his baby girl, Yvonne Elise Coty, Yvonne Coty-Cotnareanu's first American great-grandchild, a tiny lovable baby of whom he was always proud. Mike and Elise, with their little girl, settled in Madison, staying at the seaside house of Elise's father.

Mike entered law school at Cornell, but now he had family responsibilities. He dropped out to become a salesman for Coty Inc., traveling far and wide, using his good looks and engaging personality to enhance the Coty presence in department stores across the land. However, he couldn't keep up with the Madison social life at the same time. It was too much; the couple grew apart and, after five years of trying, they divorced.

Runaway Marriage: 1960

When I interviewed at Coty Inc. for the position of product manager of fragrances in 1959, Léon Cotnareanu was chairman of the board of Coty Inc. and Coty SA. After my training at Revlon by Charles Revson, whose rough manner of speaking was difficult to follow, but who was a brilliant instructor in marketing, I was ready for a management position. I had also graduated from my personal course in how to avoid the boss's misplacement of his hands. I certainly knew that no women held upper-level positions at Coty even though the company was owned by a woman. Eleanor Lambert had long been a consultant for Coty, but she had never been a Coty employee.

Having applied for the position, I was told that Mr. Cotnareanu would call me. When I went home to dress for a cocktail party that evening, the Coty secretary called to inform me that the chairman was leaving town but wanted to interview me before he left, expecting me to rush down to the factory headquarters on Fifty-fifth and Twelfth Avenue. I quickly finished dressing for cocktails and grabbed a taxi to meet Mr. Cotnareanu, knowing that if I got the job, I would be the first woman to become a product manager at Coty. He chatted briefly with me while glancing at my plunging neckline as I clutched my little black mink around my shoulders. He smiled lasciviously and suggested we continue the interview during luncheon the next day at the Oak Room of the Plaza Hotel. Suddenly, he changed his mind and decided to hire me on the spot. "Naturally you have excellent references. Charles Revson was most complimentary. He was sorry to see you leave Revlon." I was fortunate to have worked with Charles, as he insisted on being called, even if he was the toughest man I had ever met. He considered me a Southern belle with the tiny bit of accent I could not shake. My reasons for leaving Revlon were obvious. Surely someone in New York would make me feel more comfortable as a woman in my career. Yet here I was again in the same spot with Mr. Cotnareanu.

Léon knew that Dorothy McCann, wife of the chairman of the board of McCann-Erickson, had trained me there, at the world's largest advertising agency. An exceptional woman executive and film producer, she also produced first-rate radio shows that won awards for her clients, who included Xavier Cougat and the Marx Brothers. She also produced the "Death Valley Days" TV series. I had left McCann when that amazing pioneering twosome, Dorothy and her husband, "Boss" McCann, were killed in an auto accident.

In my new position at Coty Inc., I walked into my office and the first person I saw was the reincarnation of François Coty. The instant electricity seemed to cause a trembling of the building on Twelfth Avenue, as far as I was concerned. The François Coty lookalike laughed when I asked him to repeat his name later that day, and I responded flippantly, "I'll just call you Joe Jones." He knew I was teasing, and the next day when he assured me that he was Michel Coty, the company founder's grandson, we were already smitten.

We worked together as product managers, trying unsuccessfully for all of three days to remain aloof and businesslike. Within two months, Mike left for Paris to tell his grandmother that he wanted to remarry, after being divorced for only a year. Yvonne thought that another American girl would be "risky," but she never opposed anything her Michie wanted. He combined the trip to see his grandmother with visits to various Coty plants. He wrote to me from the Kurstadt Hotel in Wiesbaden to say that he was next visiting the Coty plant in Mainz. There was no time to go to the new plant in Michaelstadt, which, he joked in the letter, was "Mike's Town" in English. He also reported that the market in Germany for Coty products was quite good.

Our secret runaway marriage in January 1960, within three months of setting eyes on one another, took place at the justice of the peace office in Goshen, New York. In New York City, we then retained our own apartments, but we needed one for us to live in. We installed three telephone lines in "our" apartment and adjusted the rings so that the wrong person did not answer the phone.

During those early times, Mike and I set our goal: we wanted to be the reincarnation of François and Yvonne Coty. We felt there was nothing we couldn't do. We lived so much with the memories and accomplishments of François that we hoped to recreate his most prestigious, high-end products again. We wanted to carry out what young Yvonne and François had begun, and being romantics, we were sure it was possible if we worked together.

It may have been a trick of the mind for me to feel so close to François, who had been gone all those years and whom I had never met, but I felt that he guided me through my work. His well-known marketing treatments were frequently solutions to the problems that I encountered in the fragrance line. In 1960, I enjoyed working with my new, secret husband, utilizing my training on behalf of the famous François Coty, whose memory I revered.

A board meeting not long after we returned from our secret runaway marriage was quite an experience, since no one, of course, knew that we were married, and we needed to keep it that way so that I would not lose my job. At the meeting, Philippe Cortney instructed me, as product manager of the fragrance division, which already constituted 60 percent of Coty's gross sales, on how to improve sales. When Mike described how he could improve the new products division, Philippe created a scene to indicate that none of the Cotys had any knowledge of business. To our surprise, Philippe stood up, removed his shoe, and banged it on the corner of the board table. I was seething in my chair at this treatment of my husband. Fortunately, we had allies on the board, and they eased the tension. This was my Khrushchev-style introduction to Coty's executive-boardroom culture, soon after the Russian premier had shocked the public by acting in the same manner.

We were getting away with our hilarious deception about our marriage, but not for long. Within three months, mention of our secret marriage appeared in Dorothy Kilgallen's New York gossip column. This altered my career plans immediately, since married executives could not work together at Coty, according to the rules that Léon had established. I no longer went to the office.

Meeting Yvonne

After our runaway marriage was made public, Mike was given time for us to visit Yvonne, who was living in Paris while Léon remained in the United States. The end of 1960 was approaching, and I could no longer put off the difficult decision of what I would wear for my first meeting with Mike's grandmother in Paris. It had to be the perfect outfit, as Yvonne Coty (we never referred to her by her current last name) was one of the fashion icons of Paris and had been for many years. She was known never to leave her home wearing anything but a Lanvin, Dior, or Chanel original. "What am I going to wear to meet this person who will be vital to my happiness?" I thought. Suddenly it came to me that she had been a milliner, and

Roland Coty and his three sons, Henri, Mike, and Frank. (Elizabeth Z. Coty Collection)

since I couldn't afford an expensive outfit before departing the U.S., I engaged a creative hat designer in New York to make a small black silk velvet skullcap. She surrounded it with a beautiful silver sable, à la Jackie Kennedy. This enabled me to afford a simple black suit and accessories and consider myself well dressed.

Upon our arrival at Rond-Point in the middle of Paris, I had to walk up a long flight of stairs while Yvonne was waiting at the top, observing me as I moved along. Her daughter, Christiane, stood behind her, with Anna, the housekeeper, towering over them both.

I studied Yvonne. She was a startling figure with her beautifully coiffed titian hair, flawless skin, and a Lanvin size-ten figure. Even at age seventy-eight, her olive-green eyes were penetrating. She smiled when we met, and I stumbled over what to call her, asking what she would prefer. She responded, "Yvonne or perhaps Midou." I queried, "Midou?" She smirked at her daughter, apparently mocking her; Midou was a pet name Christiane, as a child, had given her mother. Seeing Christiane's frown, I knew that I had made an enemy of her with my first words to her mother. Yvonne had sliced her own daughter in the back by offering me use of the name Midou. Mike was smiling as he realized what was passing among the three women, although he wanted to laugh out loud. Meanwhile, "Midou"

Yves Michel Coty and Elizabeth Zerkel Coty aboard ship going to Paris in 1960, after their marriage in New York. (Elizabeth Z. Coty Collection)

graciously mentioned during our twilight meeting at her muraled bar that I had made a charming picture when I arrived. I breathed a big sigh; Mike smiled and looked smug, as it was important to him that I make the right impression on his grandmother.

The first event awaiting Mike and me was a formal dinner party in our honor. Green-coated butlers stood behind each guest at Yvonne's dinner table, their white gloves seeming to slither before me, bringing course after course, each one previewed in print on cards engraved with Yvonne's insignia. These menus were set on individual holders in front of each guest. I ate the fish listed, along with many other delicious dishes whose French translation escaped me. I learned later that Yvonne, being quite a gourmet, always had menus printed for her parties, and she personally supervised the selection and preparation of the food.

I carefully rehearsed a French phrase to show my appreciation of the lovely dinner party in our honor. Back in my room, I had a handwritten list of French words. I said to Yvonne, "C'est délicieux, votre poison." Eyebrows lifted, and there followed an awkward moment before I cringed and Mike started laughing. This sent the small group around us into gales of laughter. What had I done? I had said the French word for "poison," which is the same as it is in English, instead of the French word for "fish"—poisson.

Our second night in Paris was extraordinary. I witnessed my new grandmother hauled off in the cage of a police "paddy wagon." The experience seemed unreal. News of the anti-French uprising in Algeria had reached Paris, and people were parading arm in arm up and down the street shouting, "Algérie Française!" ("French Algeria!") The four of us, in the meantime, were leaving Yvonne's five-story apartment for dinner at her favorite oyster restaurant, Chez Resche, a simple eating place for workers. Patrons ascended a long, narrow staircase to a plain room with wooden benches on either side of bare wood tables. It was not a place you would expect a gracious French woman wrapped in her sable coat to patronize.

The conscientious French police stopped us in front of Rond-Point, to enquire who we were. When Granné stated her name, they were astonished. She was the person they were looking for: the majority owner of Le Figaro, *an unpopular daily at the time because of its editorials about the Algerian situation. The police lifted her into the back of the van. I added to the excitement by crying. Mike tried to reason with the officers, but it was an impossible situation. As they drove off, Yvonne called to him through the wire, "Michie!" We grabbed a taxi and followed as fast as we could.*

When we reached the police station, Léon promptly made telephone calls to everyone he could think of, from her lawyers to the premier of France. The situation, considering her advanced age, was ghastly. Surprisingly, though, the calmest person at the police station was Yvonne. Her sense of humor and her grace had once more carried her through tense moments. To Mike and me, who were ignorant about the French political climate, Algeria was nothing compared to the attempted incarceration of the richest woman in France. She was free within the hour, and we taxied back to ascend the long stairway to the oyster restaurant.

Dinnertime at Rond-Point took place in the huge dining salon with Yvonne and Jeff, her pug dog, who was peaceful and docile only with his mistress. Otherwise, he chewed at everyone's heels. Family members were observed wearing Band-Aids following

Yvonne's dinners. Yvonne never knew; she marched ahead into her regal dining room each evening saying, "Come along, Jeff." Little did she realize everyone was shaking the snarling pug off pant legs and precious stockings, not to mention bleeding skin. Jeff received many a clandestine kick when Yvonne wasn't looking.

Roland Coty's second wife, Antoinette Mouchet, was a lovely, chic Parisian blonde who was well informed about Parisian customs and proved a great help to me. When I met her during that first trip to Paris, she was living, apart from Roland, in an apartment with their ten-year-old son, Yvon Coty, when he was not away at boarding school. Antoinette wanted her son to see Granné often, so when he was home, she brought Yvon to lunch at Rond-Point every day. Before luncheon, Granné frequently chastised her behind the scenes on various subjects. At such times, all other family members present would shuffle awkwardly out of earshot. Poor, beautiful Antoinette's anxiety resulted in the habit of self-defacement, scratching her arms with long fingernails until they bled.

These luncheons were difficult for me since the only French I knew was "Il fait beau," meaning, "It's beautiful today." My new husband was busy reintroducing himself at the headquarters of the family perfume business and reacquainting himself with its factories and

Henri Coty, Mike Coty, Henri's wife, and Frank Coty in a Paris nightclub about 1960. (Elizabeth Z. Coty Collection)

operations, so I had to fend for myself, mutely, at many of Granné's luncheons with Antoinette and Yvon. Luckily, the weather was quite "beau" that winter, making our six-month stay at Rond-Point a little more palatable.

Christiane always arrived in time for the cocktail hour, which had become a daily ritual at Rond-Point in postwar France. She had a new "friend" following her divorces from Paul Dubonnet and William Saurin, whom we called the Sausage King.

Marcel Laurent, Roland's pilot-mechanic, was yet another

Henri dances with his wife in Paris, about 1960. (Elizabeth Z. Coty Collection)

observer of the continuing family melodrama. Among the grandsons, he earned the nickname "the dog walker," which was one of his duties. He needed more Band-Aids than anyone else in the family because Christiane also owned a pug dog.

Roland, banished from Yvonne's house, arrived in Paris with our wedding present charmingly wrapped in blue paper with gold stars on it to match the painted china tea set inside. The pattern was gold on the inside and dark blue on the outside, bordered with gold stars, something one might find in a dollar store today. Imagine this, from the son of the onetime richest man in France.

Roland was a gambler who had always lost, at the tables and perhaps in life. But he was a very sweet man. We were so truly happy to have Mike's father travel to Paris to meet us that we were thrilled with the gift. We all laughed, and he knew then that we understood. The following year, his mother would go to court to have him judged "incompetent" so that he could not handle money, except for his small allowance.

My favorite possession is a brass, five-franc coin, worth two or three pennies in those days, that Mike's father took out of his pocket and gave to me that day when I first met him. He told me to put it on the gold charm bracelet I was wearing, in remembrance of the moment. "Here, daughter, I want you to have something valuable from your old dad as a memory of this occasion," he said. It remains on my bracelet, mingled with other souvenirs of the rest of my first trip to France to meet the Coty family.

Yvonne read one day when I was in Paris with Mike in 1961 that a famous actress from Romania was giving her last performance in Paris before retiring at eighty-two. She had seen the actress and knew of her beauty, which had fascinated François years before. In fact, Elvire Popesco had become one of the numerous mistresses housed on François's own private floor at Hotel Georges Cinq. It occurred to Yvonne, even knowing of the relationship between the actress and her François, that her grandson Mike and his new bride might enjoy this rare theatrical occasion.

Popesco had ranked with Lillie Langtry and Sarah Bernhardt in the Belle Epoque theater. She had made one movie during François's lifetime, Ma Cousine de Varsovie, in 1931. Perhaps François had financed the movie for her, loving to make his mistresses happy. Tickets for her grand finale were only for the "insiders" of Paris society, and Yvonne Coty-Cotnareanu had no problems arranging seating in the center row. Was it because of François or because of the Romanian connection with Léon?

Roland, Elizabeth, and Mike in Paris, 1960. (Elizabeth Z. Coty Collection)

I shall never forget the evening. Elvire Popesco certainly showed no age and she gave an excellent performance in French. She had fled to France like so many performing artists and painters after the Russian Revolution and the First World War. Popesco had become the Comtesse de Foy by marriage and had conquered the Parisian public with her style and talent. She was called "Queen of the Boulevard" and "Notre Dame of the Theater." I did not know at the time that she had recently played Letizia Bonaparte in a film about the Battle of Austerlitz or that she had starred in over thirty movies--all this in addition to her prolific stage career as a tragedienne. Nor did I now that she had saved Paul Poiret, the couturier and parfumeur, *from terrible financial failure by buying his mansion in Mezy.*

Madame Popesco had been advised we were in the audience and summoned François's grandson and me to her dressing room after the performance. The great Popesco told us she had been François's mistress the longest. Twelve years, she bragged, considering it an honor. "I shall never forget," she assured Mike. "He was a man who asked nothing for himself but who gave love freely and took joy in making me happy and optimistic." I remember exactly what I was wearing: a sleeveless brocade silk dress, dappled with crystals and pearls, and a Cartier bracelet Granné had pitched to me while she was on the ladder in her jewelry room, selecting her own adornment.

During this first visit to Rond-Point, I became fascinated with every aspect of such unimaginable wealth. The jewelry room included a dark-red velvet ladder to reach the hundreds of red-velvet-lined drawers that ran from floor to ceiling. The drawers overflowed with millions of dollars worth of designer jewelry. Boucheron, Chanel, Cartier, Van Cleef, Fabergé, Buccelatti—no prominent designer was ignored. I placed several of Granné's tiaras on my head, and each equaled anything I had seen in the British Royal Crown jewel collection on display at the Tower of London.

One of the most prized possessions that I received from Yvonne was the Romanoff necklace previously owned by Empress Alexandra of Russia. It had fifty-two cabochon emeralds—almost fifty-five carats—on a platinum chain, linked together with alternating spacers of natural pearls and roundels of diamonds. Hanging from the necklace was a pair of square-cut emeralds (two and one-half carats) and a ninety-five-carat Indian-faceted emerald, shaped, as my friends said, like an American football. Its final destiny was the hands of a prominent jeweler who wined and dined my husband to just the right point and who took the piece apart to sell the jewels separately. Who cares about sentiment or heritage, beauty or design?

Le Baron

One weekend in 1962, in response to a phone call from Yvonne in Paris, Mike and I traveled from New York to her farm in Warrenton, Virginia, named Le Baron. Yvonne had told us that she was planning to sell this property. It was already developed in 1812 when George Settle, of Barren County, Kentucky, executed a deed of release to John M. and Edward Settle of Fauquier County, Virginia, acknowledging their purchase of the old home place, "The Cottage." Léon and Yvonne Cotnareanu "of New York and Paris," according to the deed of purchase, bought the estate in 1941 and named it Le Baron. The Cotnareanus visited Le Baron at intervals and entertained extensively there. It was not until 1972 that Mr. and Mrs. George W. Offutt would purchase it and name it Canterbury Farm.

Yvonne had not only purchased a historic house with extensive

Yvonne and Léon with her three grandsons—Frank, Henri, and Mike—in Warrenton, Virginia, in the 1950s. (Elizabeth Z. Coty Collection)

Yvonne and Léon in Warrenton. (Elizabeth Z. Coty Collection)

stables, but she had added nine farms to the property. No matter which view she gazed at through her windows, it was on her property, on both sides of the Rappahannock. From the entrance to the master bedroom on the second floor, one could enjoy a spectacular view of the Virginia countryside. The Charolais cattle no longer grazed there, and the horses and geese had already been sold when we arrived. Yvonne had loved Le Baron, her fourth home in America, because she felt safe there and humbled by the charming warmth of the Southern people. Mike and Frank had loved it, too, as a place for the boys to unwind from their strict Jesuit schools and also from New York, where there had always been Léon or the governess to tell them what to do. I was distressed to see the estate in Warrenton finally leave the Coty family.

Yvonne's main request that weekend was that we look over the estate to make sure that the servants had left it in good order. What a large assignment! We were to survey the contents of a twenty-eight-room house filled with the finest English antiques. Since François's time, Yvonne had kept sizable quantities of her possessions, especially clothes for any occasion, in each of her residences.

That first day we entered closets fitted from ceiling to floor with huge glass-front drawers, complete with a rolling stepladder. Carefully folded clothes created patterns of color visible through the glass drawers. We were fascinated with the luxury surrounding us. The horror came when we noticed a swarm of moths flitting about in the air. I screamed in anger because I knew, without checking further, what we would find. We spent our weekend calling Paris and searching for anything that could be saved. Yvonne expressed sorrow, believing it was inevitable that the little flying beasts would be the ruin of her beautiful American wardrobe. She said there were also trunks to be cleaned out, and she told us to take anything we wanted that the moths had spared.

We opened drawer upon drawer, perhaps fifty or more. The contents were such that, even with the years of neglect, there remained magnificent silks and furs. I must have over fifty signature scarves from designer stores, some yards long and twenty inches wide in heavy silk of many colors and weaves, and some squares a yard wide—designs from Hermès, Nina Ricci, Le Must de Cartier, Gucci, and Jean Desses. One unforgettable bright red, heavy silk scarf from India is one and one-half feet wide by eight feet in length with designs in pure gold thread and large tassels that could probably be sold separately as art objects. Today it seldom leaves its nest in my own vault.

The men's scarves in silk would be considered antiques today. These were found to have escaped the insect invasion. Then came the shock of opening the big steamer trunk with its drawers on one side and three deep compartments on the other. I had never seen furs like the ones that I beheld therein. A coat in Brazilian otter had a pastel mink collar and matching cuffs. A pure white ermine cape was lined in soft black wool cashmere. The muffs of sable, fine gray chinchilla, dark Lacoda seal, and ermine to match lovely small hats, all in perfect condition, provided another surprise. I was brave enough to carry the muffs on several special evenings, attracting a number of stares, even from men.

Cold, Cold Canada

Months passed until finally Mike was made president of Coty Canada, "to give the old company a bit of new blood and marketing ideas," according to Léon. He sent us to Montreal, where we lived for two years. I was suspicious of this move, because we were so far away from the home office.

From a beautiful apartment in Montreal, we traveled 33,000 miles throughout Canada, removing fifteen years of old merchandise from shelves. In Montreal, though not officially employed, I demonstrated makeup application on television, selecting ladies from live audiences, and I advised young women on how to use Coty cosmetic products. Mike meanwhile gave Coty Canada a new look.

At last we found the time to return to Paris. Yvonne was in Geneva, but with her permission we stayed at her Rond-Point apartment, and it felt like heaven. We were just settling in when the giant doorbell of the courtyard gates sounded. We heard shouting, and the next morning Pierre told us of Monsieur Cotnareanu's adventure with the gatekeeper's wife. She had shouted to Monsieur Léon that he could not come in with his mistress, as Monsieur Michel and his bride were in residence. Léon had intended to bring his mistress to Yvonne's suite for their stay in Paris, something that we were amazed to learn had been done previously. Because of our arrival, Master Léon and his mistress had to march a few blocks down and pay for the privilege of staying in Paris's finest hotel, the Plaza Athenée. We couldn't stop smiling.

Coty Sold by Cotnareanu

Back in cold, cold Canada, in the early stages of my pregnancy, I received a call that my uncle had died, and I immediately departed for Pittsburgh. Between flights in New York, I phoned the New York Coty office to ask how things had been. "Miss Elizabeth, things are terrible. Haven't you heard? Didn't you know? Mr. Cotnareanu is selling Coty to Pfizer, a Canadian pharmaceutical company."

With my heart in my mouth and fury and fear increasing so fast I worried I would lose the baby, I telephoned Mike at our home in Canada. While I continued on to Pittsburgh, Mike flew to France that night to confront Yvonne. After all, she had always promised that the company would go to Roland's boys.

Yvonne cried, saying that she had signed the papers the night before and Léon had already left with them for New York. Léon and his brother Philippe managed to get Yvonne, now an eighty-one-year-old, brokenhearted woman, to agree to sell the company and all its assets, including sixty factories located all over the world, for $30 million. That was a paltry amount, even in 1963. My brother-in-law Henri Coty explained to me later that it was $30 million for the Coty family, $2 million for Léon, and $1 million for Philippe.

As the company was being sold, Mike and I were given five days to leave Canada, turn in our cars, ship our furniture, and seek our fortunes elsewhere. Pfizer had agreed with Léon that no Coty could work in the company again, making this stipulation an official part of the agreement to sell. I blamed Léon for this, but our opinions and wishes made no difference. One of the final ironies was that Pfizer had bought the Coty plant in North Carolina, next to my home state of Virginia. Coty products had been manufactured and distributed in America from a dedicated facility in Sanford, North Carolina, on a 258-acre site. In over 430,000 square feet of buildings, almost 273,000 were devoted to manufacturing, 140,000 to warehousing and distribution, and 18,400 to administration. The Sanford plant had been in operation from before the time I joined Coty in New York. I had imagined Mike and myself living in Virginia, with him in charge of that plant, among his many international duties. None of it was to be.

During this critical period, Mike and I received a call while on a golf course in Barbados. We knew it must be a matter of serious concern, because we were traveling far and wide and someone must have made a heroic effort to find us. On the road from Versailles to Paris, Roland had wrapped his car around a tree. Henri, his eldest son, was called to come get his wallet, but there was little else left to retrieve.

Our child was to be born in six months, and the two expectant parents searched for a new life after being released from the company we had expected to be ours forever. Even with this realization, we were unaware just how deeply the sale would affect our world. After traveling through seven Southern states, we settled in Virginia. We found an elegant Georgian-style mansion in Albemarle County and bought horses for our new country life. My birthplace, Luray, Virginia, was only an hour away. Thinking of Le Baron Farm and Yvonne, we bought French Charolais cattle from Canada, 31/32 percent pure, since it was illegal to import purebloods from France. We began crossbreeding them with the local Angus. Although we traveled and enjoyed our lovely rural life, nothing erased our bitter disappointment over Yvonne's broken promise that Mike would run Coty as François had done. Mike's disappointment was profound.

Léon's role in Yvonne's decisions was too powerful. She yearned for him physically and was quite lonely without him. She enjoyed the formal way he treated her, with his Eastern European savoir faire. His brilliance and his pompous airs entranced her. Yvonne, a lovesick woman, endured without a whimper Léon's unfaithfulness to her and his management and use of her fortune for his own ends. This handsome and intelligent woman of distinguished background was humiliated by both her husbands; each had been known to *have his mistress of the moment to dinner with Yvonne. At the end, she submitted to Léon's determination to sell the company, even though he had become her unfaithful and mostly absent husband. Now she grieved with us. People continue to ask why Yvonne turned her fortune, her belongings, and her life over to Léon Cotnareanu.*

Yvonne Coty-Cotnareanu's Death

Yvonne died in Paris in 1965, a lonely woman. She knew that Léon had not only taken the company away from the family, especially Mike, the only Coty who had worked extensively for the company, but he had sold Coty Inc. and Coty SA to Pfizer with the stipulation that no Coty could ever work for the company. By the time of her death, Yvonne was as brokenhearted as François had been. She died without Léon, at Rond-Point. He was off with his current mistress, who was the age of Yvonne's youngest grandchild. Yvonne put up with it, and as Geraldine Leo Feder, Léon's niece, said, "What woman of her class and time in Paris did not die alone? The men were always out of town or out on the town. It is to be expected and borne by all of us."

Yvonne may have died alone, but she had married and matured with François Spoturno dit Coti, the man who had become France's first billionaire. He loved perfume, women, and himself more than he loved the money or any one woman. Claiming that perfume was a love affair with one's self, François Coty continued his affair all his life; his ego and sensuality sent him into the arms of many women. Coty's legacy, however, far surpasses his reputation as a lover and France's first billionaire. When a man writes about perfume and creates it the way he did, making one of the greatest fortunes of his era, he should not be forgotten. He rhapsodized: "Fragrances there are that tantalize, entreat, caress—others that sing of conquest and triumph—some that send up the incense of worship and some that sigh of infinite sadness. She whose entangling charm disturbs the sons of men will give it richer allurement in her choice of perfume—and she whose soul is questing will surround herself with the fragrance of inspiration."

Because of his achievements in the world of *parfumerie*, François Coty bore a name recognized by women and by businessmen the world over. His name made a difference on five continents, but he lived for his own dreams of a greater France. The last of the effective dilettantes with voracious interests, François, with Yvonne's help, fulfilled the boast of his calling card and much, much more—François Coty: Industrialist, Artist, Technician, Economist, Financier, Social Scientist.

Epilogue

Keep striving for your goals. Always remember that by working to increase the company's strength, it is your own fortune you are building. . . . You are—we all are—the best.

François Coty at 1925 Coty SA meeting

The fortune was gone in much less time than it took François to make it. He had started accumulating the fortune when he was thirty, and he died thirty years later with just 600 pounds in an English bank—that anyone was ever able to find. Just before his death, his children had hired lawyers to file injunctions against his further spending at Louveciennes or d'Artigny. His money was draining away on projects such as constructing half an acre of tropical greenhouses for perfume experiments, serviced by expensive, labyrinthine passages. They were too late; he had lost or given away all of his billions through philanthropy or formalized bequests. Of course, Yvonne, because of Léon's cleverness and Philippe Cortney's legal talent, had gotten millions from the half of his holdings that she was due according to French law. Since she did not die until she was eighty-three, it took years for François's rightful heirs to "enjoy" (I use the word loosely) the portion that came to them.

Although Christiane had managed to become executor of Yvonne's estate, Léon remained in charge of all Yvonne's business affairs and properties. At Yvonne's request, he inherited from her the lush three-bedroom apartment in Geneva with its magnificent white and pink jade collection, Aubusson rugs, sunken living area, and exceptional view of Lake Geneva. Though he had always distanced himself from Yvonne's grandsons in New York, he clutched their futures in his hands even after her death.

Just two days after Yvonne's funeral, Christiane told her nephews, "I've got $40 million. Roland, if he were alive, would have gotten half of it. Each of you four boys will get $5 million

279

in cash or property—that's $20 million." Christiane then sold François's properties for about $72 million. She sold the five-story Rond-Point apartment for $3 million. Léon and his brother Philippe had already sold most of the art in that apartment through Jansy in Paris, with Yvonne's permission. Then someone in the family remembered that Yvonne had favored adopting her grandsons, but this had been opposed by Léon, and it certainly would not have been in the interests of Christiane.

The fight over the sale of these properties lasted three weeks. The only sane and calm person in the room during these fights was Jean-Jacques Vignault. He should have been named Granné's executor, but he only represented Roland's son, Yvon. In a brilliant move, his mother, Antoinette, had retained this loyal, gifted man to protect her son's interests.

Only God in his wisdom can possibly know where such a fortune could have flown just in the time that I knew the Coty family. Roland is blameless, only because he never stole any of the money that should have been his anyway. Not only did he never take the reins, he knew it was fruitless, and he would have gambled his inheritance away if Granné had not legally divested him of it.

After his liberation, Henri worked to help his fellow surviving French inmates. He started a motion picture company, after which he bought French automobiles for his fellow prisoners so that they could travel across Europe as his representatives. We used to joke that Henri owned 225 cars. This project indicates that Henri was living in his grandfather's tradition—grandiosely and in the media. He also worked to reestablish the importance of the Coty name and business.

Henri partnered with France III TV in Corsica to produce a video emphasizing the Corsican aspect of François's life as a perfumer. He also produced a television program on Napoleon. His documentary of the prison camp about Dora-Ellrich is used, along with an accompanying book, in French schoolrooms. Wanting to teach and inform, like his grandfather before him, Henri wrote in a Paris Match *article, "I have wanted the new generations after 1945 to better understand the dangers of totalitarianism, of racism and the annihilation, the crimes, the massacres and the deportations that these things have wrought." His film, featuring interviews with survivors, was the first made by a detainee and received an award as an "exceptional documentary." After the coverage of the film, the French press launched a publicity drive to attract memoirs of other members of the French Resistance. Henri was active in the Association of Dora-Ellrich Prisoners until his death.*

Coty Products Lose Their Cachet

When Yvonne and Léon moved to America, Jean Despres became their closest French associate. In the 1940s, he initiated drugstore sales of Coty products in New York because it would cause Coty profits to soar immediately. Léon Cotnareanu and Philippe Cortney, who ran Coty for Yvonne, wholeheartedly supported him in this effort. In May of 1983, Bernard Lee wrote about Jean Despres in *Beauty Fashion.* "There was a time when we would sell perfume in huge gallons to pharmacies, and they would pour out individual drams to sell to customers, but soon we had adequate packaging in America. To achieve this wide success in the United States, contacts were made, not just at the great department store chains, but at small stores, five and dime stores, dress shops and drugstores across the country from county to county. Jean was on the road constantly, crisscrossing the country, taking the 20th Century Limited, calling on every major department store, making contacts with drug chains, wholesalers, independents from coast to coast. [Despres] opened warehouses in San Francisco, Chicago and Los Angeles, and wrote the first sales training manuals."

Another sales device Coty Inc. developed was tying promotions to holidays or particular seasons. Capitalizing on François Coty's old tradition of "sets," multiple items relating to a single scent or theme were packaged together and then sold as a single unit. Coty created a new idea in Christmas gifts, with a few spectacular presentations selling for one hundred to two hundred dollars each. Coty soon produced less expensive sets to meet the volume business as thousands of retail outlets, including lower-end city and country drugstores, caught on to the concept. These holiday sets were among the first of their kind. Jean Despres remembered orders for 10,000 Christmas sets, a startling figure at the time, according to Bernard Lee.

The move to drugstore sales resulted in big money for the company but loss of prestige for the product. Bernard Lee recalled in the *Coty Review* that the policies of department stores limited sales. By contrast, drugstores "had longer hours, were free to be more aggressive and seized upon fragrances as advertising leaders," he wrote. "And they discovered something wonderful. Even the chains did not have to cut prices to sell perfume in volume and on a quality level. . . . The growth of our industry in drugstores was assured."

By 1960, Coty's L'Origan, L'Aimant, Paris, and Emeraude had reigned for thirty years as the four best-selling fragrances in the United

States. To Americans today, this seems amazing, since Coty products that use the name prominently on the packaging now appear, if at all, on dusty bottom shelves of drugstores. Fragrances have gone full circle, from the pharmaceutical bottles and heavy aroma that offended François Spoturno in Raymond Goëry's apothecary to the most expensive, elegant, sought-after scents in their equally refined flasks and packaging—and then back again where they started, down to the bottles that I cannot even call flagons.

The American Coty

Mike and I had settled in Albemarle County in 1964 to raise a Virginia daughter, the tenth-generation Virginian in my family. It was obvious, though, that after raising Charolais cattle for a while, a young man of thirty-three needed a vocation even if the IRS made it futile. Mike needed to have a place of business to get him out of the house. It was a case of "don't keep them down on the farm," a reverse of the song. He therefore invested in real estate. This included 80,000 acres in West Virginia, as well as part of a project in Albemarle County, where I helped him design twenty-three houses. He could, however, have done much better without the in-town executives and their martini luncheons. A Coty by birth, he needed no extraneous temptations.

After seven years, the inevitable daily cocktails increased to hours, and romance deteriorated. Finally, after an autumn Hunt Country Ball, a "best friend," a houseguest, was joined by Mike in her guest bedroom. The Protestant in me reacted without thinking of the ultimate loss to my child of home, family, and inheritance.

In January of 1973, the Cristoforo Colombo *was sailing from New York, the first ship out to anywhere, and nine-year-old Patrice, her puppy Bijoux, and I sailed to Algeciras, Spain, where we experienced the largest mosquitoes known to man. A day after our arrival, we made our way along the Andalusian coast of the Mediterranean Sea to the exclusive Marbella Club, where we were installed in grand fashion. There were transatlantic calls and talk of "forgive and forget." That was almost impossible, but "who knows," I thought.*

I cannot speak about it even today in the first person. Inaction by Elizabeth meant divorce and remarriage by Mike within a few short months. In 1974, another call to me in Marbella from Charlottesville reported Mike's sudden death, when he was forty-two years old. He, like François, had an aneurysm.

Since my teenage daughter, Patrice Charloe, and her half-sister,

Yvonne Elise Coty (daughter of Elise Kullman and Mike), were heirs of Yvonne Coty, I left Marbella for Paris, Switzerland, and Virginia to represent these two minors, to little avail. It did not help that their father had remarried just seven months before his death.

Coty Buyout

After I returned to Spain, I threw myself back into my "priceless" free magazine, the Marbella Times. *Mike's death only made me more determined than ever to revive the memory of François Coty. The great perfume magnate had been dead forty-five years, but the company, even after the tragic sale to Pfizer in 1963, could be reconstituted. I longed to again "reach" the Coty public whose purchases had in the early days created the largest fragrance and cosmetics company in the world.*

Having been the wife of Yves Michel Coty and an officer in the Coty fragrance business in New York, I tried in 1987 to make a leveraged buyout of Coty Inc. from Pfizer, not really even understanding the phrase. After setting up the Coty Foundation in Marbella, I set about raising money for the buyout. Through my contacts I was able to get commitments from the Investment Trust in London, the oldest trust company in England, and the Banque Nationale de Paris. I also had commitments from the Finarab Investment Company in London. Through Charles Daughtery I had made good contacts with Banker's Trust of New York.

In 1986, Pfizer had reported that the Coty Division employed about 1,020 people in the United States, of which approximately 535 were nonstaff plant employees. While Pfizer claimed they were not offering the Coty Division for sale, they estimated it was worth a minimum of $200 million. Elizabeth Coty estimated that, in 1986, U.S. sales accounted for at least 96 percent of Coty's net sales of $153.6 million. There were about $12 million in net sales in Canada and Puerto Rico. Shocking to her was that in all other countries, Coty products had been licensed to distributors in exchange for royalties based on sales, bringing in about $8.5 million net that year.

Pfizer had corresponded with Elizabeth, who set herself up at New York's River Club in March 1987. Patrick J. Martin of Banker's Trust, London, wrote her that same month: "As I mentioned to you during our meeting, we are very excited about the prospect of this great family business reuniting with its founding heritage. . . . We are prepared to support the Coty Foundation in its attempt to form a group of investors that would provide the financing for the acquisition of Coty."

During our second negotiation, we agreed to raise the price $100 million more than Pfizer had originally valued the corporation. I was given an insurance check for $25 million as a down payment to Pfizer. When I presented the check, the insurance company's president sat beside me in the finance director's office at Coty Inc. in New York City, then the offices of Pfizer.

Pfizer made us wait three weeks for their decision. Finally, we were called in to what we thought would be the meeting to seal the deal. Mr. Edgreen, my senior lender, and I were stunned to hear that Pfizer had "never sold a division." Coty Inc. had been a registered company in Delaware since 1913, and now Pfizer used the excuse that Coty was just a division of their company and their policy was to never sell divisions. I was furious at having remained in New York for seven months at my own expense to complete the buyout for the Coty descendants. In 1992, Pfizer sold Coty to Benckiser, a German pharmaceutical company with no recognized fragrance experience at the time.

After Benckiser bought Coty, mass distribution of all their cosmetics grew to account for 63 percent of cosmetics sales worldwide at chain drugstores: Wal-Mart, Kmart, Walgreen's, and Rite Aid in America and Kaufhof, Carrefour, and Boots in Europe. High-end or luxury cosmetics products that were sold through department stores, duty-free shops, and prestige beauty-care shops accounted for only 37 percent of cosmetics sales worldwide a century after Coty went into business in 1904.

The yearly worldwide cosmetics market between 1998 and 2004 was in the $80 billion range. Fragrances accounted for a whopping 20 percent; color cosmetics about 16 percent; and personal-care products, such as skincare and toiletries, represented the balance. François Coty, more than any other individual in the industry, was the talent, energy, and wisdom behind the promotion of quality fragrances and cosmetics to teach women how to enjoy making themselves attractive.

In 1934, the year François died, the word "perfume" was synonymous with the Coty name the world over. Because of him, women everywhere, at all economic levels, could spend time on themselves, enhancing their appearance and the way they felt about themselves. Coty provided this opportunity because of his worship of women and his intense interest in beauty.

Le Figaro's Paul Morand, a friend of Yvonne Coty, wrote in 1900 that designer Coco Chanel was "the exterminating angel of 19th century convention" for women. Coty, however, was the harbinger of any woman's appreciation of herself, which at the turn of the twentieth century was a new idea. A woman, enhanced in her own mind by Coty perfume and scented cosmetics, was more than a seductress, more than a representative of fashion: she was herself enhanced. Coty products reinforced this new female self-esteem.

Coty empowered women at a time when legislatures the world over were still refusing to do so. He understood that he was doing this, and he supported suffrage for women and their participation in the governmental process. He also illustrated his professional as well as personal appreciation of women by his practices toward his female employees the world over.

François was on the mark when he said, "It is essential that Coty perfumes be the expression of a woman's soul." The advertisements, brochures, guides, and marketing plans that he produced or supervised are a preview to the women's liberation movement decades years later.

The French billionaire with more passion, more creative ability, and more personality than any other public man in France between the two world wars is now forgotten. François Coty paid for his genius and courage and his philosophy. History has ignored him, even though Coty Inc. under Benckiser is called the largest perfume company in the world since they added celebrity scents.

The Spoturno residence in Ajaccio, attached to Napoleon's birthplace, should be a historic landmark in the ancient city. There was family money to preserve it as late as the 1960s when interest in historic sites, and in Ajaccio, had begun to penetrate Corsica, but Coty's descendants were unaware of the Spoturno association with the building at that time.

The Château d'Artigny resembles the man who created it—powerful and grandiose. To design and build a château of the grandeur of Louis XV's age, with the modern efficiency envisioned and achieved by François Coty, would be impossible today. In its reincarnation as a luxury hotel, the Château d'Artigny commemorates François Coty. The Prix François Coty is awarded for the best fragrance of the year at a grand event celebrated at the Château d'Artigny each fall.

The pavillon at Louveciennes, where Coty died, has been purchased by the Dumeste Foundation to commemorate François and Yvonne Coty, along with La Comtesse Du Barry and the architect Nicolas Ledoux. The beautiful apartment buildings at Rond-Point are gone, and the Avenue Raphael house is now hidden behind infill building. Suresnes, a town that Coty put on the map, has lost most of its large collection of Coty buildings. Pfizer, which bought Coty Inc. in 1963, continued to make perfume in the Cité des Parfums until the 1970s, when they sold the real estate to Agfa-Gevaert. Some buildings deteriorated; some were demolished. Ironically, the remnant of one of Coty's buildings is now the René Sordes Museum; Sordes was Coty's competitor. The museum preserves a magnificent collection of photographs of the city of Suresnes that Coty caused to be developed. Exhibitions pay homage to Coty's contribution to France from time to time, but such fitful remembrances are, on the whole, disappointing.

Despite or perhaps because of the downfall of the name Coty in parfumerie, the eldest of François's great-grandsons determined to go into the perfume business. Through the generosity of a family friend, Madame Anne-Marie d'Estanville, who provided $100,000, Stephane Coty, Henri's son, created two fragrances, Ruban Noir *and* Ruban Vert. *He produced and marketed them under the name Stephane Coty at 18, avenue des Champs-Elysées, Paris. Benckiser, having bought Coty Inc. from Pfizer, brought a successful suit against Stephane for using his own family name, and his perfume had to be taken off the market in France. At the last minute, Russian perfume marketers arrived, so impressed with Stephane's fragrances that they bought and transported his inventory to Russia, where they sold it. Stephane or his attorneys should have used the precedent set by a contemporary of François who, though unrelated to him, set up a perfume business called Coty. The courts ruled in the upstart's favor so long as he attached his first name to the name Coty on his bottles of perfume and advertisements. The label Stephane Coty should have pleased the court. After all, Stephane is a real Coty.*

In 1982, Yvon, Roland Coty's youngest son, was similarly disappointed when he tried to create perfumes using his own name. He, too, was advised not to pursue the venture. Instead, he bought Roger-Vivier, a perfume company. In 1987, he sold it to Edwin Alfine, who had been an executive with Chanel.

By the time of his 1934 death, François Spoturno dit Coti was deserted by friends, family, and most of the intimates that he had befriended, supported, or mentored, except for Maurice Hanot d'Hartoy, who had his own reasons for hanging on to François. The question is still asked today of family members in a few places in the Americas, the Far East, or Europe: "Whatever happened to the name Coty on perfumes and powders?" The response is, "Your grandmother will remember, if you ask her."

Acknowledgments

Elizabeth Coty's interest in a biography of François Coty and the Spoturno family of Corsica began passively in 1960, the first time she went to Paris with her new husband. There she met Yvonne Coty and visited with the family at Rond-Point des Champs-Elysées. When she went to Spotorno and Noli, Italy in 1965, she became enchanted with the medieval history of the Spoturno family and their immigration to Ajaccio, Corsica. In Spotorno, city-hall officials were helpful, especially Giuliano Cerrutti, who read ancient Italian. This launched Elizabeth into a series of trips to Italy, Corsica, and France until 1980. In La Rochelle, France, Francine Maeck, Jeanne Moorsom, and Didier Beraud, former assistant director of the Bibliothoque Nationale, provided invaluable help.

After a number of stops and starts over the years, Elizabeth met Mariano Castaneiro in 1980 in Charlottesville, Virginia. An Argentine from Buenos Aires, Mariano was working on a Ph.D. in international affairs at the University of Virginia. He told Elizabeth that the Coty perfume empire was discussed in his textbooks. When she related a smattering of her knowledge about the family and the business and her interest in writing a book, he emphatically said, "Do it!" Finally, there is a book.

Elizabeth is indebted to many people who through the years have shared their knowledge of the Spoturno dit Coti family and Coty *parfumerie.* Stephane Coty, the eldest great-grandson of François Coty, traveled to Ajaccio to find François's birth certificate, clarifying an often-published incorrect birth date. François had been given the birth date of his stillborn younger brother, François-Henri, in much publicity related to his life and times. Finding François's verified birth certificate with his full name and birth date was an inspiration. Other family members cooperated in the writing of this book: Michel Coty's daughters Yvonne Elise Coty-Mancini and Patrice Coty Batcheller as well as her husband, David Batcheller; Roland Coty's youngest son, Yvon, his mother, Antoinette Mouchet Coty, and Antoinette's

287

eldest son, Claude Mouchet; Rolande Dubonnet, Christiane Coty Dubonnet's daughter, and her son Eric Nascimbeni and his wife; Marcos de Morelos, son of Lorenzo, Conde de Morelos, and France (Françoise), the daughter of François Coty and Henriette Dieudé; and José Morelos, eldest son of France, whom Elizabeth Coty met by chance in the United Arab Emirates in 1985.

In the early 1980s, the assistant editor of the *Daily Express* in London, Alan Frame, gave Elizabeth access to Reuters, where she searched through British newspapers back to 1900, obtaining copies, back-up material, and direction. She gained access through Michel Coty's best friend at Coty Inc., Pierre Croquez, to his 1950s research in the New York Public Library. At that time, Croquez was one of the eighty contemporary perfumers who created fragrances for fragrance companies and factories.

Roulhac Toledano began to participate in the project in 2002 and help for her came from Alain Rabier, the Coty family's administrative director of Château d'Artigny; René Traversac, the 1960 purchaser of the château; and his son Pierre Traversac; and their administrative director, Patrice Puvilland. The following responded to inquiries: André Gillet, Jean Miot, and Jacques Baigneres, of *Le Figaro;* Marguerite Hitier, of the Ministry of Foreign Affairs, Paris; Philippe Chaveneau, son of the managing director of the Morgan Bank in Paris, André Chaveneau; the staff at Agri on rue de Castiglione, Paris; Jean Beysset, at the office of the Legion of Honor; the Julienne Dumeste Foundation at Louveciennes; Alain Froger, Eric Peres, and Marc Boss, of Louveciennes; Marie-Pierre Deguillaume, at the René Sordes Museum; Anne Devroye Stilz, at Château Sainte-Hélène in Nice; Jean Noel Jeanneney, of the Bibliothèque Nationale de France, Paris; Claire Béchu; Marie-Frédérique Bergeaud; Bernard d'Hartoy, son of Maurice d'Hartoy, and his granddaughter Agnès Vivier; Roland Rachel and Marie-Christiane Moine, of CARAN; Catherine Vincent-Dolor, at Lalique, Paris; and Marie-Claude Lalique, of Paris, recently deceased. Patrick Sarran shared information leading to his own book on the Château d'Artigny. Appreciation goes to Gerard Proust, of Tours; Jean Kerleo, of Versailles; Sabine La Brosse, of Prouvoust; the staff at the Musée Mauriac; and French authors and friends Jacqueline and Maurice Denuzière and Katherine Hermary Veielle, who gave us appropriate contacts throughout France.

The authors want to thank colleagues, friends, and acquaintances in Corsica whose interest, knowledge, and assistance have made it possible to finish the manuscript: Alain Venturini, of Ajaccio; Simon Renucci, mayor of Ajaccio and now senator from Corsica;

his assistant, Madame Santini; the Ajaccio archives staff; André Stefanaggi, of France 3, Ajaccio; author and researcher Paul Sylvani; and Georges Cianfarani, who owns the Grand Hotel in Calvi, which Christiane Spoturno dit Coti established. The staff at the public library of Spotorno, Italy, clarified the family history.

In New York, assistance came from the staff, including Robert Foy and Alexandra Saxe, at the New York Public Library; the Donnell Library Center, at 20 West Fifty-third, which holds the World Languages Collection; the Science, Industry, and Business Library, at 188 Madison Avenue; the Central Library, on Fifth Avenue; and Richard Kinsel, historian of Coty affairs in New York, formerly curator of Coty Inc., owned by Benckiser.

Thanks go to the staff at the Library of Congress in Washington, D.C.: the European Reading Room staff at the Jefferson Building; the Newspaper and Current Periodical Reading Room staff at the Madison Building; and the Copyright Publication Information Office and the Legal Department.

Many people responded to Elizabeth's requests for information: Frank Sellin and Roberto and Irina Trigani at the University of Virginia; Allison Webster at the University of Kentucky Press; Michael Bradfield in Washington; Judah Gribetz in New York; Alvin Lindsay, former president of International Flavors and Fragrances; Victoria Rodriguez Thiessen of Sotheby's, London; author Joseph McLean Gregory; Madeleine France, who provided books on perfumes; Carmela Schaufler of New York, who provided her master's thesis on Coty; Rea S. Hederman of New York City, who encouraged Elizabeth; and Annette Green, president of The Fragrance Foundation in New York City. Elizabeth corresponded with Ghislaine Picchiottino, a Coty scholar and author of a book on Coty as an industrialist, over what form the biography might take.

Anne-Emmanuelle Grossi of Ajaccio, professor at the University of Avignon, spent weeks in the libraries and city halls of Ajaccio and Paris, making it possible to finish the book. She also provided translations of some French epigrams, as did Roland Simon. Her parents, Anne-Marie and André-Antoine Grossi, rallied to help as well. André Madec-King, director of the Alliance Française of Charlottesville, assisted with translations from the French, and her knowledge of her native Brittany and French history proved invaluable. Marie-Reine Thomas of Charlottesville, Laurence Devillairs of Besançon and Paris, Margaret Keith of Paris and Selma, Alabama, and Louisa Dixon of Besançon and Staunton, Virginia, translated essential documents and pursued French sources. Similarly, Michel Gauthier, an architect of Clermont-

Ferrand and Middleburg, Virginia, translated political information. Mary Miller, reference librarian at the Charleston, South Carolina County Public Library, and Athena Michaels, with John Wiley and Sons, provided essential materials. Brunie Mayor of New York City handled German translations and located rare books at the New York Public Library.

Much appreciated has been reading and editing by Blanche Krubner in both French and English and help with editing and notes by Phillip Honenburger of Orange, Virginia. Readers Jim Johnston, Daniel Meador, and Noel Parmentel helped. Thanks go to Jim Barnes of the Reference Department at the Thomas Jefferson Regional Library in Charlottesville, Virginia and the Reference Room staff at the University of Virginia. Rosemarie Fowler served as research assistant in France and the United States and provided a residence in New Orleans for work at Tulane University. University of Virginia professors Adam Watson and Hans Schmitt, both now deceased; Ambassador Randolph Bell of Richmond, Virginia; and his wife, Karla, assisted on the history of France between the wars and the search for resistance information. Thanks go to Warren Robbins for an office in his Foundation for Cross Cultural Communications and his assistant, Brad Simpson, for help in Washington, D.C. Laura Denyes provided assistance with graphic design and Coleman Kitchin helped with computer technology.

In the United States and Canada, thanks go to Geraldine Leo Feder, Léon Cotnareanu's niece; Donna Marie Quinn, of Nantucket; and Jeanine Cooper. Sylvain Gingras provided information about La Seigneurie du Triton outside of Montreal. Janet and Bruce Fein of the Alliance Française of Charlottesville contacted the Cotnareanu descendants for us. Angela Comnene and Lavinia Mascan of Ottawa, Canada; Christina Ioana Zarifol Illias; and Lelia Kanavariotis Washburn of Athens and Washington, D.C. contributed research on the Moldavian roots of the Cotnareanu family.

Purposely left to last but not least are two men essential to this presentation. The first person to help Elizabeth, beginning when she was living in Spain and commuting to France and England, was her cousin Jared Loewenstein, veteran curator and director of the Reference Department at the Alderman Library at the University of Virginia. He has continued to assist throughout the project. Henri Coty, the eldest grandson of François Coty and the only one to remember his grandfather, with whom he lived for five years, worked in Paris, Corsica, Germany, and New York to reestablish the Coty legend in perfume, until his death in late 2006. His documentaries and recorded interviews with Elizabeth, and his lunch at the Crillon with Roulhac just months before his death, helped to clear up contested points relating to François Coty's complex and conflicted life. Henri Coty did not authorize, read, or approve the manuscript, except for the preface.

Notes

Preface

1. Maurice de Waleffe, "Derrière le cercueil de Coty," *La Nouvelle Corse* (August 5, 1934).

2. Ghislaine Picchiottino, *François Coty, un Industriel Corse sous la IIIe République*, 223.

3. Justinius, *De François Coty à Fernand Pouillon: Un Homme de Loi se Souvient* (Paris: Debresse, 1978), 21.

4. Chandler Burr, *The Perfect Scent* (New York: Henry Holt, 2008), xxi.

Chapter 1

1. Arthur Train Jr., "François Coty and the War of Words and Ink," *World Today* (February 1932).

2. Bernard Lee, "Days of Perfume and Roses," *Beauty Fashion* (May 1983).

3. Train, 461.

4. "Coty in Accord on French War Debt to U.S.," *New York Times,* July 1, 1926.

5. François Monteagle, "Les débuts de *L'Ami du Peuple* de François Coty, une experience médiatique et politique extreme, 1928-1931" (master's thesis, University of Paris, 2002).

Chapter 2

1. The medieval village of Coti is just off the Ajaccian Gulf, inland at Porticcio and the Tour de Capannelle. It was sacked in the sixteenth century by the Moors.

2. As recently as January 30, 1954, the newspaper *Chronique de la Vieille Corse* featured the Bonaparte-Spoturno-Ornano connection. The article was written to clarify the differing backgrounds between the president of the Republic of France, René Coty, and François Coty, France's first billionaire, known as the Emperor of Perfume. The president's ancestors sprang from mainland France, and he was a native of Le Havre.

3. She was also known as Madame Felix Bacciochi.

4. The Hôtel de Ville was built in 1826 after the designs of Alphonse

de Gisors, just across the treelined avenue Du Premier-Consul from the Spoturno house.

5. Later they moved to La Plage.

6. Anna Maria had four brothers, only one of whom lived in Corsica at the time.

7. *L'Ami du Peuple*, May 13, 1933.

8. Municipal archives of Ajaccio, Corsica, 1894 and 1897.

Chapter 3

1. Yvonne Goldberg, *La Medaille en France de Ponscarme à la fin de la Belle Epoque* (Paris: Hôtel de la Monnaie, 1967), 56.

2. Picasso had arrived in Paris from Barcelona in that year.

3. Bennett had left New York for Paris in 1877..

Chapter 4

1. Fabienne Pavia, *The World of Perfume* (New York: Knickerbocker, 1995), 34-36.

2. Elisabeth Barillé and Catherine Laroze, *The Book of Perfume* (Paris: Flammarion, 1995), 80.

3. Jacqueminot, born in Nancy in 1787, had shown exemplary courage in the Battles of Austerlitz (1805) and Wagram (1809), among others, all in the service of Napoleon. He appealed to François: a brave soldier and leader, a successful elected official, a rebellious hero to the people of Paris, and, most important, a man with a name that the public knew well. It has also been published that Raymond Goëry worked for a pharmacist named Jacqueminot on the avenue de la Motte-Piquet, and it was there that François first recognized his own talent. Thus one story goes that he named his first perfume after the pharmacist. See Picchiottino, 43, 54, 65.

Chapter 5

1. The Le Baron and Dubois families, well-known engravers of medals and coins, were then reaching the acme of their profession. Between 1918 and 1926, Albert-Eugène, Edouard, Joseph-Marie, Paul-Gustave, Pierre-Marie, and Jules-Georges Le Baron were awarded the Legion of Honor for their engravings.

2. Some sources say that Baccarat's bottle for *La Rose Jacqueminot* was only made for later editions of the perfume, but this is incorrect.

3. *Ambre Antique* is of the soft amber classification and *L'Origan* is under the floral spicy amber classification, according to L'Osmothèque Society.

4. Regarding the princesses' preference for Coty products, see Robert K. Massie, *Nicholas and Alexandra* (New York: Anthem, 1967).

5. Legras and Company was established in 1864.

6. Sylviane Humaire. "Les flacons à parfum de Lalique," *Le Figaro* (October 27, 1986).

7. Mary Lou Utt, Glenn Utt, and Patricia Bayer, *Lalique Perfume Bottles* (New York: Crown, 1990), 31.

8. Ibid., 23-24.

9. Yvonne continued a cordial business relationship with Lalique, even after her divorce from François. Her ex-husband had died by the time the Lalique firm was commissioned as the primary interior designer for Yvonne's oceangoing yacht, the *Alphée*.

Chapter 6

1. The villa became part of Coty's Cité des Parfums in 1915.

2. A Roman villa was established at nearby Mont-Valérien during the Gallo-Roman epoch. Some seventeen centuries later. Napoleon wanted to fortify Mont-Valérien because the Prussians had occupied it in 1815. François found the association with Rome and with Napoleon an enhancement of the place. See Nicolas Viasnoff, "Senteurs et Parfums," *Suresnes Magazine* no. 127 (April 2002).

3. Hebe Dorsey, *"The Belle Epoque in the Paris Herald," International Herald Tribune* (1986).

4. Paul Poiret, *King of Fashion: The Autobiography of Paul Poiret* (Philadelphia: Lippincott, 1931).

5. Incidentally, Marc Lalique (the successor of René) created the first postwar Worth perfume in 1945. This perfume was named *Requête*.

6. Patrick Sarran, *Empereur D'Artigny* (Tours: Nouvelles République, 1990), 23.

Chapter 7

1. Pavia, 69, 80-81.

2. Sarran, 19.

3. Lee, *Coty Review*.

Chapter 8

1. Paul Lucchini, *Par les Rues d'Ajaccio: Dictionnaire Historique et Anecdoctique* (Ajaccio: La Societé d'Historie d'Ajaccio, 1992), 103.

2. Corsican newspapers seldom recognized Coty's name change.

Chapter 9

1. Cyril Conolly and Jerome Zerbe, *Les Pavillons: French Pavilions of the Eighteenth Century* (New York. Macmillan, 1962).

2. Ibid.

3. Marlise Simons, *New York Times,* February 15, 1996.

4. *New York Times,* July 13, 1931.

5. Emile Buré, "Obituary of François Coty," *L'Ordre* (July 27, 1934).

Chapter 10
1. Sarran, 19.
2. Claude Bellanger, *Histoire Générale de la Presse Française* vol. 3 (Paris: Presses Universitaires de France, 1972).

Chapter 11
1. Germaine Martin, *Revue de Paris,* August 15, 1926. Quoted in William L. Shirer, *The Collapse of the Third Republic* (New York: Simon and Schuster, 1969), 165.
2. Bernard d'Hartoy to Elizabeth Coty, 2003, Paris.
3. Ibid.

Chapter 12
1. *Le Figaro* (March 31, 1923).
2. Sisley Huddleston, "A French Hearst," *The Living Age* (Boston: October 1928).
3. See chapter 19.

Chapter 14
1. *New York Times,* May 8, 1934.
2. Picchiottino, 273.
3. Coty's grandmother Anna Maria Belone Spoturno was also buried in the little cemetery at Montbazon.
4. *Le Matin,* July 26, 1934.

Chapter 17
1. Larry Collins and Dominique Lapierre, *Is Paris Burning?* (New York: Simon and Schuster, 1965), 38.

Chapter 18
1. Linda Clark, "François Coty: A Forgotten Contributor to Modern Management Techniques" (thesis, Appalachian State University, Boone, N.C.).
2. The Eleanor Lambert Archive, The Costume Institute, Metropolitan Museum of Art.
3. Ibid.
4. "The Most Prized Fashion Award," *Vogue* (February 1960).

Chapter 19
1. Collins and Lapierre.

Bibliography

Books

Barillé, Elisabeth. *Coty: Parfumeur and Visionary.* Translated by Mark Howarth. Paris: Assouline, 1996.

Barillé, Elisabeth, and Catherine Laroze. *The Book of Perfume.* Paris: Flammarion, 1995.

Behr, Edward. *The Good Frenchman: The True Story of the Life and Times of Maurice Chevalier.* New York: Villard, 1993.

Bellanger, Claude. *Histoire Générale de la Presse Française.* Vol. 3. Paris: Presses Universitaires de France, 1972.

Ben-Sasson, H. H., ed. *A History of the Jewish People.* Cambridge, Mass.: Harvard University Press, 1976.

Bernard, Leopold. *Les Odeurs Dans les Romans de Zola.* Paris, 1887.

Bernard, Phillippe, and Henri Dubief. *The Decline of the Third Republic, 1914-1938.* Cambridge: Cambridge University Press, 1993.

Berstein, Serge, and Pierre Milza. *Histoire de la France au XXe Siècle, T. II: 1930-1945.* Paris: Complexe, 1991.

Burr, Chandler. *The Perfect Scent: A Year Inside the Perfume Industry in Paris and New York.* New York: Holt, 2007.

Callil, Carmen. *Bad Faith: A Forgotten History of Family, Fatherland and Vichy France.* New York: Knopf, n.d.

Caorsi, Luigi. *Noli, Alla Ricerca Del Passato.* Civitas Nauli: Centro Storico Culturale, 1999.

Choltitz, Dietrich von. *Brennt Paris.* N.p., 1951.

———. *Soldat unter Soldaten.* Zurich: Europa-Verlag, 1951.

Clarke, Linda. "François Coty: A Forgotten Contributor to Modern Management Techniques." PhD diss., Appalachian State University, John A. Walker College of Business, 1998.

Cohen, William B., ed. *The Transformation of Modern France.* New York: Houghton Mifflin, 1997.

Collins, Larry, and Dominique Lapierre. *Is Paris Burning?* New York: Simon & Schuster, 1965.

Connolly, Cyril, and Jerome Zerbe. *Les Pavillons: French Pavilions of the Eighteenth Century.* New York: Macmillan, 1962.

Cornwall, John. *Hitler's Pope: The Secret History of Pius XII.* New York: Viking, 1999.

Coston, Henry. *Dictionnaire de la Politique Française.* Paris: Henry Coston, 1967.

———. *Dictionnaire des Pseudonymes.* New corrected edition. Paris, 1965.

Cotnareanu, Léon. *The Alternative: Culture and Peace.* New York: Dodd, Mead, 1941.

———, ed. *Chroniques du Figaro: Suites Françaises.* 2 vols. New York: Brentano's, 1945.

Cotnareanu, Yvonne. *La Croisière de l'Alphee.* N.p., 1933.

Coty, François. *Contre le Communisme.* Paris: Bernard Grasset, 1928.

———, preface. *Les Ecuries d'Augias: Les Campagnes "de L'Ami du Peuple" en 50 Dessins.* By Chancel. Paris: Leroy et Hervé Baille, 1929.

———. *Le Péril Rouge en Pays Noir.* Paris: Bernard Grasset, 1931.

———. *La Réforme de l'état.* Paris: Bernard Grasset, 1931.

———. *Savon Nos Colonies, Montrouge.* Paris: Bernard Grasset, 1931.

———. *Tearing Away the Veils: Financiers Who Control the World.* Translated by Eugene Nelson. New York: Sanctuary, 1940.

———. *Wiege zu Reichtum und Ehre.* Berlin: A. Bock, 1933.

Dawes, Nicholas M. *Lalique Glass.* New York: Crown, 1986.

De LaCretelle, Jacques. *Face l'Evénement: Le Figaro, 1826-1966.* Paris: Hachette, 1966.

Deniel, A. *Bucard et le Francisme.* Paris: J. Picollec, 1979.

Dilasser, Bernard, Lucia Orsoni, and Risterucci Angelina. *François Coty, Le Napoleon de la parfumerie moderne.* Ajaccio: France 3, 2000. Documentary.

Dingli, Laurent. *Louis Renault.* Paris: Flammarion, 2000.

Durvelle, J-P. *The Preparation of Perfumes and Cosmetics.* Translated by Ernest J. Parry. London: Scott, Greenwood & Son, 1923.

Earle, Edward Mead. *Modern France.* Princeton: Princeton University Press, 1951.

Erickson, Carrolly. *Josephine: A Life of the Empress.* New York: St. Martin's Griffin, 1998.

France 2001. Clermont-Ferrand: Michelin, 2001.

Gohier, Urbain. *Mon Jubilé.* Paris: Baudinière, 1934.

Graziani, Antoine-Marie. *Pascal Paoli, Père de la Patrie Corse.* Paris: Tallandier, 2002.

Huddleston, Sisley. *Paris Salons, Cafes, Studios: Being Social, Artistic and Literary Memories.* New York: Blue Ribbon Books, 1928.

Isherwood, Christopher. "The Last of Mr. Norris, Goodbye to Berlin." In *The Berlin Stories*. New York: New Directions, 1954.

Jenkins, Alan. *The Twenties*. New York: Universe Books, 1973.

Jones-North, Jacquelyn Y. *Commercial Perfume Bottles*. West Chester, Pa.: Schiffer, 1987.

———. *Perfume, Cologne and Scent Bottles*. West Chester, Pa.: Schiffer, 1986.

Justinius. *De François Coty à Fernand Pouillon: Un Homme de Loi Se Souvient*. Paris: Debresse, 1976.

Kaufmann, Emil. *De Ledoux à Le Corbusier: L'Origine et Developpement de L'Architecture Autonome*. Translated by Guy and Ruth Ballangé. Paris: La Villette, 2002.

Kedward, Harry Roderick. *In Search of the Maquis: Rural Resistance in Southern France, 1942-1944*. Oxford: Clarendon, 1993.

———. *Occupied France: Collaboration and Resistance, 1940-1944*. Oxford: Blackwell, 1985.

Kennan, George F. *Russia and the West under Lenin and Stalin*. Boston: Little, Brown, 1960.

Kupferman, Fred. *François Coty—Journaliste et Homme Politique*. 2 vols. PhD diss., Paris-Sorbonne, 1965.

———. *Pierre Laval*. Paris: Masson, 1976.

Lang, André. *Pierre Brisson: le journaliste, l'écrivain, l'homme*. Paris: Calmann-Levy, 1967.

Large, David Clay. *Between Two Fires: Europe's Path in the 1930s*. New York: Norton, 1990.

Latzarus, Louis. *Un Ami du Peuple: M. Coty*. Paris: Valois, 1929.

———. *La Politique: Notes et Maximes*. Paris: Hachette, 1928.

Lefkowith, Christie Mayer. *The Art of Perfume*. New York: Thames and Hudson, 1994.

———. *Paul Poiret and His Rosine Perfumes*. New York: Stylissimo, 2007.

Le Galliene, Richard. *The Romance of Perfume*. New York: R. Hudnut, 1928.

Loiseaux, Gérard. *La Littérature de la Défaite et de la Collaboration (d'après Phénix ou Cendres? de Bernhard Payr)*. Paris: Publications de la Sorbonne, 1984.

Lucchini, Paul. *Par les Rues d'Ajaccio: Dictionnaire Historique et Anecdoctique*. Ajaccio: La Societé d'Historie d'Ajaccio, 1992.

Manevy, Raymond. *Histoire de la Presse en France, 1914-1939*. Paris: Corréa, 1945.

Manhatten, Avro. *The Vatican in World Politics*. New York: Gaer, 1949.

Marchand, Pierre, ed. *Corse-du-Sud*. Paris: Guides Gallimard, 1993.

Massie, Robert K. *Nicholas and Alexandra*. New York: Anthem, 1967.

Maurois, André. *Miracle of France*. Translated by Henry L. Binsse. New York: Harper, 1948.

Maxence, J-P. *Histoire de Dix Ans (1927-1937)*. Paris: Gallimard, 1937.

Micaud, Charles A. *The French Right and Nazi Germany, 1933-1939: A Study of Public Opinion*. New York: Octagon, 1964.

Milza, Pierre. *Fascisme Français*. Paris: Flammarion, 1987.

Monéry, André. *L'Ame des Parfums*. Paris: Quillet, 1924.

Monteagle, François. "Les débuts de *L'Ami du Peuple* de François Coty, une experience médiatique et politique extreme, 1928-1931." Master's thesis, University of Paris, 2002.

Mortimer, Tony L. *Lalique*. Paris: Atlas, 1990.

Mussolini, Benito. *My Autobiography*. Foreword by Richard Washburn Child. New York: Scribner's, 1928.

Negulesco, Jean. *Things I Did and Things I Think I Did*. New York: Simon & Schuster, 1984.

Ophuls, Marcel. *Le Chagrin et la Pitié* (The Sorrow and the Pity). Documentary.

Paoli, Robert. *Les Couleurs d'Ajaccio*. Paris: Pélican, 2002.

Pavia, Fabienne. *The World of Perfume*. New York: Knickerbocker, 1995.

Picchiottino, Ghislaine. *François Coty, Créateur de la Parfumerie Moderne: Mythes, Légendes et Réalité*. Paris: Université de Paris, 2000.

———. *François Coty, un Industriel Corse sous la IIIe République*. Ajaccio: Albiana, 2006.

Pipes, Richard. *Russia under the Bolshevik Regime*. New York: Knopf, 1993.

Poiret, Paul. *King of Fashion: The Autobiography of Paul Poiret*. Philadelphia: Lippincott, 1931.

Ravon, Georges. *Memoir of Life as a Journalist*. Paris: Flammarion, 1956.

Raymond, Gino. *Historical Dictionary of France*. Lanham, Md.: Scarecrow Press, 1998.

Rebatet, Lucien. *Les Décombres*. Paris, 1942.

Rees, Philip. *Biographical Dictionary of the Extreme Right Since 1890*. New York: Simon & Schuster, 1990.

Regismanset, Charles. *Philosophie des Parfums*. Paris, 1907.

Rémond, René. *Les Droites en France*. Paris: Aubier, 1982.

Roussel, Christine. *Lucien Romier (1885-1944): Historien, Economiste, Journaliste, Homme Politique*. Paris: France-Empire, 1979.

Sagaren, Edward. *The Science and Art of Perfume*. New York: McGraw Hill, 1945.

Sarran, Patrick. *Empereur D'Artigny*. Tours: Nouvelle République, 1990.

Schom, Alan. *Napoleon Bonaparte*. New York: Harper, 1997.

Shirer, William L. *The Collapse of the Third Republic.* New York: Simon & Schuster, 1969.

———. *The Rise and Fall of the Third Reich.* New York: Simon & Schuster, 1960.

Silvani, Paul. *Un Siècle de la Vue Corse.* Ajaccio: Albiana, 2000.

Sternhell, Zeev. *Neither Right nor Left.* Berkeley: University of California Press, 1986.

Sweets, John F. *Choices in Vichy France: The French under Nazi Occupation.* New York: Oxford University Press, 1986.

———. *Politics of Resistance in France, 1940-1944.* Dekalb: Northern Illinois University Press, 1976.

Taylor, A. J. P. *The Struggle for Mastery in Europe 1848-1918.* New York: Oxford University Press, 1971.

Taylor, Theo. *Corsica: The Rough Guide.* London: Penguin Books, 1994.

Utt, Mary Lou, and Glenn Utt. *Lalique Perfume Bottles.* With Patricia Bayer. New York: Crown, 1990.

Valois, Georges. *L'homme contre L'argent: Souvenirs de Dix Ans 1918-1928.* Paris: Valois, 1928.

Vignes Rouges, Jean des [Jean Taboureau]. *Un Chevalier de L'idéal: Maurice D'Hartoy.* Paris: Pélican, 1927.

Vuitton, Henry L. *La Malle aux Souvenirs.* Paris: Editions Mengès, 1984.

Wiser, William. *The Crazy Years: Paris in the Twenties.* New York: Atheneum, 1983.

———. *The Twilight Years: Paris in the 1930s.* New York: Carroll and Graf, 2001.

Newspaper Articles

Buré, Emile. "Obituary of François Coty." *L'Ordre,* July 27, 1934.

Burr, Chandler. "In the Lab, Creating the Essence That Entices Consumers to Buy." *New York Times,* February 23, 2008.

Dorsey, Hebe. "The Belle Epoque in the *Paris Herald.*" *International Herald Tribune,* 1986.

Dubernard, Maurice-Christian. "Antisémites d'hier et d'aujourd'hui." *Le Pays Libres,* February 8, 1941.

France-Soir, May 1954.

Humair, Sylvain. "Les flacons à parfum de Lalique." *Le Figaro,* October 27, 1986.

Il Pensiero Latini, February 21, 1926.

La Dépeche de Toulouse.

L'Ami du Peuple, September 1928; November 18, 1928; January 8, 1933; May 13, 1933, July 31, 1933

Latzarus, Louis. "La Journée Brisset." *Le Figaro,* April 13, 1913.

Le Combattant (Ajaccio, Corsica), May 14, 1920.

Le Figaro, "Directeur, François Coty, Coty Changes Name of Newspaper," May 13, 1929.

———, March 1, 1922; March 27, 1923; March 31, 1923; August 15, 1926; April 15, 1927; November 20, 1926; November 30, 1926; December 1, 1926; February 7, 1934; December 8, 1958.

L'Illustration, August 4, 1934.

London Daily Express, March 12, 1931; December 12, 1931.

London Daily Herald, "Coty's Illegitimate Children Win Perfume Fortune from Stepmother, Yvonne Coty Cotnareanu," April 22, 1955.

London Daily Mirror, April 23, 1955.

London Daily Observer, "Ami Du Peuple Passes," May 3, 1934.

London Daily Telegraph, "Fortune from Perfume: M. Coty's Rise to Fame," July 26, 1934.

———, March 12, 1933; July 8, 1934.

London Evening News, July 9, 1934.

London Evening Standard, April 12, 1953; December 13, 1954.

London News Chronicle, "Coty Loses His Last Paper," May 3, 1934.

London Sunday Chronicle, "Family Sues Mother [Henriette Dieudé] for Millions," December 13, 1953.

London Times, April 25, 1936.

———, "Coty, Scent Manufacturer and Newspaper Owner, Dies," July 27, 1934.

Mondet, N. Review of *Contre le Communisme. L'Economiste* (January 1928): 72-81.

New York Herald Tribune, "Coty's Ex-Wife Wins Point in Fight against Banks on Perfume Fortune," July 8, 1934.

New York Times, "Attacks Against Hungary in Coty's Paper Cause Boycott," September 19, 1928.

———, "B. E. Levy Elected Chairman of the Board of Coty Inc.," July 16, 1934.

———, "Boycott of Coty Perfumes by Hungary Because of Adverse Criticism in His Newspaper Still Effective," February 3, 1929.

———, "Charges of Fraud Interrupt Sale of Art from Coty Estate, Paris," December 2, 1936.

———, "Corporate Reports," April 10, 1934; May 9, 1934.

———, "Coty Attacks Austrians in Paris *Figaro* for Laziness: Reaction by Austrians—Boycott of Coty Products," October 2, 1927.

———, "Coty Attacks French Moving Picture Stand Toward American Films in His Newspapers," April 18, 1929.

————, "Coty Finances France-Japan Flight of M. Doret and J. Le Brix," July 13, 1931.

————, "Coty Gives $100,000 to French Hospital in New York," January 20, 1929.

————, "Coty in Accord on French War Debt to U.S.," July 1, 1926.

————, "Coty Inspired Versailles Meeting of National Assembly to Create Sinking Fund," August 3, 1926.

————, "Coty Leases Three Floors in Building on West 55th Street," January 4, 1923.

————, "Coty Loans France One Million Francs to Defray Expenses of Olympic Team," July 24, 1927.

————, "Coty Makes Largest Gift to Hospital Drive," February 5, 1929.

————, "Coty Ordered to Pay $5,200,000 to Ex-Wife," December 3, 1931.

————, "Coty Receives Divorce Decree," May 16, 1929.

————, "Coty Salon Redecorated," March 31, 1966.

————, "Coty's Ex-Wife Asks Lien on American Assets in Delaware," May 8, 1934.

————, "Coty's Ex-Wife Wins Point in Stock Suit," October 12, 1934.

————, "Coty's Former Wife Sues for Coty Inc. Stock," June 27, 1934.

————, "Coty's Former Wife Yvonne Le Baron Cotnareanu Sues for Alimony Payments," June 12, 1934.

————, "Coty's Illness Reported," June 18, 1934.

————, "Divorced Wife Says Coty Instigated Suit," May 1, 1934.

————, "French Election of Coty in Corsica Annulled," April 11, 1924.

————, "French Freemasons Assailed by Deputy," March 31, 1934.

————, "Jonathan F. Woods Wins $1,144,084 Verdict Against Coty on Drafts and Acceptances," April 27, 1934.

————, "Letter to Coty from Mussolini Published by French Left Press, Which Finds Sinister Meaning in Contents," January 16, 1932.

————, "Map Shows France Partitioned in 1935," September 2, 1931.

————, March 31, 1929; July 26, 1934.

————, "New Salon Opens in Air of Splendor," July 10, 1941.

————, "Tribute to Coty from D. Costes for Aiding Transatlantic Flight," November 1, 1930.

"Newspaper Deal." *London Evening Standard,* February 17, 1950.

"Newspaper Lease: Future of the *Figaro.*" *London Daily Telegraph,* February 7, 1950.

Reveil de la Corse, December 4, 1920.

Sartène Enchaîné, January 7, 1921.

Weber, Eugen. "The Most Dubious Battle." Review of *The Road to Verdun: World War I's Most Momentous Battle and the Folly of*

Nationalism, by Ian Ousby. *New York Times Book Review* (August 25, 2002).

World Today, "François Coty and the Launching of *L'Ami Du Peuple,*" October 1930.

Magazines, Quarterlies, and Pamphlets

"Actualité Beauté." *L'Esprit de Famille* (1994).

All Products. *Coty Dans le Monde.* 1953.

"Big Beauty Business." *Fortune* (August 1930): 41-43, 98-100.

"Biosphere." *Time Magazine* (August 23, 1999): 63-66.

"Cosmetics: The American Woman Responds." *Fortune* (August 1930): 29-32.

Cotnareanu, Philippe. "La rechute économique aux Etats-Unis." Paper presented at the Conference of the Centre polytechnicien d'études économique, Paris, July 4, 1938.

Coty, Elizabeth Z. "Coty Inc.: History and Future." Unpublished report.

———. "The Long 'C' Coty." Paper presented to Pfizer, USA, 1987.

Coty, François. "Coty & Chicago." *Living Age* (February 1, 1927).

———. "Settling with America." *Living Age* (1931).

Coty, François. "Tares in the Wheat." *Living Age* 318 (July 28, 1923): 151-53.

Coty manuscript notes, miscellaneous family archives, documents, and large photograph books of estates designed and built by François Coty in France.

Coty Review (1937-).

Coty SA. *Coty Est Dans Toutes les Langues un Nom Prestigieux.* N.d.

"Dans les Affaires: François Coty, un Grand Nom dans la Parfumerie." In *Le Mémorial des Corses,* edited by Francis Pomponi. Ajaccio: Gleizal, 1982.

De Beauvoir, Simone. "Oeil Pour Oeil." *Les Temps Modernes:* 813-30.

de Waleffe, Maurice. "Derrière le cercueil de Coty." *La Nouvelle Corse* (August 5, 1934).

Duquesnoy, Isabelle. "Parfums des Etés Perdus." *Corsica* (August 2004).

"Elizabeth Arden: Queen." *Fortune* (August 1930): 37-41, 92.

Huddleston, Sisley. "A French Hearst." *Living Age* (October 1928).

Kupferman, Fred. "François Coty, un Politicien au Parfum." *Historama* 48 (February 1988): 44-48.

Lee, Bernard. "Days of Perfume and Roses." *Beauty Fashion* (May 1983).

"The Lure of Perfumes." *Fortune* (August 1930): 32-35.

"M. Coty, Mr. Levy." *Fortune* (August 1930): 35-37, 97-100.

McKee, Douglas. "American School in Paris's History, 1946-1979." www.asparis.org/history2.html.

Marcus, H. Stanley. "America Is in Fashion." *Fortune* (November 1940): 80-84.

"The Most Prized Fashion Award." *Vogue* (February 1960).

Musée de Suresnes-René Sordes. *La Cité-Jardins, Ville de Suresnes.*

Rémond, Renée. "Les Anciens combattants et la politique." *Revue Française de Science Politique* (1955): 290.

"Richest Frenchman, Women and Solidarité Française." *Literary Digest* (April 11, 1931),

Schor, R. "Xénophobie et l'extrême droite: L'Exemple de 'L'Ami du Peuple' (1928-1937)." *Revue d'Histoire Moderne et Contemporaine* 23 (1976).

"Senteurs Parfums, Expositions, Ateliers, Conferences: Les Secrets des Parfumeurs Suresnois." *Suresnes* 127 (April 2002): 14-19.

Touraine 24 (October 1987).

Train, Arthur, Jr. "François Coty and the War of Words and Ink." *World Today* (February 1932).

Viasnoff, Nicolas. "Senteurs et Parfums." *Suresnes* 127 (April 2002).

Vignault, Jean-Jacques. "Un Grand Parfumeur, François Coty." *Parfums, Cosmétiques et Arômes* 54 (December 1983).

Lawsuits

Coty Inc. v. Hearn Department Stores, Inc., Supreme Court New York County (1935).

M. Vincent & autres v. M. Spoturno-Coty & autres, Civ. 34.03.1987. D. 1987.489.

Magnum Import Company, Inc. v. Spoturno Coty, 265 U.S. 159, 163; 43 S. Ct. 531; 67 Law. ed. 922 (1923).

Magnum Import Company, Inc. v. Coty; Cohn, Trading as Caclen Import Company v. Coty; Baum et al., Trading as Beautex Company v. Coty; Ivory Novelties Trading Company, Inc. v. Coty.; Magnum Import Company, Inc. v. Houbigant, Inc., 978, 979, 982, 981 U.S. (1923).

Prestonettes, Inc. v. Coty, 264 U.S. 359 (1924).

Spoturno Coty v. Société anonyme Heim et l'Etat français, 8 Tribunal de grande instance de Paris (1976).

Sources of Information

American Cemetery of Suresnes

Association of the Friends of the Museum of the Order and the Liberation
Paris

Bibliothèque Forney
Paris

Bibliothèque Institut de France
Paris

Bibliothèque Municipale
Ajaccio

Bibliothèque Nationale de France
Site François Mitterand
Paris

Bibliothèque pour Tous
Ajaccio

Bibliothèque Sainte-Genevieve
Paris

Centre d'Accueil et de Recherche des Archives Nationales
Paris

Centre de Documentation Juive Contemporaine

Centre Historique des Archives Nationales
Paris

Columbia University Digital Knowledge Ventures
"The Architecture and Development of New York City" Web site
Developed by Andrew Dolkart
Departmental Archives
South Corsica

France 3
Ajaccio

Grand Chancellery of the Legion of Honor
Paris

Harvard Library

Institut Supérieur du Parfum, de la Cosmétique et de l'Aromatique
Versailles

International Conservatory of Perfumes
Versailles

The Klarsfeld Foundation
Paris

Library of Congress
European Reading Room (Jefferson Building); Law Reading Room
  (Madison Building)
Washington, D.C.

Matteoli Commission Report

Metropolitan Museum of Art
The Eleanor Lambert Archive
The Costume Institute
New York City

Musée de Grasse, France

Musée de Suresnes-René Sordes, France

Musée de la Monnaie
Medals of Alphée Dubois
Paris

Musée Fesch
Ajaccio

Musée International d'Art Naif Anatole Jakovsky
Nice

Société Française des parfumeurs
Versailles

Stanford University
Hoover Institution Library and Archives
Cotnareanu correspondence with Henri Bergson
Palo Alto

United States Holocaust Memorial Museum Library
Washington, D.C.

University of Nice Library
Letters Section

Index